**Nominated for 3 EISNER AWARDS including
Best New Series and Best Ongoing Series**

"For fans of literature (from classics to contemporary) this series is worth a read. . . .
The Unwritten is **a roller-coaster ride through a library, weaving famous authors
and characters into a tale of mystery** that is, at once, oddly familiar yet highly original."
– USA TODAY

"*The Unwritten* makes a leap from being just a promising new Vertigo title to being on-track to
become the best ongoing Vertigo book since *Sandman*. And given that Vertigo has delivered
the likes of *100 Bullets*, *Y: The Last Man*, and *Fables* since *Sandman* ended,
that's saying something… A-"
–THE A.V. CLUB

"In a time where periodical comics are often being ignored in favor of waiting for the collected
edition, Carey and Gross haven't forgotten how a strong periodical can keep people's interest.
This is a serial that makes me want to read it monthly, because I just have to know
what happens next. Now that's good stuff."
– COMIC BOOK RESOURCES

the
Unwritten
THE WOUND

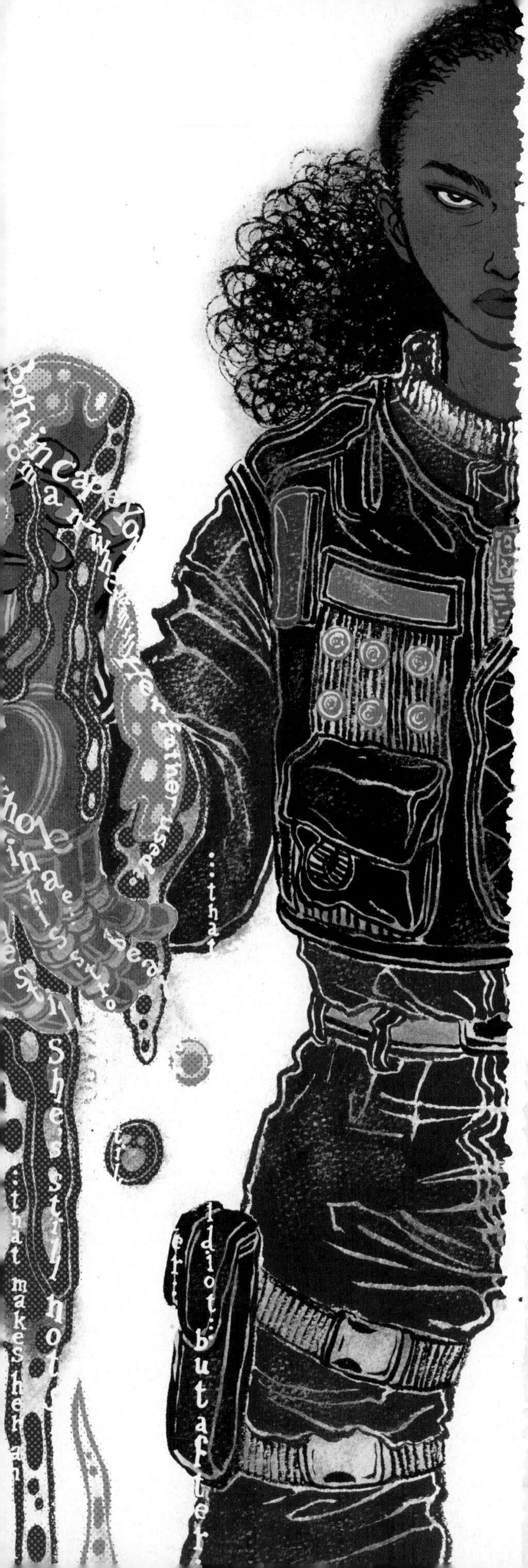

...that
She's still hot
...that makes her an
idiot... but after

the Unwritten

THE WOUND

Mike Carey & Peter Gross   Script – Story – Art

Rufus Dayglo   Finishes – issue #36

Chris Chuckry   Colorist

Todd Klein   Letterer   Yuko Shimizu   Cover Artist

THE UNWRITTEN created by Peter Gross and Mike Carey

Special thanks to Barb Guttman & Britt Sabo

UNW
v. 7

14.99
9/4/13
NKN

Shelly Bond Editor – Original Series
Joe Hughes Gregory Lockard Assistant Editors – Original Series
Rowena Yow Editor
Robbin Brosterman Design Director – Books
Louis Prandi Publication Design

Karen Berger Senior VP – Executive Editor, Vertigo
Bob Harras VP – Editor-in-Chief

Diane Nelson President
Dan DiDio and Jim Lee Co-Publishers
Geoff Johns Chief Creative Officer
John Rood Executive VP – Sales, Marketing and Business Development
Amy Genkins Senior VP – Business and Legal Affairs
Nairi Gardiner Senior VP – Finance
Jeff Boison VP – Publishing Operations
Mark Chiarello VP – Art Direction and Design
John Cunningham VP – Marketing
Terri Cunningham VP – Talent Relations and Services
Alison Gill Senior VP – Manufacturing and Operations
Hank Kanalz Senior VP – Digital
Jay Kogan VP – Business and Legal Affairs, Publishing
Jack Mahan VP – Business Affairs, Talent
Nick Napolitano VP – Manufacturing Administration
Sue Pohja VP – Book Sales
Courtney Simmons Senior VP – Publicity
Bob Wayne Senior VP – Sales

Library of Congress Cataloging-in-Publication Data

Carey, Mike, 1959- author.
  The Unwritten. Vol. 7, The wound / Mike Carey, Peter Gross.
     pages cm
  "Originally published in single magazine form in The
Unwritten 36-41."
  ISBN 978-1-4012-3806-3
  1. Characters and characteristics in literature--Comic books,
strips, etc. 2. Identity (Philosophical concept)--Comic books,
strips, etc. 3. Graphic novels. I. Gross, Peter, 1958- illustrator.
II. Title. III. Title: Wound.
  PN6727.C377U586 2013
  741.5'973--dc23
                                              2012047806

1.1394.6146

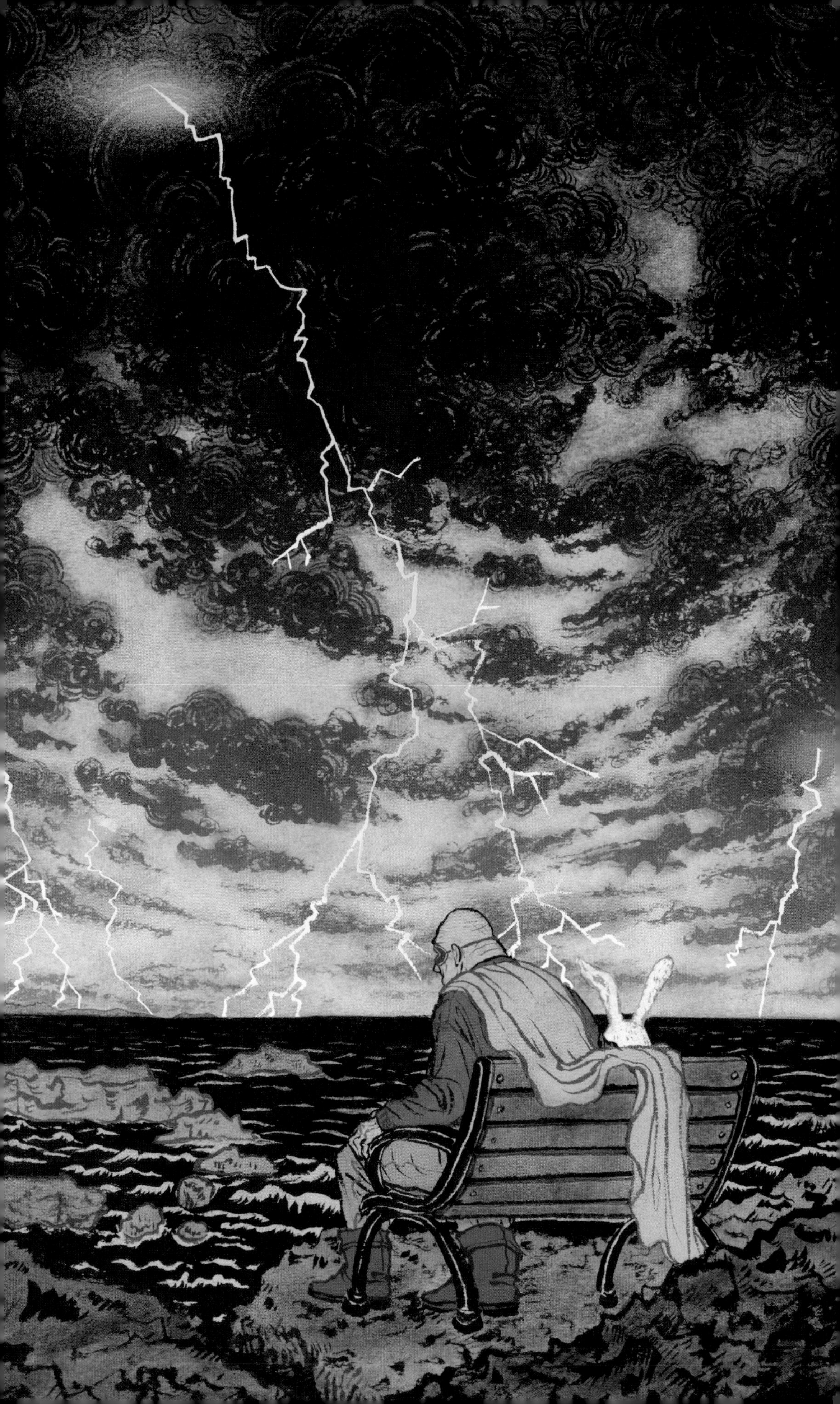

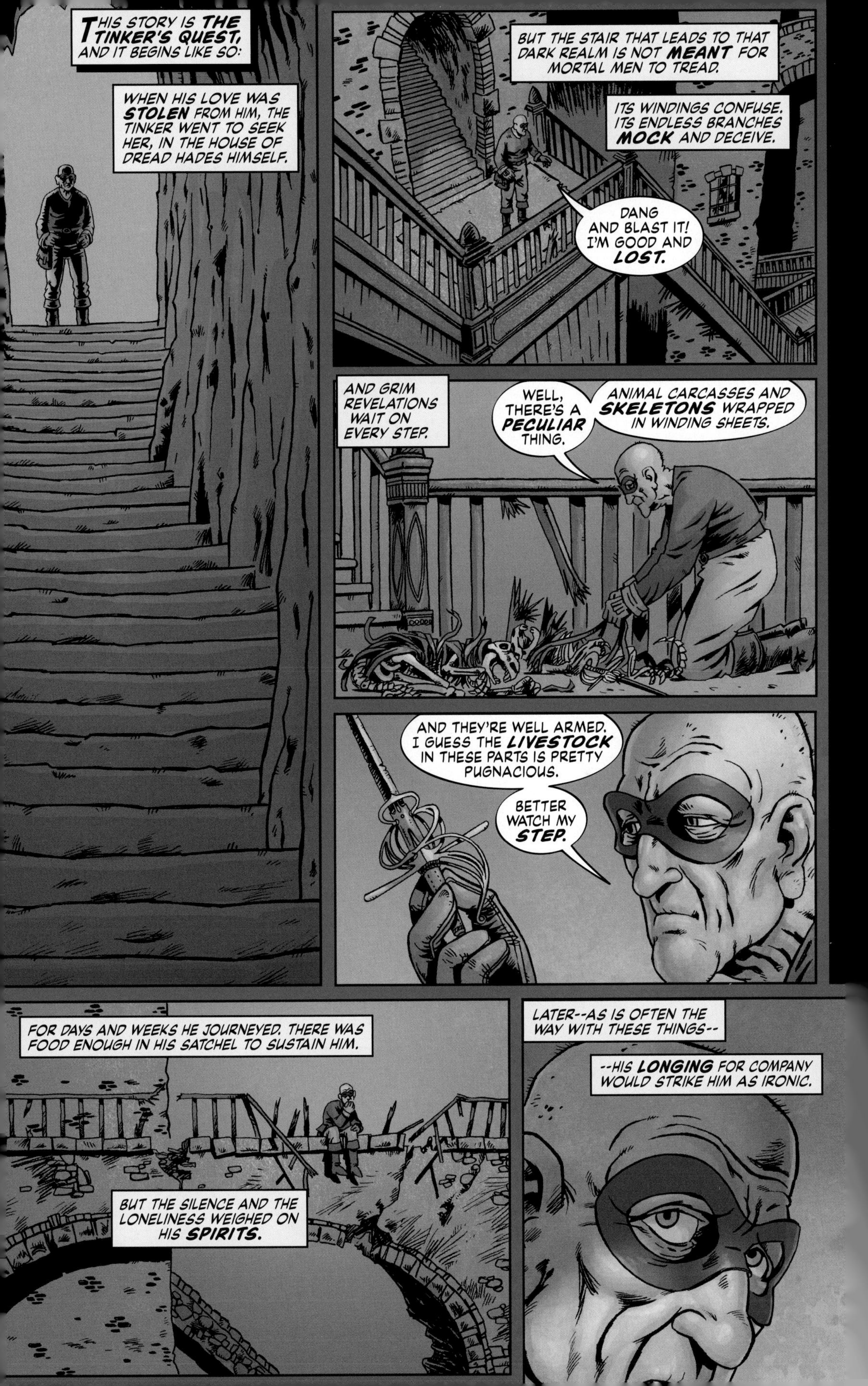
THIS STORY IS THE TINKER'S QUEST, AND IT BEGINS LIKE SO:
WHEN HIS LOVE WAS STOLEN FROM HIM, THE TINKER WENT TO SEEK HER, IN THE HOUSE OF DREAD HADES HIMSELF.
BUT THE STAIR THAT LEADS TO THAT DARK REALM IS NOT MEANT FOR MORTAL MEN TO TREAD.
ITS WINDINGS CONFUSE. ITS ENDLESS BRANCHES MOCK AND DECEIVE.
DANG AND BLAST IT! I'M GOOD AND LOST.
AND GRIM REVELATIONS WAIT ON EVERY STEP.
WELL, THERE'S A PECULIAR THING.
ANIMAL CARCASSES AND SKELETONS WRAPPED IN WINDING SHEETS.
AND THEY'RE WELL ARMED. I GUESS THE LIVESTOCK IN THESE PARTS IS PRETTY PUGNACIOUS.
BETTER WATCH MY STEP.
FOR DAYS AND WEEKS HE JOURNEYED. THERE WAS FOOD ENOUGH IN HIS SATCHEL TO SUSTAIN HIM.
BUT THE SILENCE AND THE LONELINESS WEIGHED ON HIS SPIRITS.
LATER--AS IS OFTEN THE WAY WITH THESE THINGS--
--HIS LONGING FOR COMPANY WOULD STRIKE HIM AS IRONIC.

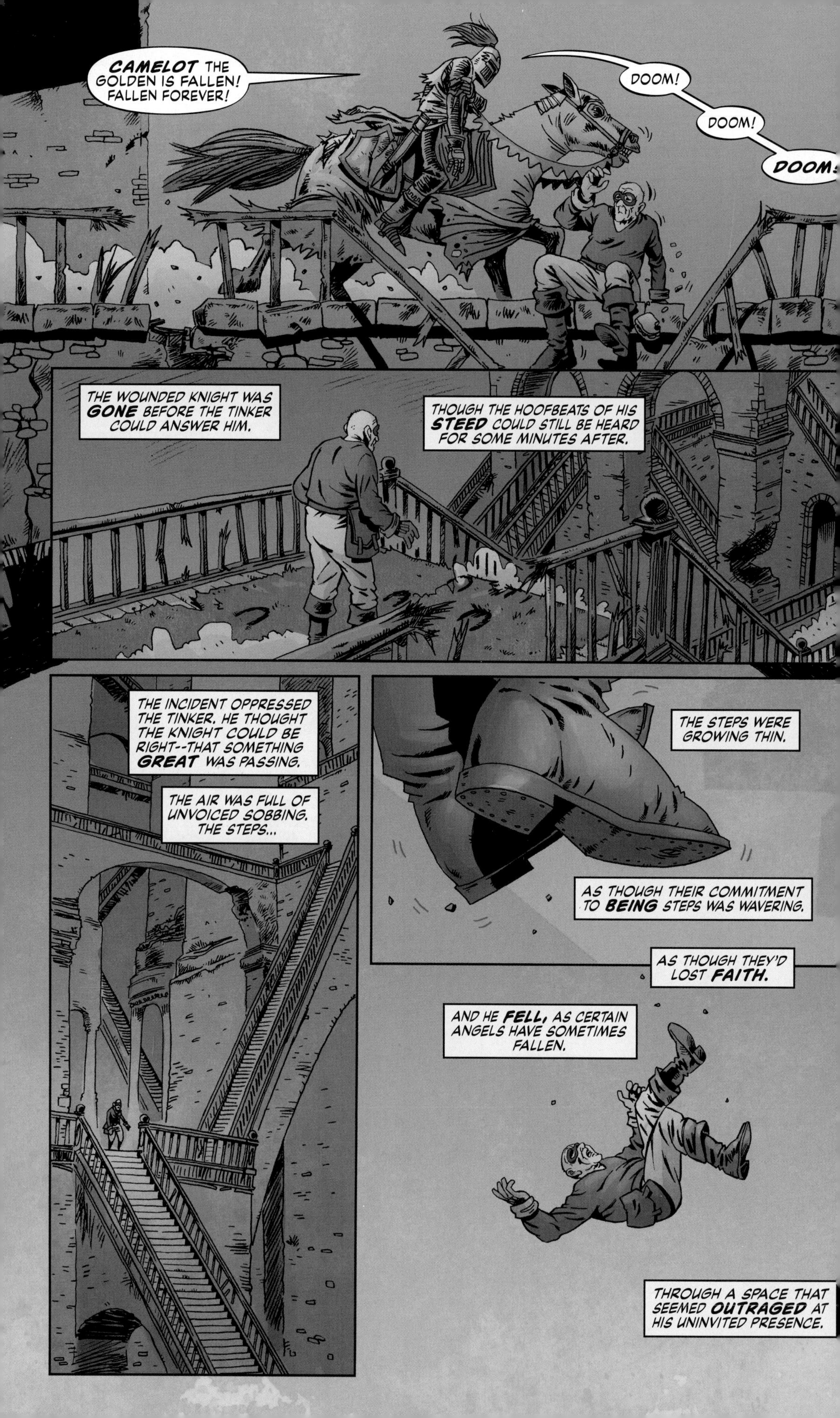

CAMELOT THE GOLDEN IS FALLEN! FALLEN FOREVER!
DOOM!
DOOM!
DOOM!
THE WOUNDED KNIGHT WAS GONE BEFORE THE TINKER COULD ANSWER HIM.
THOUGH THE HOOFBEATS OF HIS STEED COULD STILL BE HEARD FOR SOME MINUTES AFTER.
THE INCIDENT OPPRESSED THE TINKER. HE THOUGHT THE KNIGHT COULD BE RIGHT--THAT SOMETHING GREAT WAS PASSING.
THE AIR WAS FULL OF UNVOICED SOBBING. THE STEPS...
THE STEPS WERE GROWING THIN.
AS THOUGH THEIR COMMITMENT TO BEING STEPS WAS WAVERING.
AS THOUGH THEY'D LOST FAITH.
AND HE FELL, AS CERTAIN ANGELS HAVE SOMETIMES FALLEN.
THROUGH A SPACE THAT SEEMED OUTRAGED AT HIS UNINVITED PRESENCE.

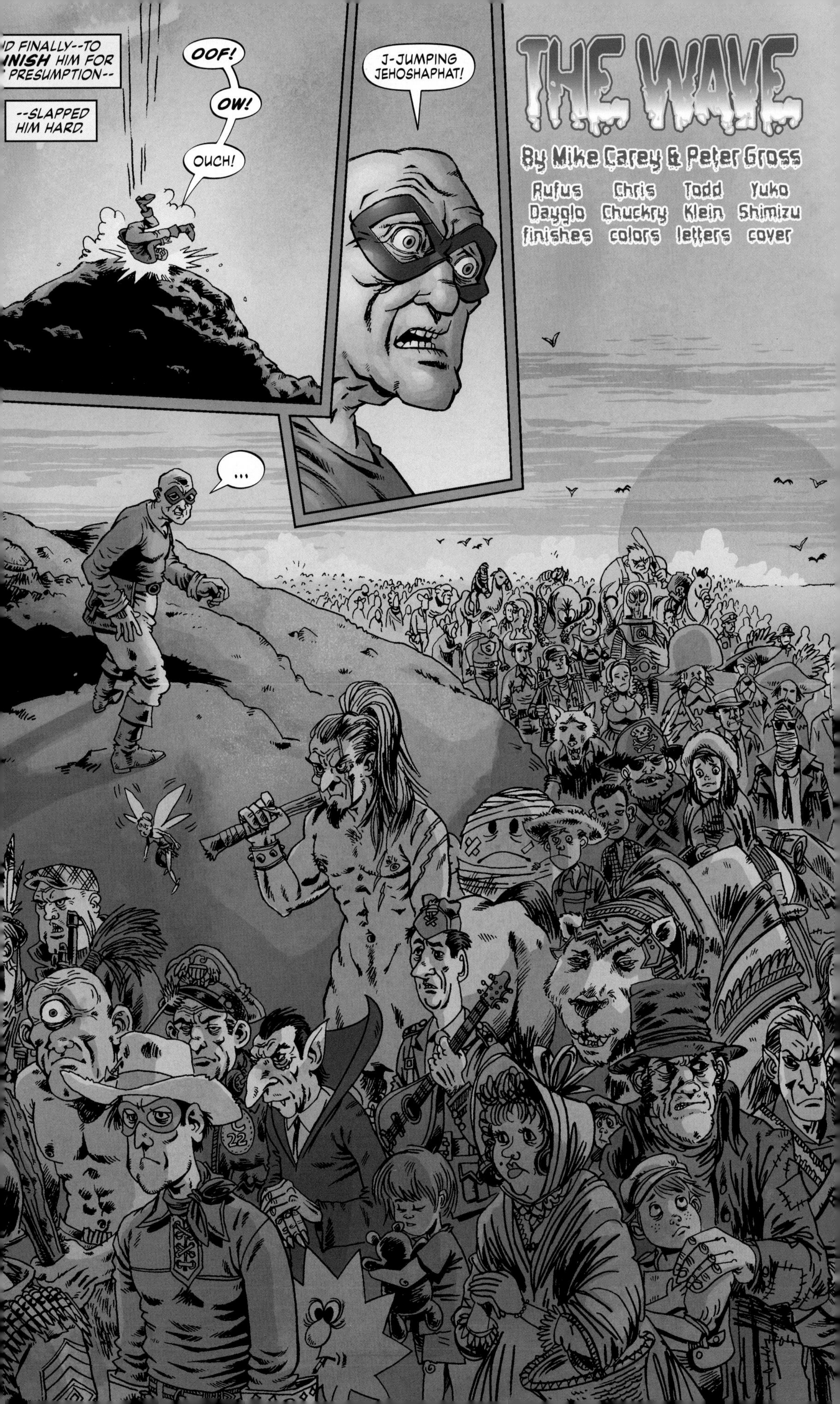

D FINALLY--TO INISH HIM FOR PRESUMPTION--
--SLAPPED HIM HARD.
OOF!
OW!
OUCH!
J-JUMPING JEHOSHAPHAT!
THE WAVE
By Mike Carey & Peter Gross
Rufus Dayglo finishes
Chris Chuckry colors
Todd Klein letters
Yuko Shimizu cover
...

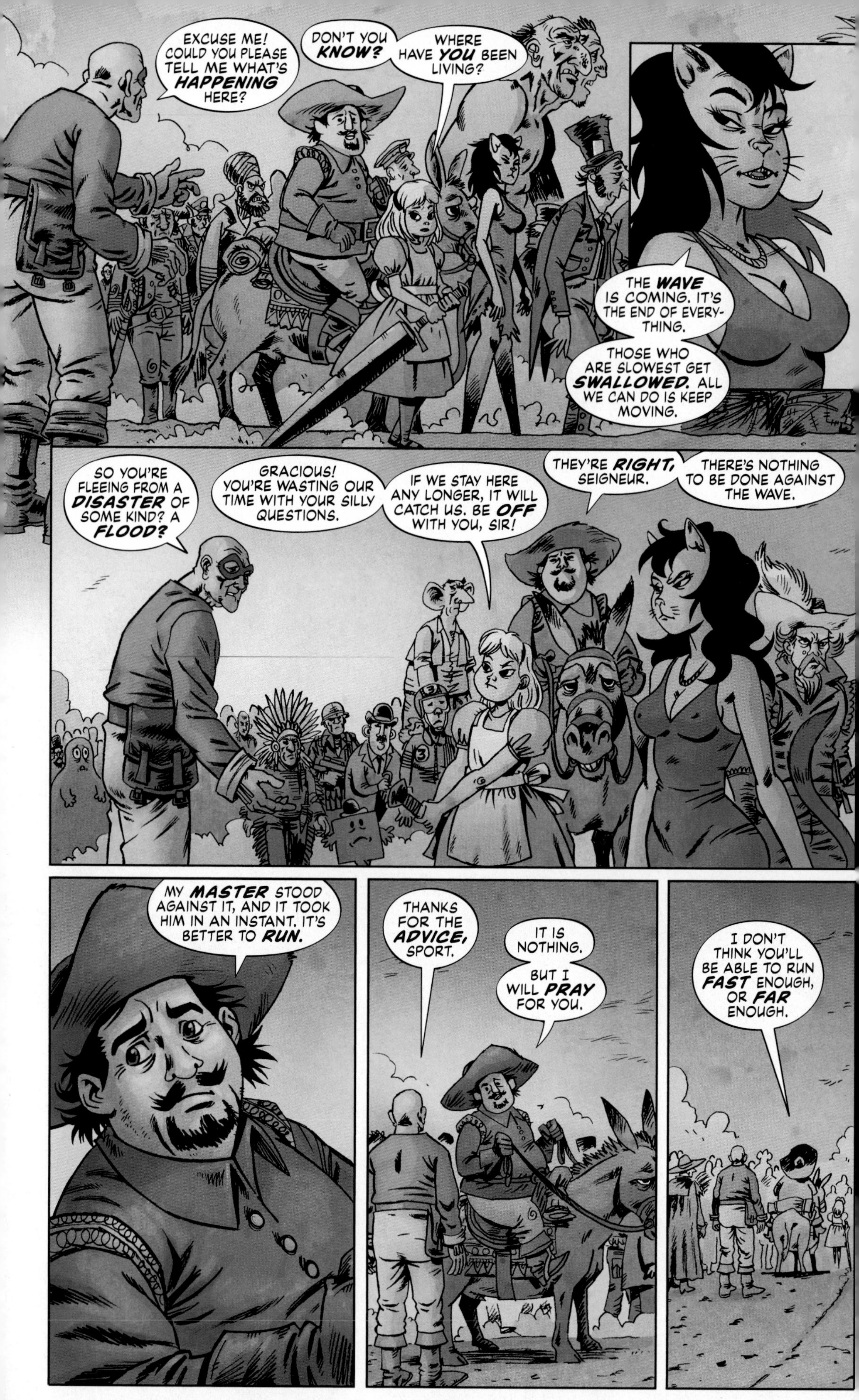

EXCUSE ME! COULD YOU PLEASE TELL ME WHAT'S HAPPENING HERE?
DON'T YOU KNOW?
WHERE HAVE YOU BEEN LIVING?
THE WAVE IS COMING. IT'S THE END OF EVERY-THING.
THOSE WHO ARE SLOWEST GET SWALLOWED. ALL WE CAN DO IS KEEP MOVING.
SO YOU'RE FLEEING FROM A DISASTER OF SOME KIND? A FLOOD?
GRACIOUS! YOU'RE WASTING OUR TIME WITH YOUR SILLY QUESTIONS.
IF WE STAY HERE ANY LONGER, IT WILL CATCH US. BE OFF WITH YOU, SIR!
THEY'RE RIGHT, SEIGNEUR.
THERE'S NOTHING TO BE DONE AGAINST THE WAVE.
MY MASTER STOOD AGAINST IT, AND IT TOOK HIM IN AN INSTANT. IT'S BETTER TO RUN.
THANKS FOR THE ADVICE, SPORT.
IT IS NOTHING.
BUT I WILL PRAY FOR YOU.
I DON'T THINK YOU'LL BE ABLE TO RUN FAST ENOUGH, OR FAR ENOUGH.

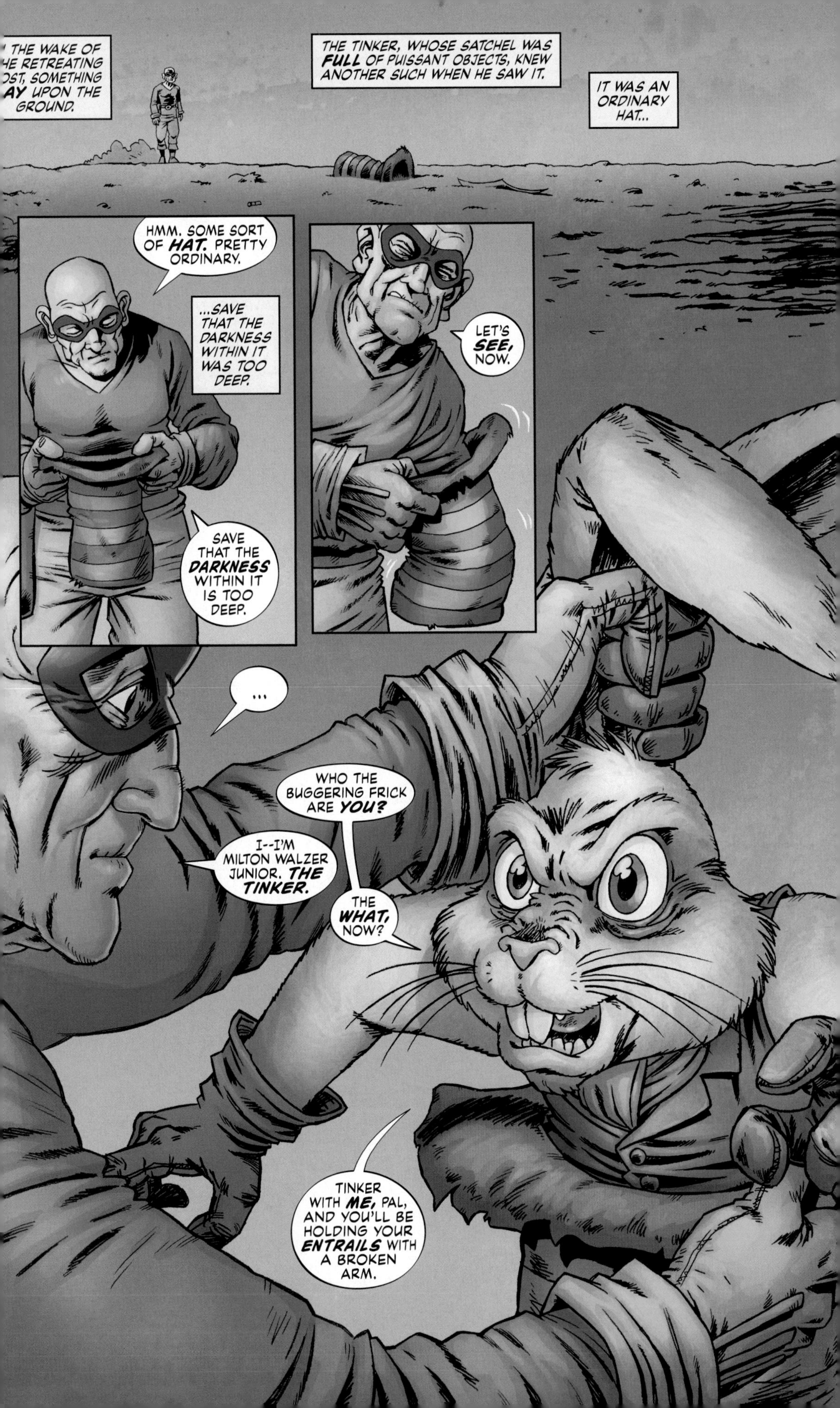

THE WAKE OF HE RETREATING OST, SOMETHING AY UPON THE GROUND.
THE TINKER, WHOSE SATCHEL WAS FULL OF PUISSANT OBJECTS, KNEW ANOTHER SUCH WHEN HE SAW IT.
IT WAS AN ORDINARY HAT...
HMM. SOME SORT OF HAT. PRETTY ORDINARY.
...SAVE THAT THE DARKNESS WITHIN IT WAS TOO DEEP.
SAVE THAT THE DARKNESS WITHIN IT IS TOO DEEP.
LET'S SEE, NOW.
...
WHO THE BUGGERING FRICK ARE YOU?
I--I'M MILTON WALZER JUNIOR. THE TINKER.
THE WHAT, NOW?
TINKER WITH ME, PAL, AND YOU'LL BE HOLDING YOUR ENTRAILS WITH A BROKEN ARM.

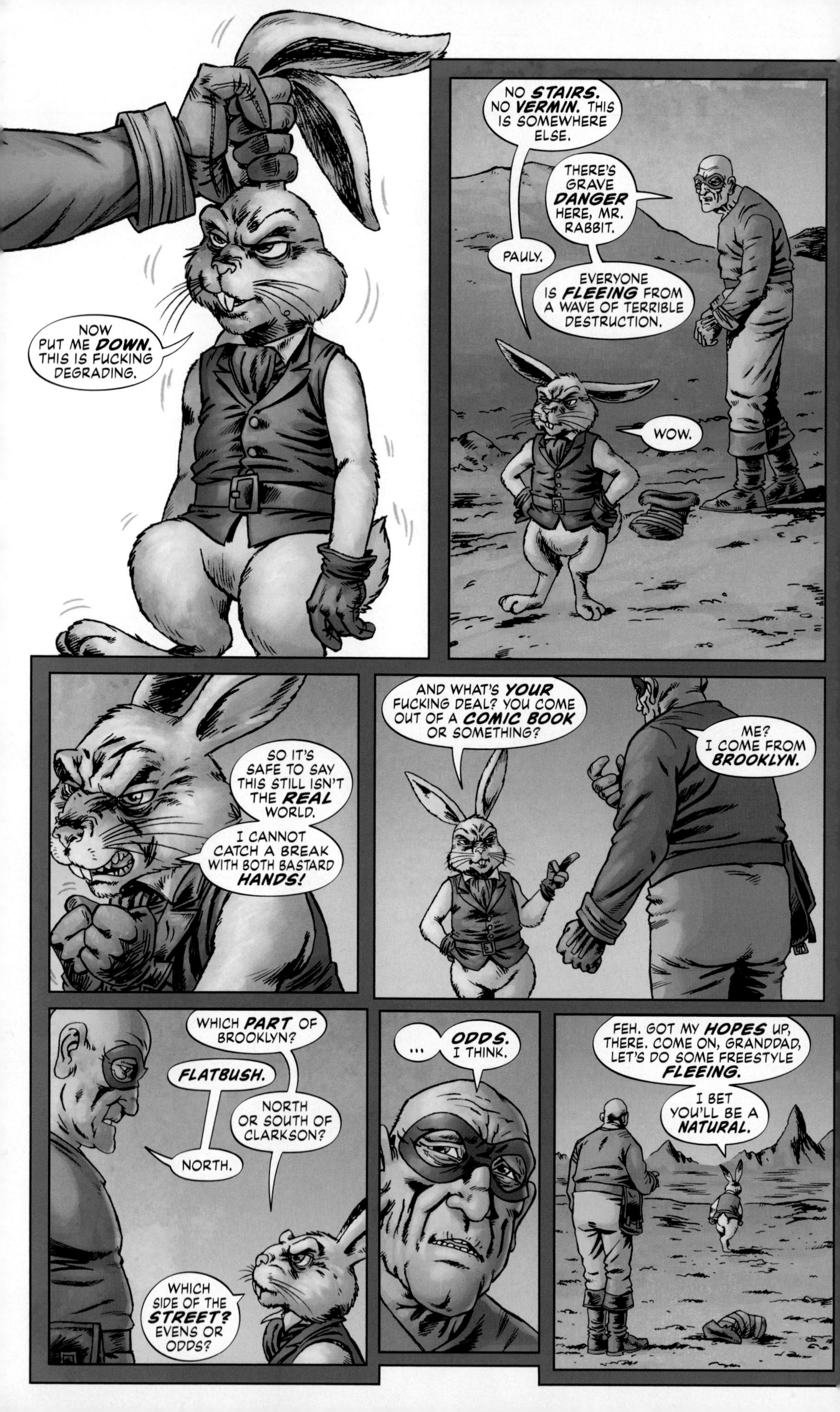
NOW PUT ME DOWN. THIS IS FUCKING DEGRADING.
NO STAIRS. NO VERMIN. THIS IS SOMEWHERE ELSE.
PAULY.
THERE'S GRAVE DANGER HERE, MR. RABBIT.
EVERYONE IS FLEEING FROM A WAVE OF TERRIBLE DESTRUCTION.
WOW.
SO IT'S SAFE TO SAY THIS STILL ISN'T THE REAL WORLD.
I CANNOT CATCH A BREAK WITH BOTH BASTARD HANDS!
AND WHAT'S YOUR FUCKING DEAL? YOU COME OUT OF A COMIC BOOK OR SOMETHING?
ME? I COME FROM BROOKLYN.
WHICH PART OF BROOKLYN?
FLATBUSH.
NORTH OR SOUTH OF CLARKSON?
NORTH.
WHICH SIDE OF THE STREET? EVENS OR ODDS?
...
ODDS. I THINK.
FEH. GOT MY HOPES UP, THERE. COME ON, GRANDDAD, LET'S DO SOME FREESTYLE FLEEING.
I BET YOU'LL BE A NATURAL.

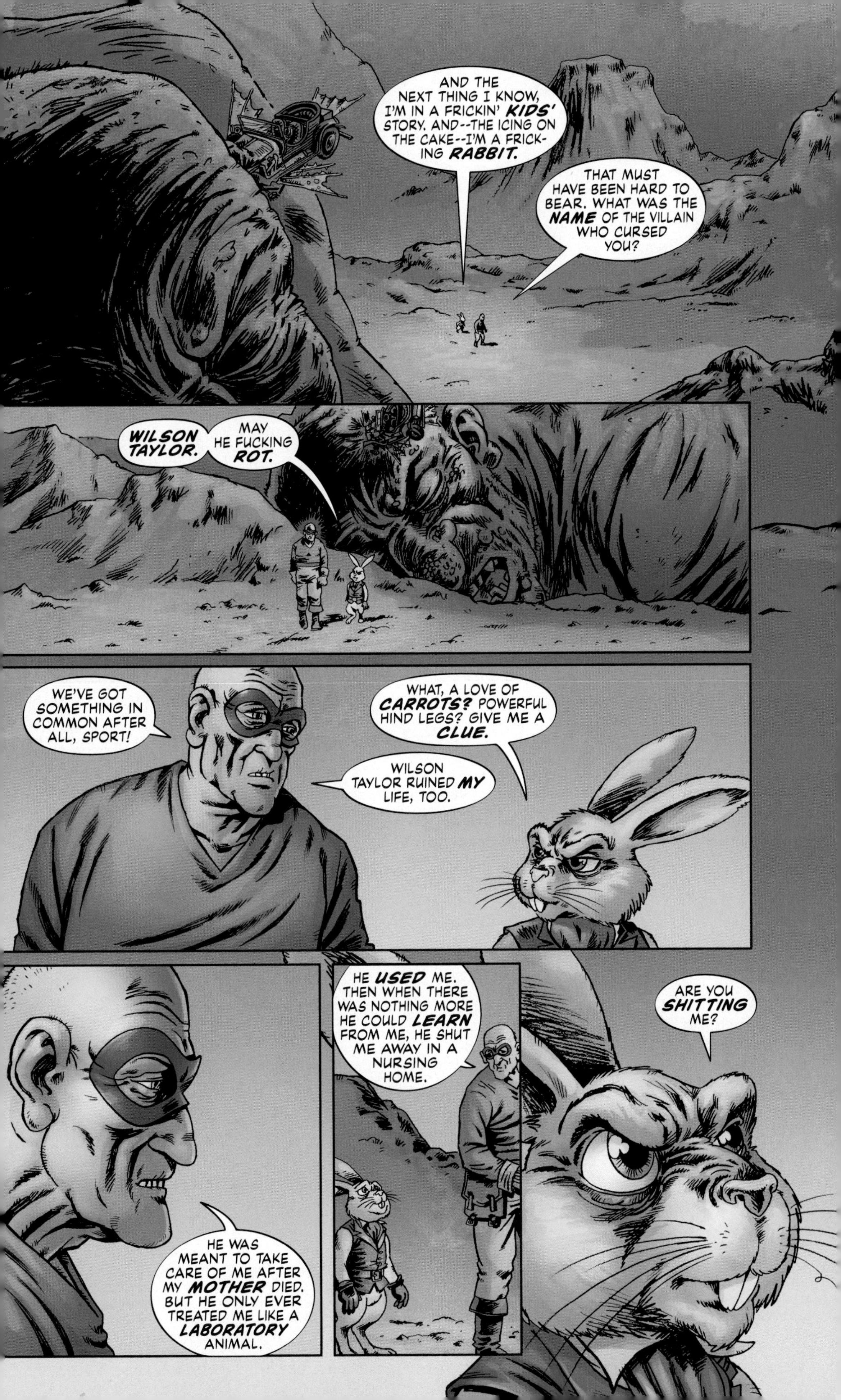
AND THE NEXT THING I KNOW, I'M IN A FRICKIN' KIDS' STORY. AND--THE ICING ON THE CAKE--I'M A FRICK-ING RABBIT.
THAT MUST HAVE BEEN HARD TO BEAR. WHAT WAS THE NAME OF THE VILLAIN WHO CURSED YOU?
WILSON TAYLOR.
MAY HE FUCKING ROT.
WE'VE GOT SOMETHING IN COMMON AFTER ALL, SPORT!
WHAT, A LOVE OF CARROTS? POWERFUL HIND LEGS? GIVE ME A CLUE.
WILSON TAYLOR RUINED MY LIFE, TOO.
HE WAS MEANT TO TAKE CARE OF ME AFTER MY MOTHER DIED. BUT HE ONLY EVER TREATED ME LIKE A LABORATORY ANIMAL.
HE USED ME. THEN WHEN THERE WAS NOTHING MORE HE COULD LEARN FROM ME, HE SHUT ME AWAY IN A NURSING HOME.
ARE YOU SHITTING ME?

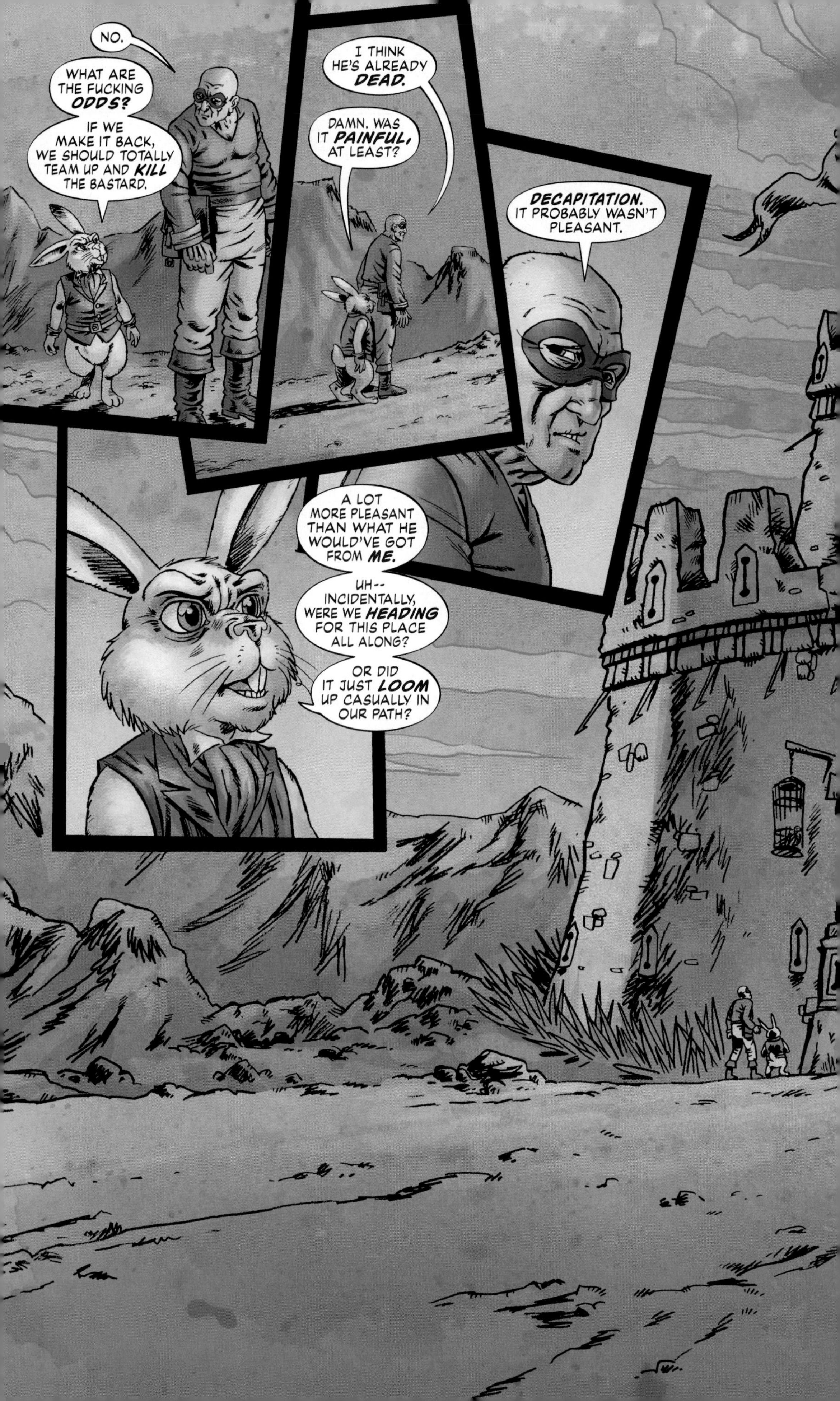

NO.
WHAT ARE THE FUCKING ODDS?
IF WE MAKE IT BACK, WE SHOULD TOTALLY TEAM UP AND KILL THE BASTARD.
I THINK HE'S ALREADY DEAD.
DAMN. WAS IT PAINFUL, AT LEAST?
DECAPITATION. IT PROBABLY WASN'T PLEASANT.
A LOT MORE PLEASANT THAN WHAT HE WOULD'VE GOT FROM ME.
UH-- INCIDENTALLY, WERE WE HEADING FOR THIS PLACE ALL ALONG?
OR DID IT JUST LOOM UP CASUALLY IN OUR PATH?

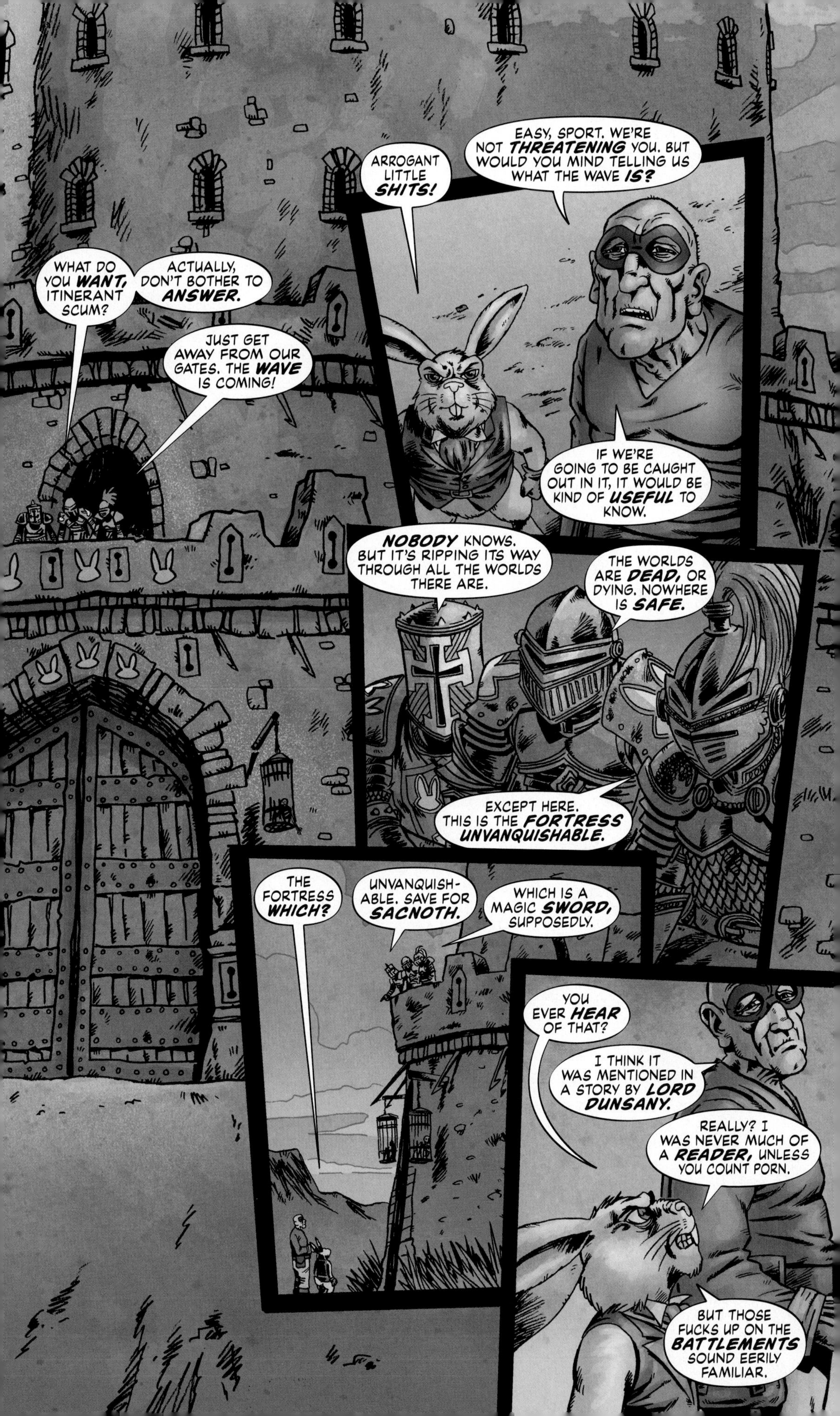
WHAT DO YOU WANT, ITINERANT SCUM?
ACTUALLY, DON'T BOTHER TO ANSWER.
JUST GET AWAY FROM OUR GATES. THE WAVE IS COMING!
ARROGANT LITTLE SHITS!
EASY, SPORT. WE'RE NOT THREATENING YOU. BUT WOULD YOU MIND TELLING US WHAT THE WAVE IS?
IF WE'RE GOING TO BE CAUGHT OUT IN IT, IT WOULD BE KIND OF USEFUL TO KNOW.
NOBODY KNOWS. BUT IT'S RIPPING ITS WAY THROUGH ALL THE WORLDS THERE ARE.
THE WORLDS ARE DEAD, OR DYING. NOWHERE IS SAFE.
EXCEPT HERE. THIS IS THE FORTRESS UNVANQUISHABLE.
THE FORTRESS WHICH?
UNVANQUISH-ABLE. SAVE FOR SACNOTH.
WHICH IS A MAGIC SWORD, SUPPOSEDLY.
YOU EVER HEAR OF THAT?
I THINK IT WAS MENTIONED IN A STORY BY LORD DUNSANY.
REALLY? I WAS NEVER MUCH OF A READER, UNLESS YOU COUNT PORN.
BUT THOSE FUCKS UP ON THE BATTLEMENTS SOUND EERILY FAMILIAR.

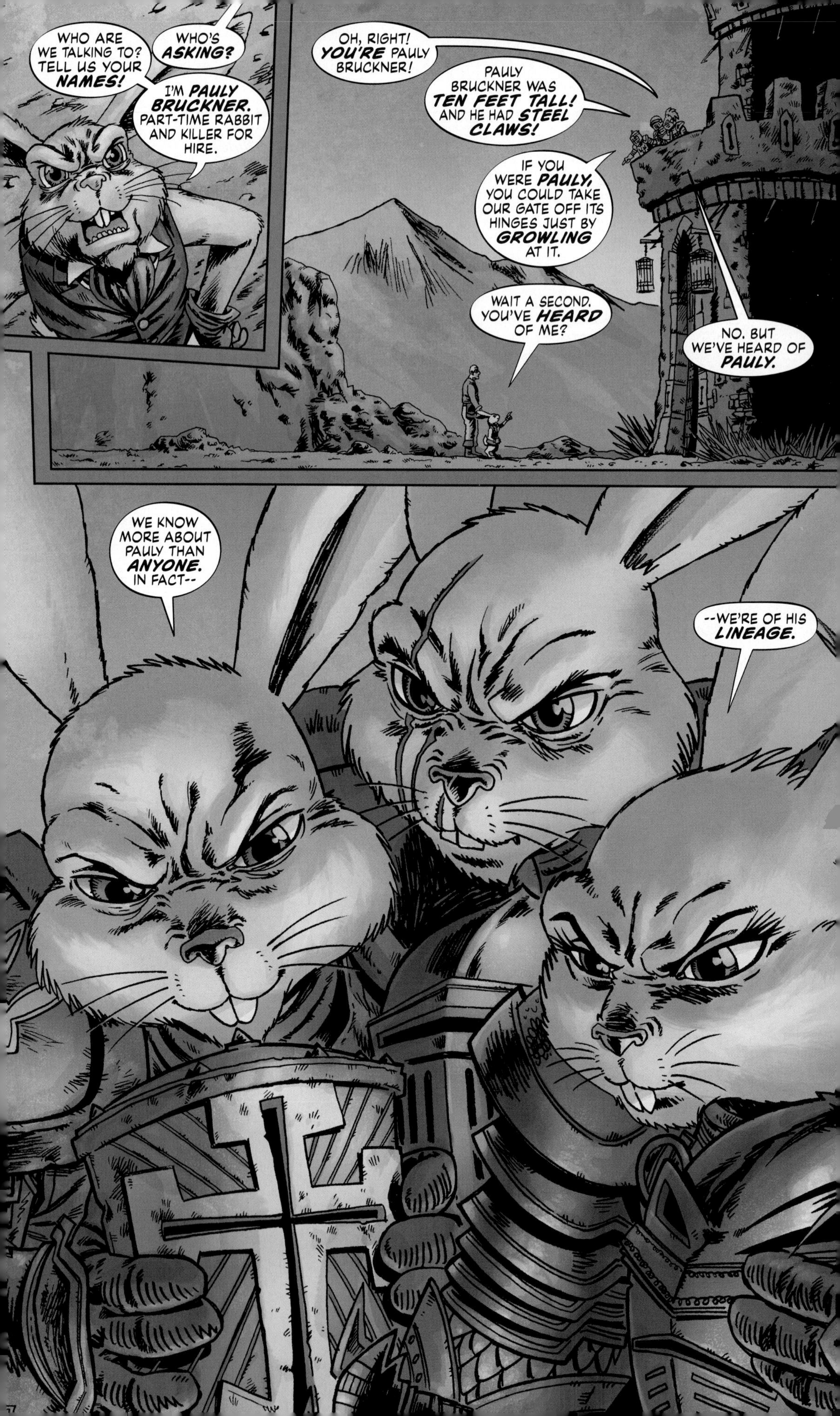
WHO ARE WE TALKING TO? TELL US YOUR NAMES!
WHO'S ASKING?
I'M PAULY BRUCKNER. PART-TIME RABBIT AND KILLER FOR HIRE.
OH, RIGHT! YOU'RE PAULY BRUCKNER!
PAULY BRUCKNER WAS TEN FEET TALL! AND HE HAD STEEL CLAWS!
IF YOU WERE PAULY, YOU COULD TAKE OUR GATE OFF ITS HINGES JUST BY GROWLING AT IT.
WAIT A SECOND. YOU'VE HEARD OF ME?
NO. BUT WE'VE HEARD OF PAULY.
WE KNOW MORE ABOUT PAULY THAN ANYONE. IN FACT--
--WE'RE OF HIS LINEAGE.

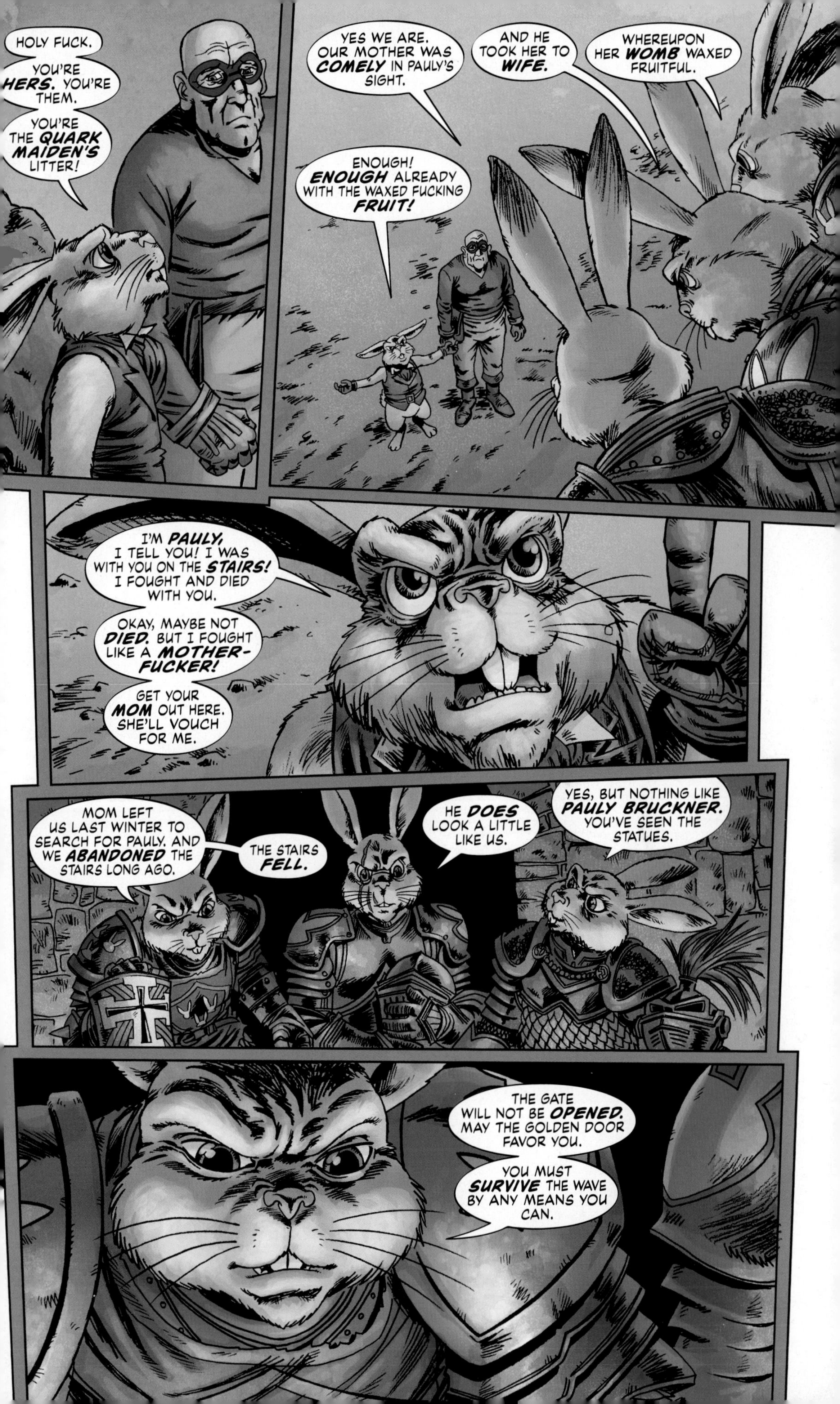
HOLY FUCK.
YOU'RE HERS. YOU'RE THEM.
YOU'RE THE QUARK MAIDEN'S LITTER!
YES WE ARE. OUR MOTHER WAS COMELY IN PAULY'S SIGHT.
AND HE TOOK HER TO WIFE.
WHEREUPON HER WOMB WAXED FRUITFUL.
ENOUGH! ENOUGH ALREADY WITH THE WAXED FUCKING FRUIT!
I'M PAULY, I TELL YOU! I WAS WITH YOU ON THE STAIRS! I FOUGHT AND DIED WITH YOU.
OKAY, MAYBE NOT DIED, BUT I FOUGHT LIKE A MOTHER-FUCKER!
GET YOUR MOM OUT HERE. SHE'LL VOUCH FOR ME.
MOM LEFT US LAST WINTER TO SEARCH FOR PAULY, AND WE ABANDONED THE STAIRS LONG AGO.
THE STAIRS FELL.
HE DOES LOOK A LITTLE LIKE US.
YES, BUT NOTHING LIKE PAULY BRUCKNER. YOU'VE SEEN THE STATUES.
THE GATE WILL NOT BE OPENED. MAY THE GOLDEN DOOR FAVOR YOU.
YOU MUST SURVIVE THE WAVE BY ANY MEANS YOU CAN.

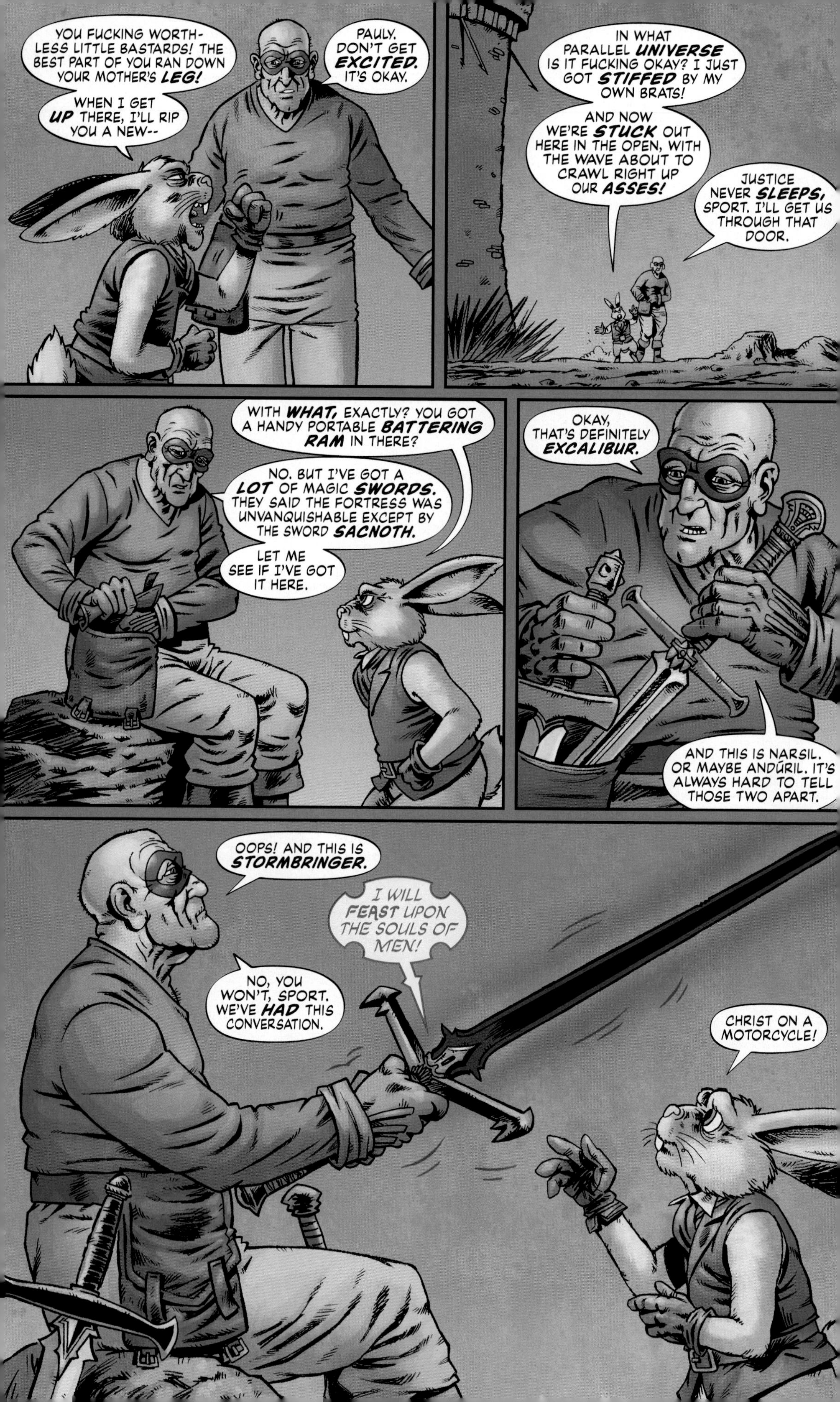
YOU FUCKING WORTH-LESS LITTLE BASTARDS! THE BEST PART OF YOU RAN DOWN YOUR MOTHER'S LEG!
WHEN I GET UP THERE, I'LL RIP YOU A NEW--
PAULY. DON'T GET EXCITED. IT'S OKAY.
IN WHAT PARALLEL UNIVERSE IS IT FUCKING OKAY? I JUST GOT STIFFED BY MY OWN BRATS!
AND NOW WE'RE STUCK OUT HERE IN THE OPEN, WITH THE WAVE ABOUT TO CRAWL RIGHT UP OUR ASSES!
JUSTICE NEVER SLEEPS, SPORT. I'LL GET US THROUGH THAT DOOR.
WITH WHAT, EXACTLY? YOU GOT A HANDY PORTABLE BATTERING RAM IN THERE?
NO. BUT I'VE GOT A LOT OF MAGIC SWORDS. THEY SAID THE FORTRESS WAS UNVANQUISHABLE EXCEPT BY THE SWORD SACNOTH.
LET ME SEE IF I'VE GOT IT HERE.
OKAY, THAT'S DEFINITELY EXCALIBUR.
AND THIS IS NARSIL. OR MAYBE ANDÚRIL. IT'S ALWAYS HARD TO TELL THOSE TWO APART.
OOPS! AND THIS IS STORMBRINGER.
I WILL FEAST UPON THE SOULS OF MEN!
NO, YOU WON'T, SPORT. WE'VE HAD THIS CONVERSATION.
CHRIST ON A MOTORCYCLE!

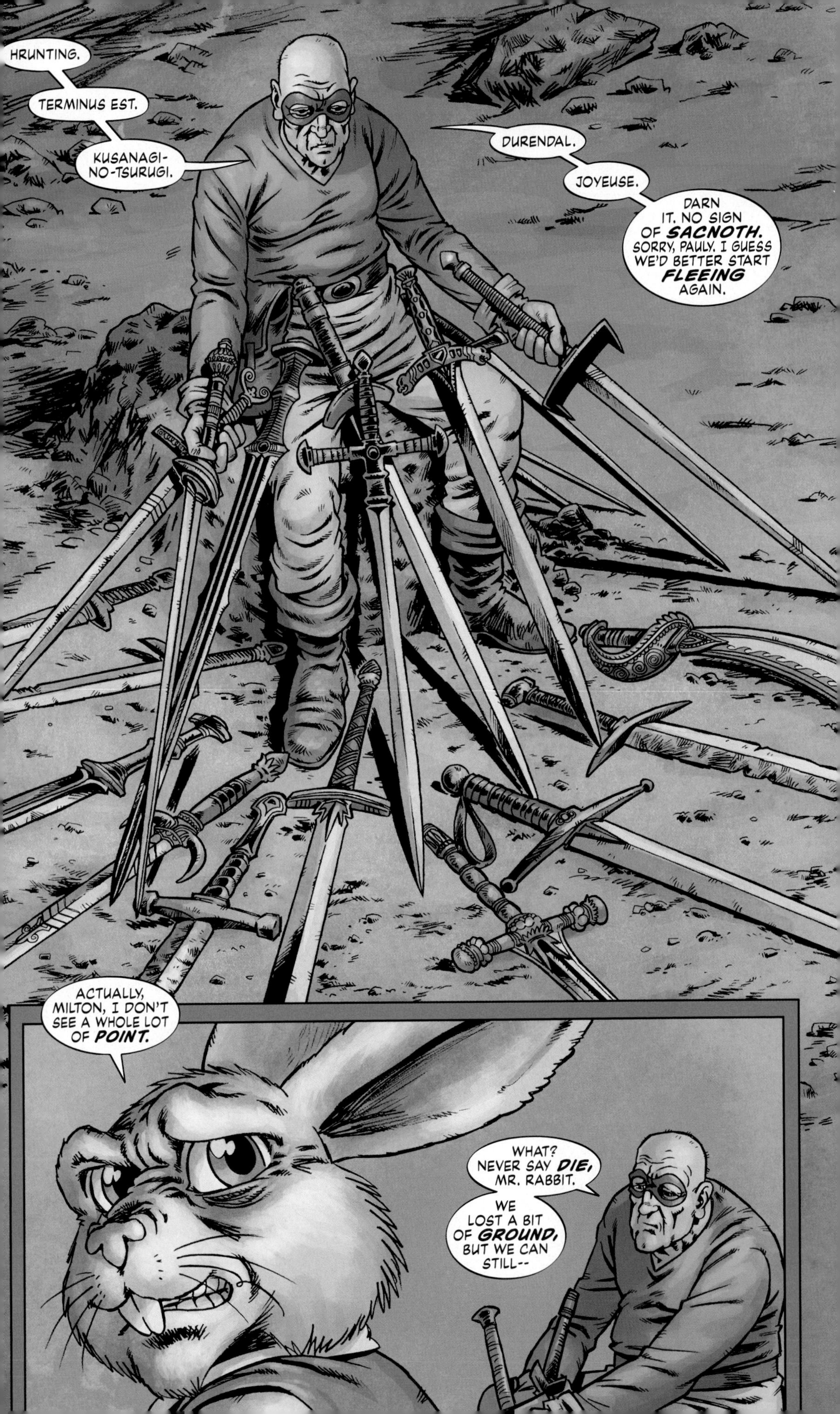
HRUNTING.
TERMINUS EST.
KUSANAGI-NO-TSURUGI.
DURENDAL.
JOYEUSE.
DARN IT. NO SIGN OF **SACNOTH.** SORRY, PAULY. I GUESS WE'D BETTER START **FLEEING** AGAIN.
ACTUALLY, MILTON, I DON'T SEE A WHOLE LOT OF **POINT.**
WHAT? NEVER SAY **DIE,** MR. RABBIT.
WE LOST A BIT OF **GROUND,** BUT WE CAN STILL--

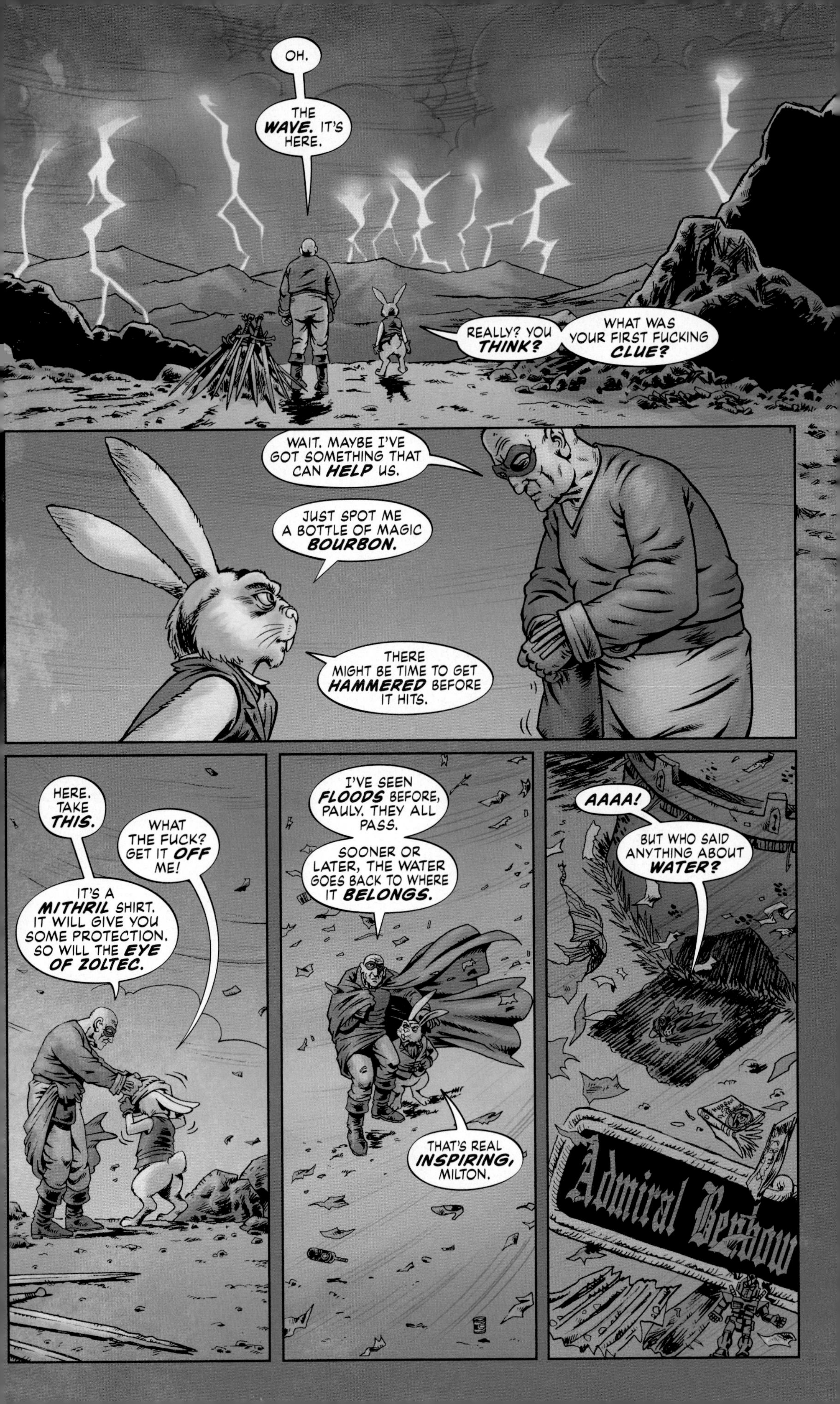

OH.
THE WAVE. IT'S HERE.
REALLY? YOU THINK?
WHAT WAS YOUR FIRST FUCKING CLUE?
WAIT. MAYBE I'VE GOT SOMETHING THAT CAN HELP US.
JUST SPOT ME A BOTTLE OF MAGIC BOURBON.
THERE MIGHT BE TIME TO GET HAMMERED BEFORE IT HITS.
HERE. TAKE THIS.
WHAT THE FUCK? GET IT OFF ME!
IT'S A MITHRIL SHIRT. IT WILL GIVE YOU SOME PROTECTION. SO WILL THE EYE OF ZOLTEC.
I'VE SEEN FLOODS BEFORE, PAULY. THEY ALL PASS.
SOONER OR LATER, THE WATER GOES BACK TO WHERE IT BELONGS.
THAT'S REAL INSPIRING, MILTON.
AAAA!
BUT WHO SAID ANYTHING ABOUT WATER?
Admiral Benbow

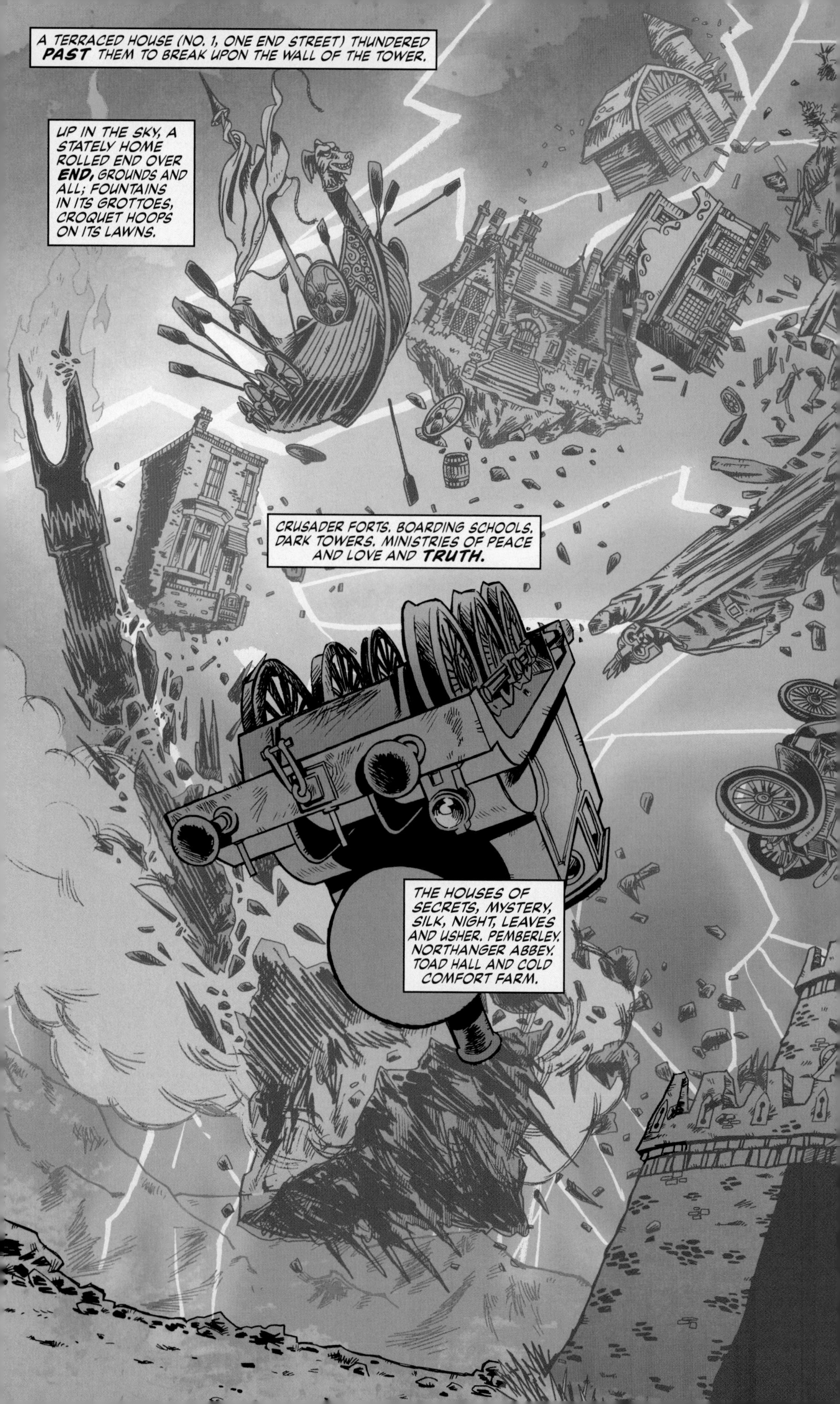
A TERRACED HOUSE (NO. 1, ONE END STREET) THUNDERED **PAST** THEM TO BREAK UPON THE WALL OF THE TOWER.
UP IN THE SKY, A STATELY HOME ROLLED END OVER **END,** GROUNDS AND ALL; FOUNTAINS IN ITS GROTTOES, CROQUET HOOPS ON ITS LAWNS.
CRUSADER FORTS. BOARDING SCHOOLS. DARK TOWERS. MINISTRIES OF PEACE AND LOVE AND **TRUTH.**
THE HOUSES OF SECRETS, MYSTERY, SILK, NIGHT, LEAVES AND USHER. PEMBERLEY. NORTHANGER ABBEY. TOAD HALL AND COLD COMFORT FARM.

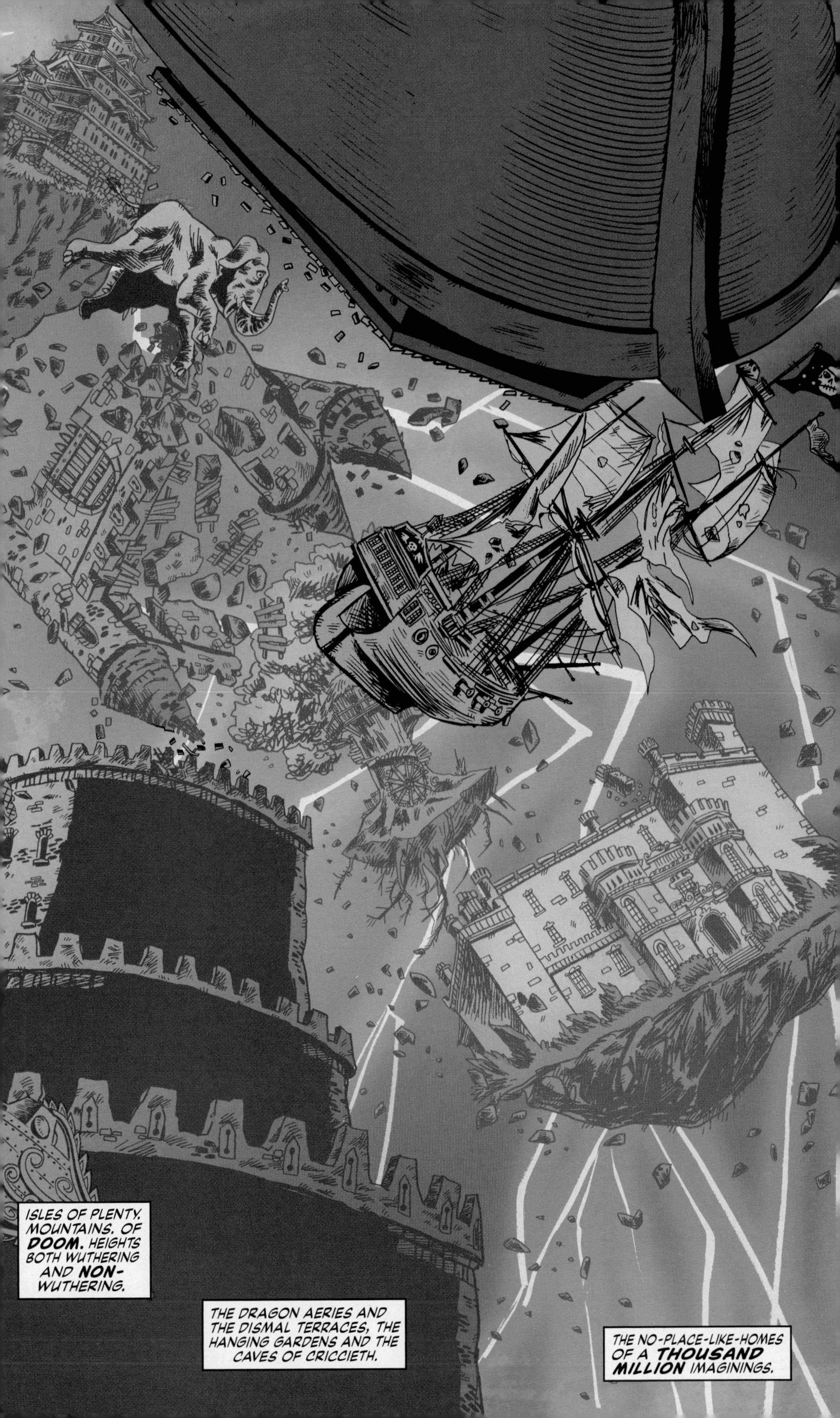
ISLES OF PLENTY. MOUNTAINS. OF **DOOM.** HEIGHTS BOTH WUTHERING AND **NON-** WUTHERING.
THE DRAGON AERIES AND THE DISMAL TERRACES, THE HANGING GARDENS AND THE CAVES OF CRICCIETH.
THE NO-PLACE-LIKE-HOMES OF A **THOUSAND MILLION** IMAGININGS.

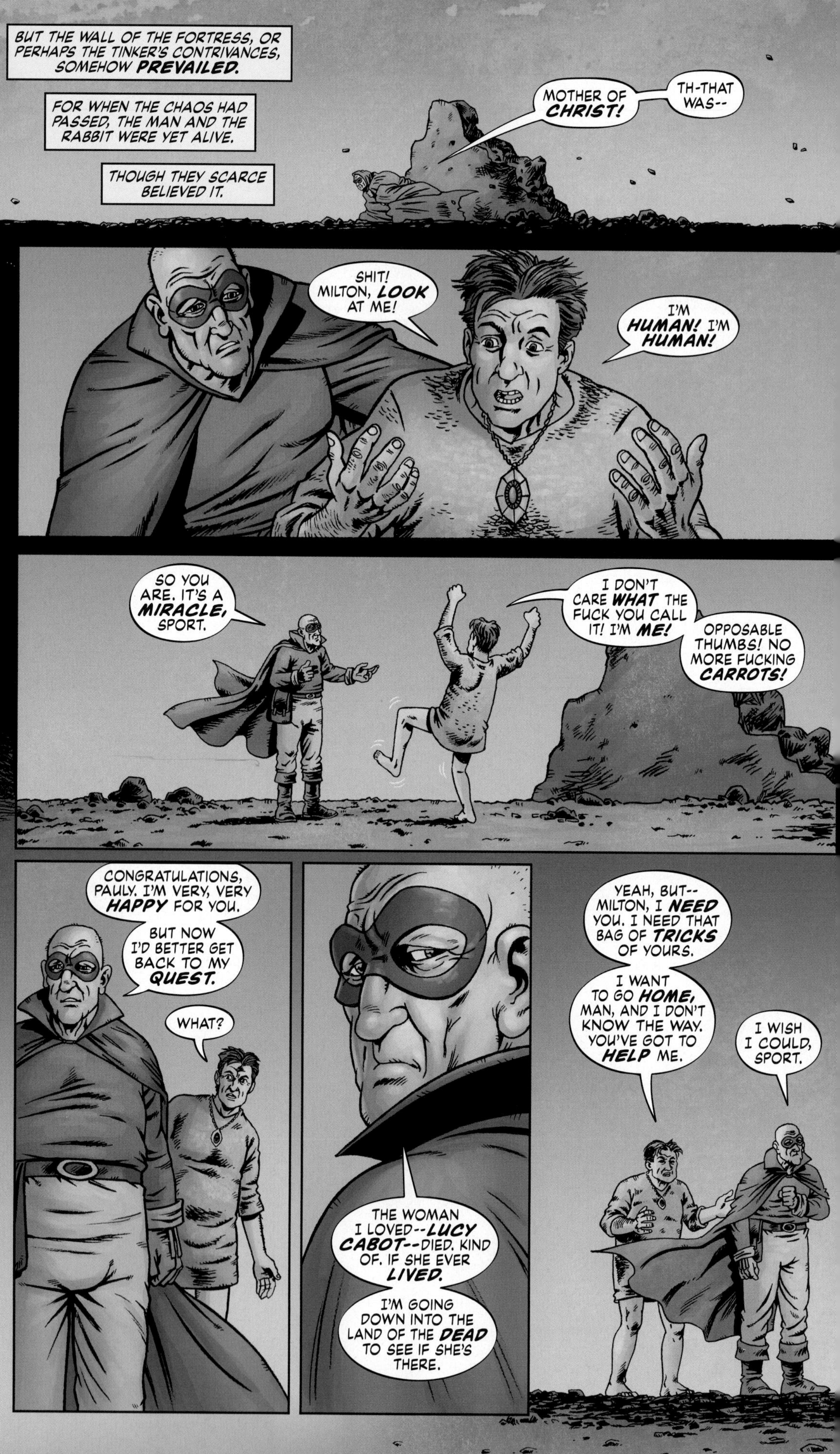
BUT THE WALL OF THE FORTRESS, OR PERHAPS THE TINKER'S CONTRIVANCES, SOMEHOW PREVAILED.
FOR WHEN THE CHAOS HAD PASSED, THE MAN AND THE RABBIT WERE YET ALIVE.
THOUGH THEY SCARCE BELIEVED IT.
MOTHER OF CHRIST!
TH-THAT WAS--
SHIT! MILTON, LOOK AT ME!
I'M HUMAN! I'M HUMAN!
SO YOU ARE. IT'S A MIRACLE, SPORT.
I DON'T CARE WHAT THE FUCK YOU CALL IT! I'M ME!
OPPOSABLE THUMBS! NO MORE FUCKING CARROTS!
CONGRATULATIONS, PAULY. I'M VERY, VERY HAPPY FOR YOU.
BUT NOW I'D BETTER GET BACK TO MY QUEST.
WHAT?
THE WOMAN I LOVED--LUCY CABOT--DIED. KIND OF. IF SHE EVER LIVED.
I'M GOING DOWN INTO THE LAND OF THE DEAD TO SEE IF SHE'S THERE.
YEAH, BUT-- MILTON, I NEED YOU. I NEED THAT BAG OF TRICKS OF YOURS.
I WANT TO GO HOME, MAN, AND I DON'T KNOW THE WAY. YOU'VE GOT TO HELP ME.
I WISH I COULD, SPORT.

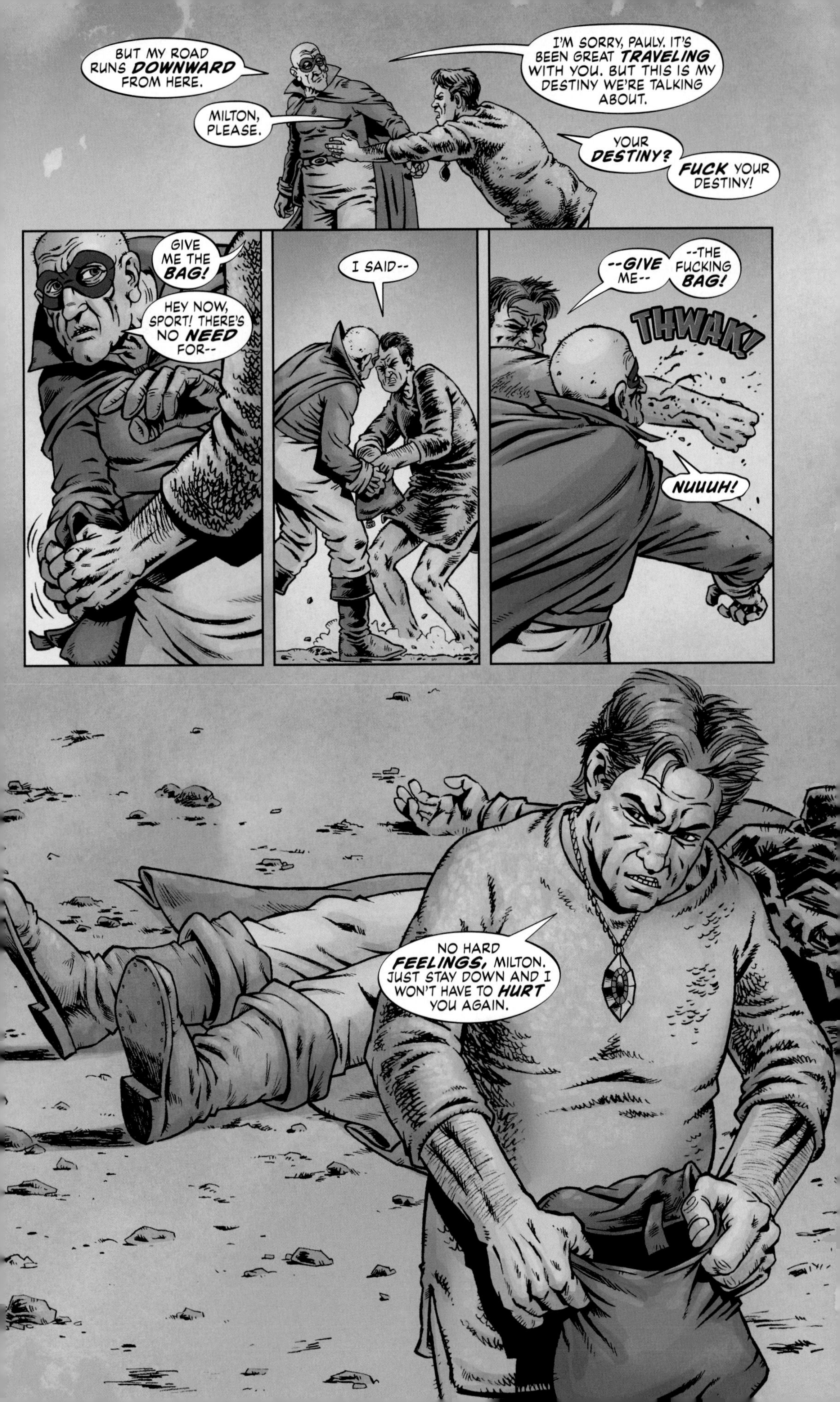
BUT MY ROAD RUNS DOWNWARD FROM HERE.
I'M SORRY, PAULY. IT'S BEEN GREAT TRAVELING WITH YOU. BUT THIS IS MY DESTINY WE'RE TALKING ABOUT.
MILTON, PLEASE.
YOUR DESTINY?
FUCK YOUR DESTINY!
GIVE ME THE BAG!
HEY NOW, SPORT! THERE'S NO NEED FOR--
I SAID--
--GIVE ME--
--THE FUCKING BAG!
THWAK!
NUUUH!
NO HARD FEELINGS, MILTON. JUST STAY DOWN AND I WON'T HAVE TO HURT YOU AGAIN.

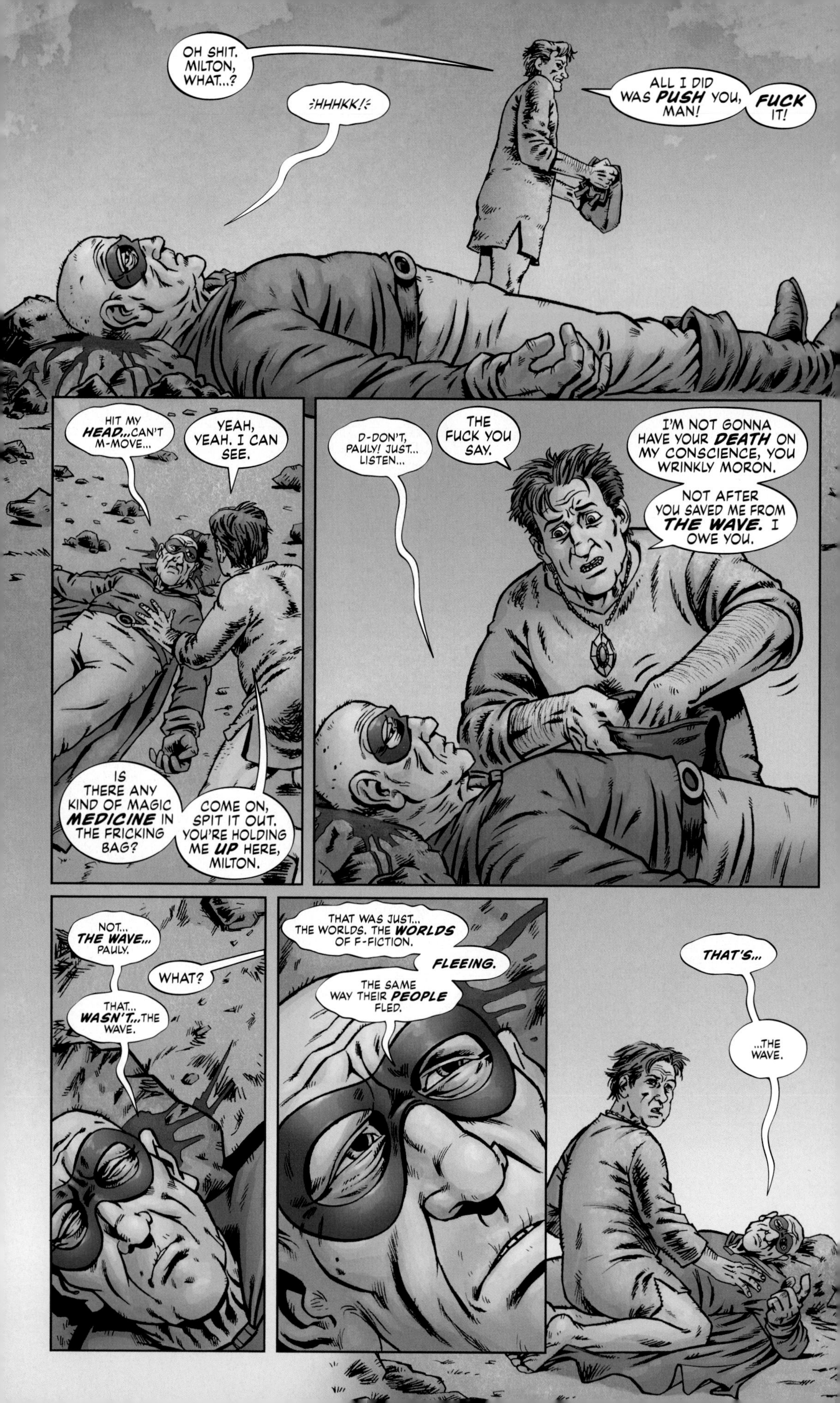
OH SHIT. MILTON, WHAT...?
ALL I DID WAS PUSH YOU, MAN!
FUCK IT!
:HHHKK!:
HIT MY HEAD... CAN'T M-MOVE...
YEAH, YEAH. I CAN SEE.
IS THERE ANY KIND OF MAGIC MEDICINE IN THE FRICKING BAG?
COME ON, SPIT IT OUT. YOU'RE HOLDING ME UP HERE, MILTON.
D-DON'T, PAULY! JUST... LISTEN...
THE FUCK YOU SAY.
I'M NOT GONNA HAVE YOUR DEATH ON MY CONSCIENCE, YOU WRINKLY MORON.
NOT AFTER YOU SAVED ME FROM THE WAVE. I OWE YOU.
NOT... THE WAVE... PAULY.
WHAT?
THAT... WASN'T... THE WAVE.
THAT WAS JUST... THE WORLDS. THE WORLDS OF F-FICTION.
FLEEING.
THE SAME WAY THEIR PEOPLE FLED.
THAT'S...
...THE WAVE.

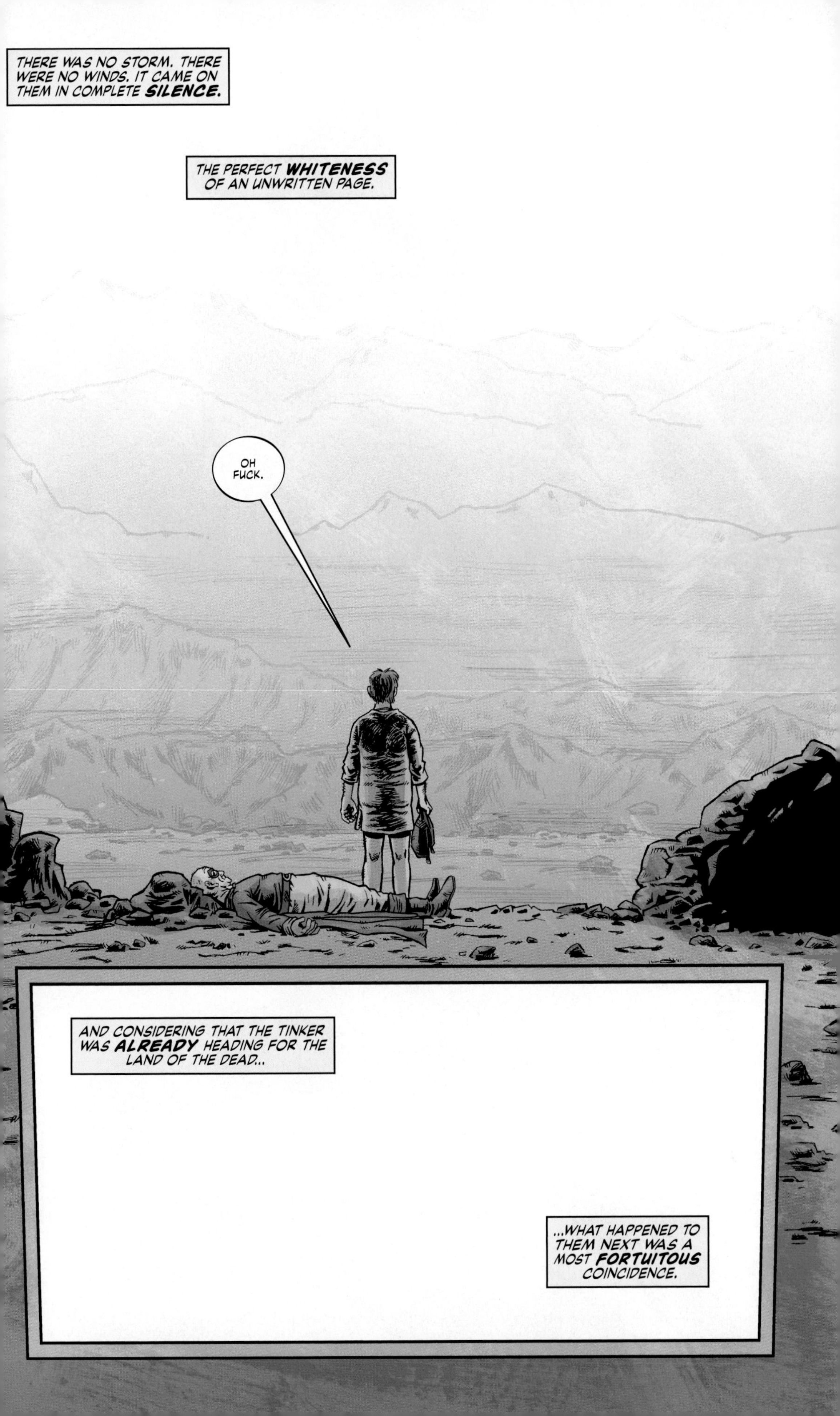
THERE WAS NO STORM. THERE WERE NO WINDS. IT CAME ON THEM IN COMPLETE **SILENCE.**
THE PERFECT **WHITENESS** OF AN UNWRITTEN PAGE.
OH FUCK.
AND CONSIDERING THAT THE TINKER WAS **ALREADY** HEADING FOR THE LAND OF THE DEAD...
...WHAT HAPPENED TO THEM NEXT WAS A MOST **FORTUITOUS** COINCIDENCE.

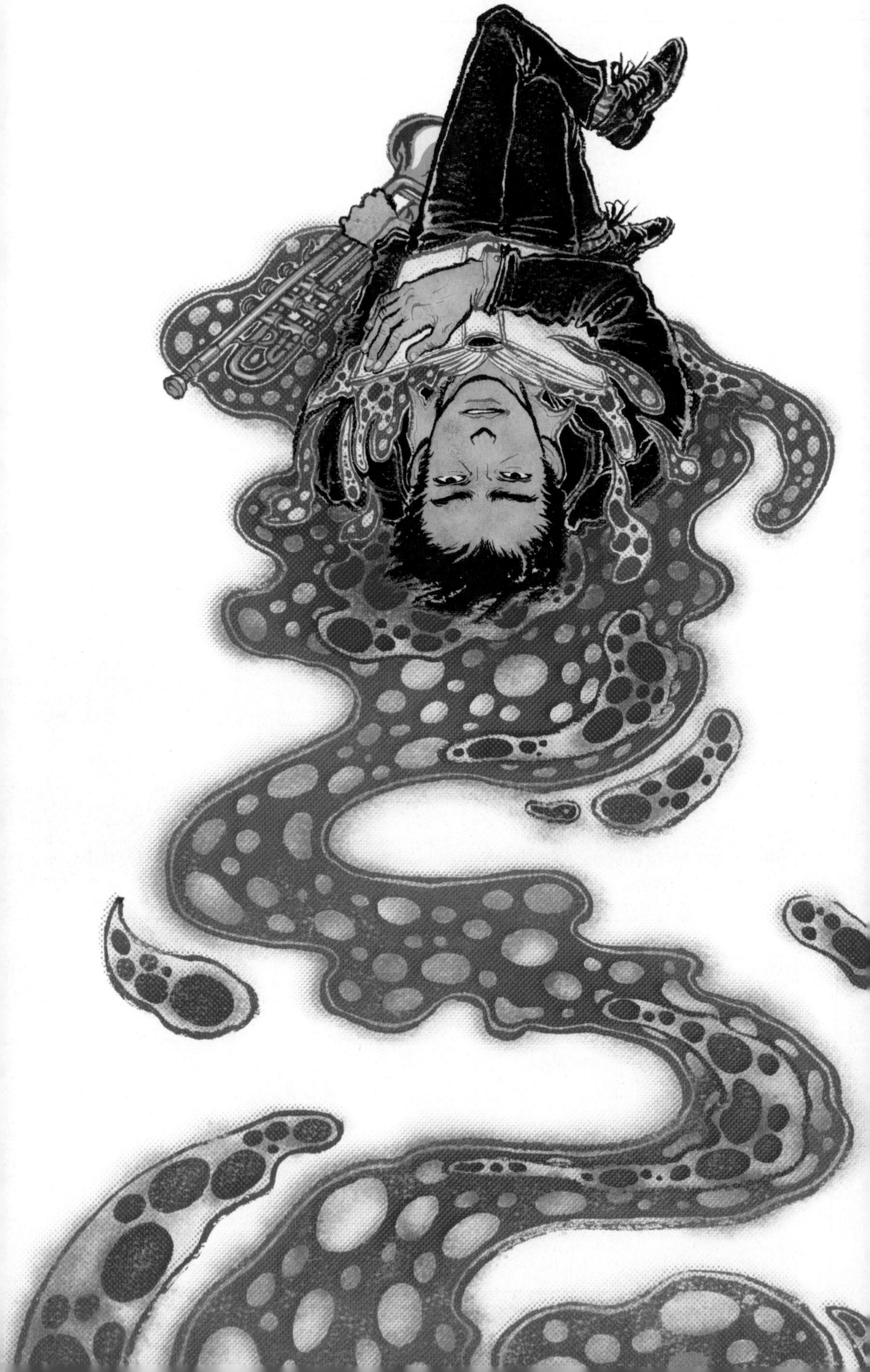

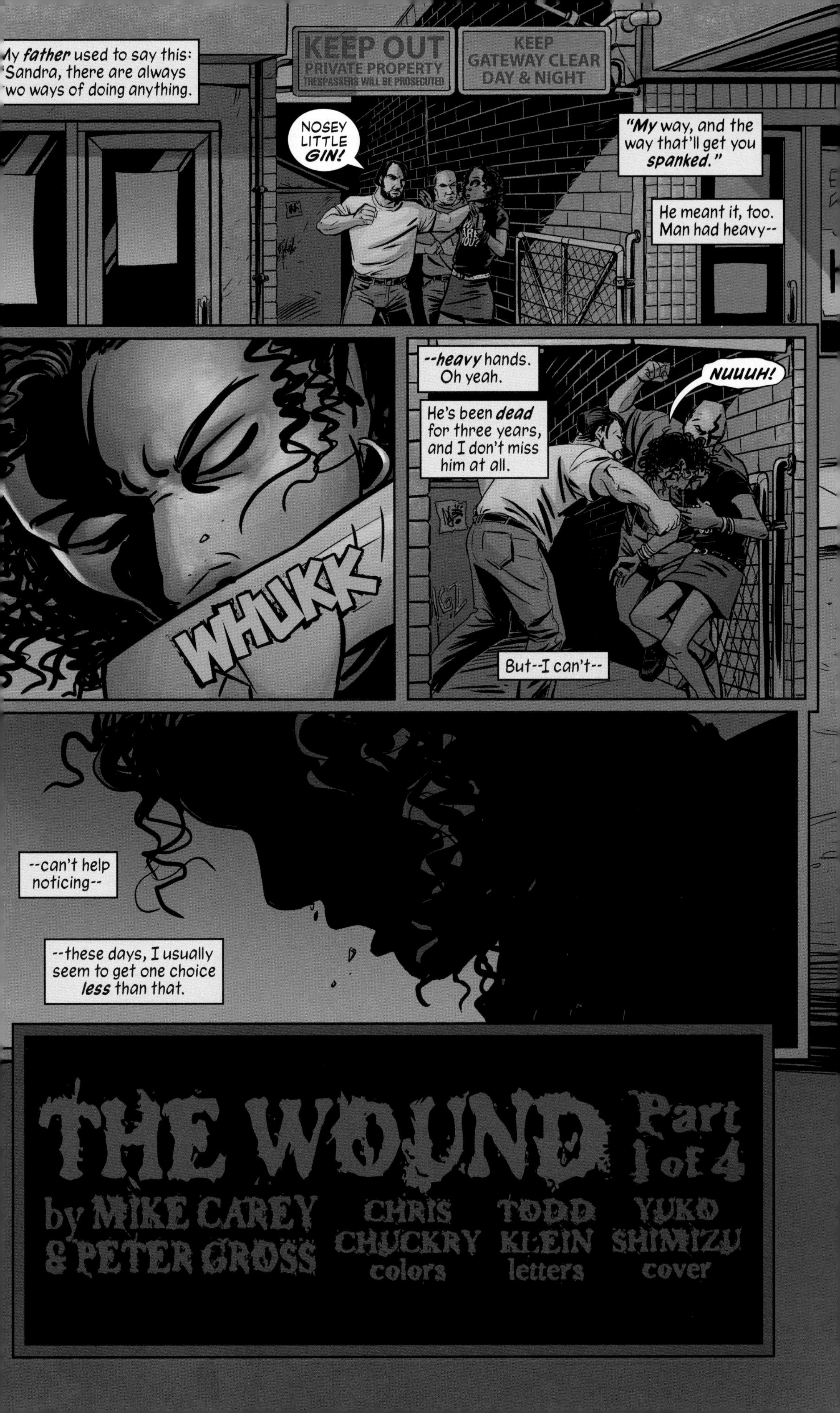
My father used to say this: Sandra, there are always two ways of doing anything.
KEEP OUT
PRIVATE PROPERTY
TRESPASSERS WILL BE PROSECUTED
KEEP
GATEWAY CLEAR
DAY & NIGHT
NOSEY LITTLE GIN!
"My way, and the way that'll get you spanked."
He meant it, too. Man had heavy--
WHUKK
--heavy hands. Oh yeah.
NUUUH!
He's been dead for three years, and I don't miss him at all.
But--I can't--
--can't help noticing--
--these days, I usually seem to get one choice less than that.
THE WOUND Part 1 of 4
by MIKE CAREY & PETER GROSS
CHRIS CHUCKRY colors
TODD KLEIN letters
YUKO SHIMIZU cover

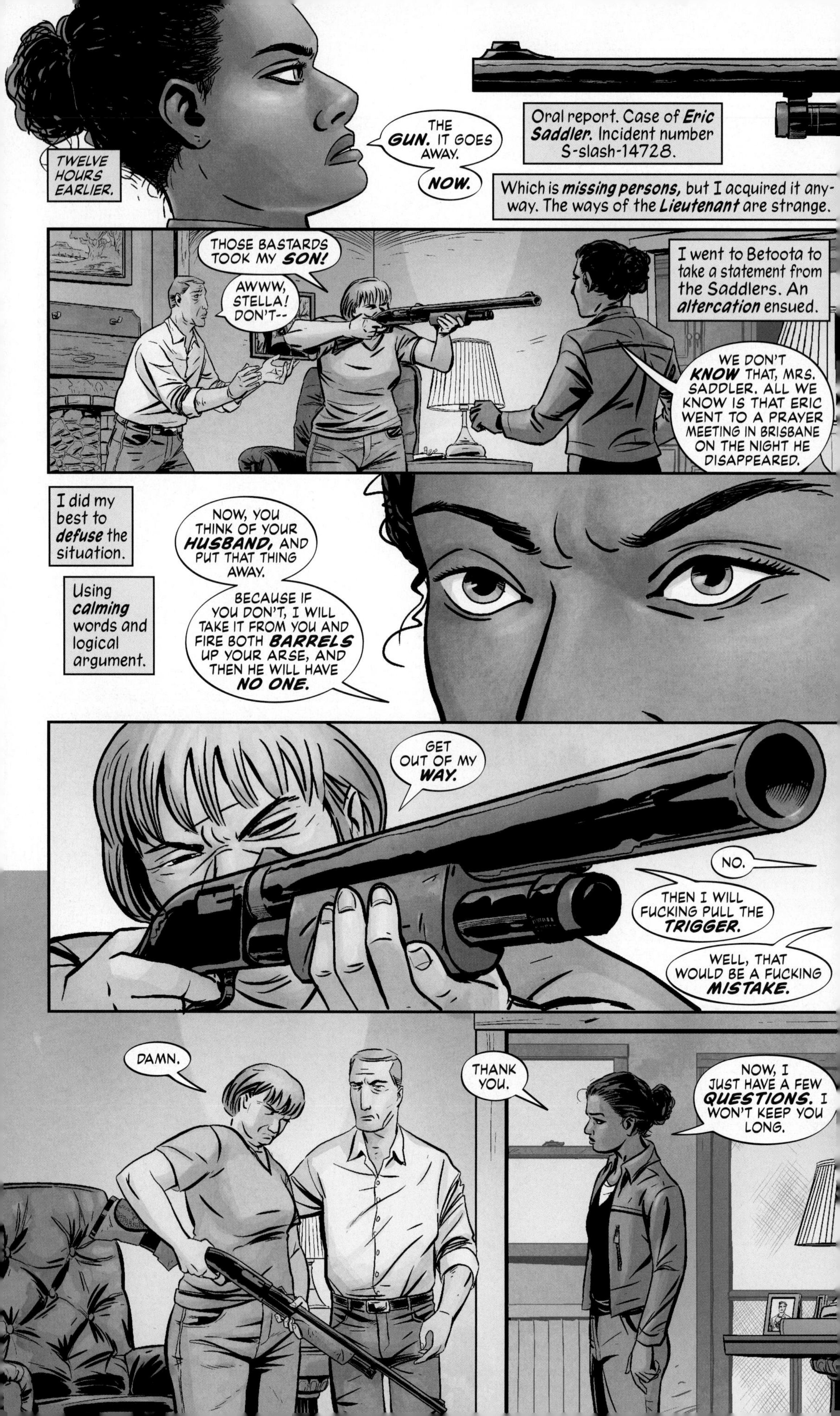
TWELVE HOURS EARLIER.
THE GUN. IT GOES AWAY.
NOW.
Oral report. Case of Eric Saddler. Incident number S-slash-14728.
Which is missing persons, but I acquired it anyway. The ways of the Lieutenant are strange.
THOSE BASTARDS TOOK MY SON!
AWWW, STELLA! DON'T--
I went to Betoota to take a statement from the Saddlers. An altercation ensued.
WE DON'T KNOW THAT, MRS. SADDLER. ALL WE KNOW IS THAT ERIC WENT TO A PRAYER MEETING IN BRISBANE ON THE NIGHT HE DISAPPEARED.
I did my best to defuse the situation.
Using calming words and logical argument.
NOW, YOU THINK OF YOUR HUSBAND, AND PUT THAT THING AWAY.
BECAUSE IF YOU DON'T, I WILL TAKE IT FROM YOU AND FIRE BOTH BARRELS UP YOUR ARSE, AND THEN HE WILL HAVE NO ONE.
GET OUT OF MY WAY.
NO.
THEN I WILL FUCKING PULL THE TRIGGER.
WELL, THAT WOULD BE A FUCKING MISTAKE.
DAMN.
THANK YOU.
NOW, I JUST HAVE A FEW QUESTIONS. I WON'T KEEP YOU LONG.

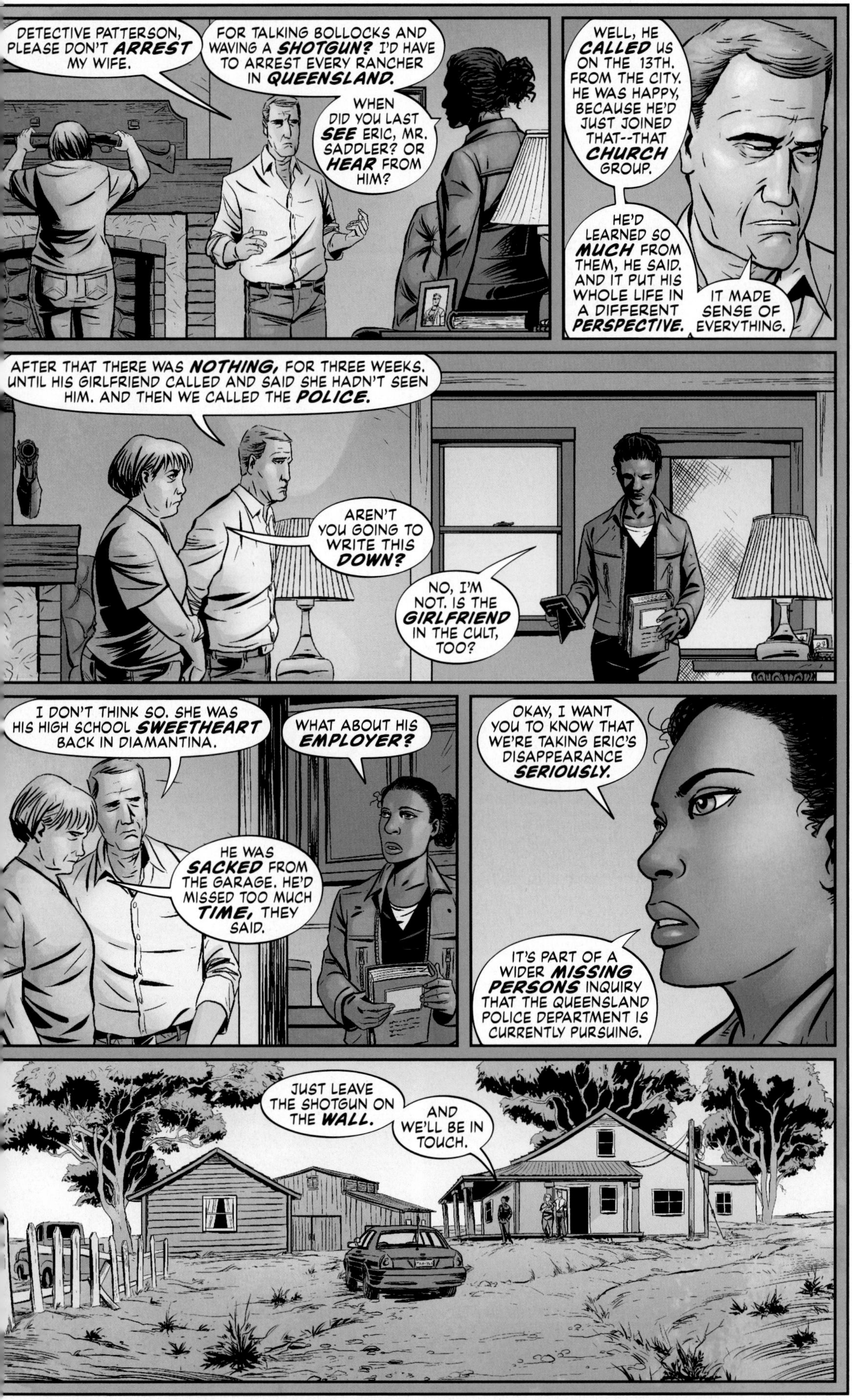
DETECTIVE PATTERSON, PLEASE DON'T ARREST MY WIFE.
FOR TALKING BOLLOCKS AND WAVING A SHOTGUN? I'D HAVE TO ARREST EVERY RANCHER IN QUEENSLAND.
WHEN DID YOU LAST SEE ERIC, MR. SADDLER? OR HEAR FROM HIM?
WELL, HE CALLED US ON THE 13TH. FROM THE CITY. HE WAS HAPPY, BECAUSE HE'D JUST JOINED THAT--THAT CHURCH GROUP.
HE'D LEARNED SO MUCH FROM THEM, HE SAID. AND IT PUT HIS WHOLE LIFE IN A DIFFERENT PERSPECTIVE.
IT MADE SENSE OF EVERYTHING.
AFTER THAT THERE WAS NOTHING, FOR THREE WEEKS. UNTIL HIS GIRLFRIEND CALLED AND SAID SHE HADN'T SEEN HIM. AND THEN WE CALLED THE POLICE.
AREN'T YOU GOING TO WRITE THIS DOWN?
NO, I'M NOT. IS THE GIRLFRIEND IN THE CULT, TOO?
I DON'T THINK SO. SHE WAS HIS HIGH SCHOOL SWEETHEART BACK IN DIAMANTINA.
WHAT ABOUT HIS EMPLOYER?
HE WAS SACKED FROM THE GARAGE. HE'D MISSED TOO MUCH TIME, THEY SAID.
OKAY, I WANT YOU TO KNOW THAT WE'RE TAKING ERIC'S DISAPPEARANCE SERIOUSLY.
IT'S PART OF A WIDER MISSING PERSONS INQUIRY THAT THE QUEENSLAND POLICE DEPARTMENT IS CURRENTLY PURSUING.
JUST LEAVE THE SHOTGUN ON THE WALL.
AND WE'LL BE IN TOUCH.

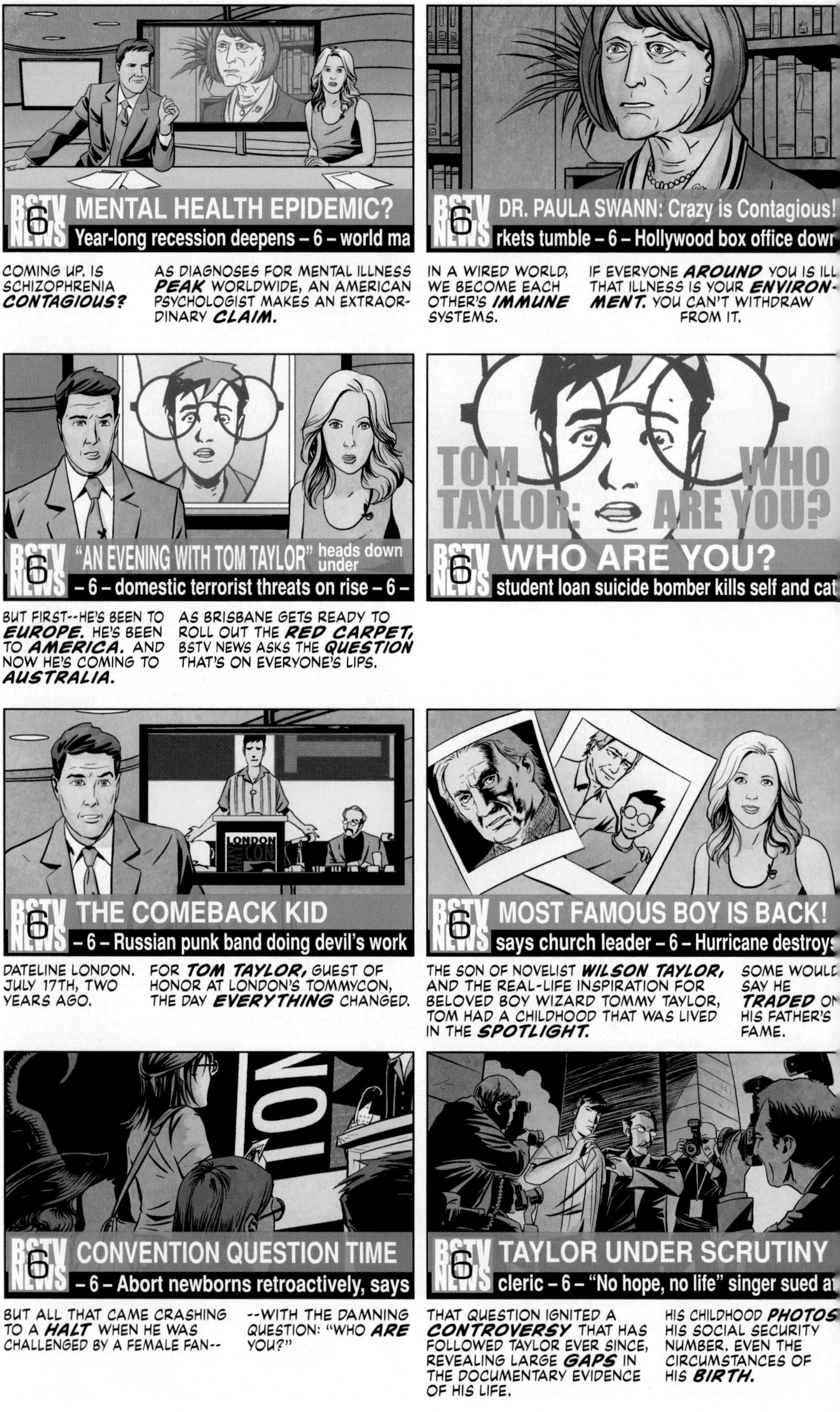
BSTV NEWS 6
MENTAL HEALTH EPIDEMIC?
Year-long recession deepens – 6 – world ma
COMING UP. IS SCHIZOPHRENIA CONTAGIOUS?
AS DIAGNOSES FOR MENTAL ILLNESS PEAK WORLDWIDE, AN AMERICAN PSYCHOLOGIST MAKES AN EXTRAORDINARY CLAIM.
BSTV NEWS 6
DR. PAULA SWANN: Crazy is Contagious!
rkets tumble – 6 – Hollywood box office down
IN A WIRED WORLD, WE BECOME EACH OTHER'S IMMUNE SYSTEMS.
IF EVERYONE AROUND YOU IS ILL THAT ILLNESS IS YOUR ENVIRONMENT. YOU CAN'T WITHDRAW FROM IT.
BSTV NEWS 6
"AN EVENING WITH TOM TAYLOR" heads down under
– 6 – domestic terrorist threats on rise – 6 –
BUT FIRST--HE'S BEEN TO EUROPE. HE'S BEEN TO AMERICA. AND NOW HE'S COMING TO AUSTRALIA.
AS BRISBANE GETS READY TO ROLL OUT THE RED CARPET, BSTV NEWS ASKS THE QUESTION THAT'S ON EVERYONE'S LIPS.
TOM TAYLOR: WHO ARE YOU?
BSTV NEWS 6
WHO ARE YOU?
student loan suicide bomber kills self and cat
BSTV NEWS 6
LONDON
THE COMEBACK KID
– 6 – Russian punk band doing devil's work
DATELINE LONDON. JULY 17TH, TWO YEARS AGO.
FOR TOM TAYLOR, GUEST OF HONOR AT LONDON'S TOMMYCON, THE DAY EVERYTHING CHANGED.
BSTV NEWS 6
MOST FAMOUS BOY IS BACK!
says church leader – 6 – Hurricane destroys
THE SON OF NOVELIST WILSON TAYLOR, AND THE REAL-LIFE INSPIRATION FOR BELOVED BOY WIZARD TOMMY TAYLOR, TOM HAD A CHILDHOOD THAT WAS LIVED IN THE SPOTLIGHT.
SOME WOULD SAY HE TRADED ON HIS FATHER'S FAME.
BSTV NEWS 6
CONVENTION QUESTION TIME
– 6 – Abort newborns retroactively, says
BUT ALL THAT CAME CRASHING TO A HALT WHEN HE WAS CHALLENGED BY A FEMALE FAN--
--WITH THE DAMNING QUESTION: "WHO ARE YOU?"
BSTV NEWS 6
TAYLOR UNDER SCRUTINY
cleric – 6 – "No hope, no life" singer sued a
THAT QUESTION IGNITED A CONTROVERSY THAT HAS FOLLOWED TAYLOR EVER SINCE, REVEALING LARGE GAPS IN THE DOCUMENTARY EVIDENCE OF HIS LIFE.
HIS CHILDHOOD PHOTOS HIS SOCIAL SECURITY NUMBER. EVEN THE CIRCUMSTANCES OF HIS BIRTH.

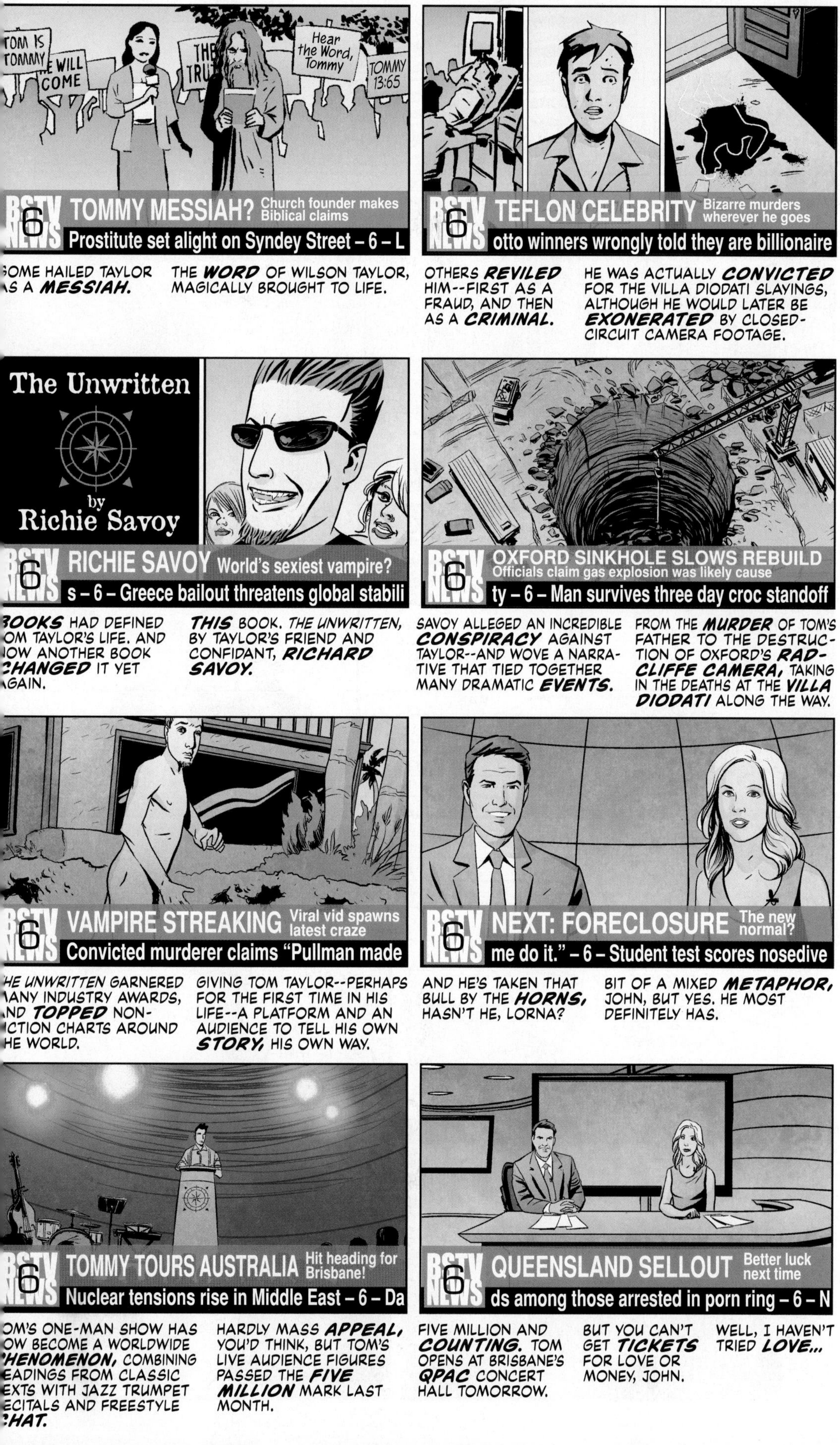

TOM IS TOMMY
WILL COME
THE TRU
Hear the Word, Tommy
TOMMY 13:65
BSTV NEWS 6
TOMMY MESSIAH? Church founder makes Biblical claims
Prostitute set alight on Syndey Street – 6 – L
OME HAILED TAYLOR S A MESSIAH.
THE WORD OF WILSON TAYLOR, MAGICALLY BROUGHT TO LIFE.
BSTV NEWS 6
TEFLON CELEBRITY Bizarre murders wherever he goes
otto winners wrongly told they are billionaire
OTHERS REVILED HIM--FIRST AS A FRAUD, AND THEN AS A CRIMINAL.
HE WAS ACTUALLY CONVICTED FOR THE VILLA DIODATI SLAYINGS, ALTHOUGH HE WOULD LATER BE EXONERATED BY CLOSED-CIRCUIT CAMERA FOOTAGE.
The Unwritten
by Richie Savoy
BSTV NEWS 6
RICHIE SAVOY World's sexiest vampire?
s – 6 – Greece bailout threatens global stabili
OOKS HAD DEFINED OM TAYLOR'S LIFE. AND OW ANOTHER BOOK HANGED IT YET GAIN.
THIS BOOK. THE UNWRITTEN, BY TAYLOR'S FRIEND AND CONFIDANT, RICHARD SAVOY.
BSTV NEWS 6
OXFORD SINKHOLE SLOWS REBUILD
Officials claim gas explosion was likely cause
ty – 6 – Man survives three day croc standoff
SAVOY ALLEGED AN INCREDIBLE CONSPIRACY AGAINST TAYLOR--AND WOVE A NARRATIVE THAT TIED TOGETHER MANY DRAMATIC EVENTS.
FROM THE MURDER OF TOM'S FATHER TO THE DESTRUCTION OF OXFORD'S RADCLIFFE CAMERA, TAKING IN THE DEATHS AT THE VILLA DIODATI ALONG THE WAY.
BSTV NEWS 6
VAMPIRE STREAKING Viral vid spawns latest craze
Convicted murderer claims "Pullman made
HE UNWRITTEN GARNERED ANY INDUSTRY AWARDS, ND TOPPED NON-ICTION CHARTS AROUND HE WORLD.
GIVING TOM TAYLOR--PERHAPS FOR THE FIRST TIME IN HIS LIFE--A PLATFORM AND AN AUDIENCE TO TELL HIS OWN STORY, HIS OWN WAY.
BSTV NEWS 6
NEXT: FORECLOSURE The new normal?
me do it." – 6 – Student test scores nosedive
AND HE'S TAKEN THAT BULL BY THE HORNS, HASN'T HE, LORNA?
BIT OF A MIXED METAPHOR, JOHN, BUT YES. HE MOST DEFINITELY HAS.
BSTV NEWS 6
TOMMY TOURS AUSTRALIA Hit heading for Brisbane!
Nuclear tensions rise in Middle East – 6 – Da
OM'S ONE-MAN SHOW HAS OW BECOME A WORLDWIDE HENOMENON, COMBINING EADINGS FROM CLASSIC EXTS WITH JAZZ TRUMPET ECITALS AND FREESTYLE HAT.
HARDLY MASS APPEAL, YOU'D THINK, BUT TOM'S LIVE AUDIENCE FIGURES PASSED THE FIVE MILLION MARK LAST MONTH.
BSTV NEWS 6
QUEENSLAND SELLOUT Better luck next time
ds among those arrested in porn ring – 6 – N
FIVE MILLION AND COUNTING. TOM OPENS AT BRISBANE'S QPAC CONCERT HALL TOMORROW.
BUT YOU CAN'T GET TICKETS FOR LOVE OR MONEY, JOHN.
WELL, I HAVEN'T TRIED LOVE...

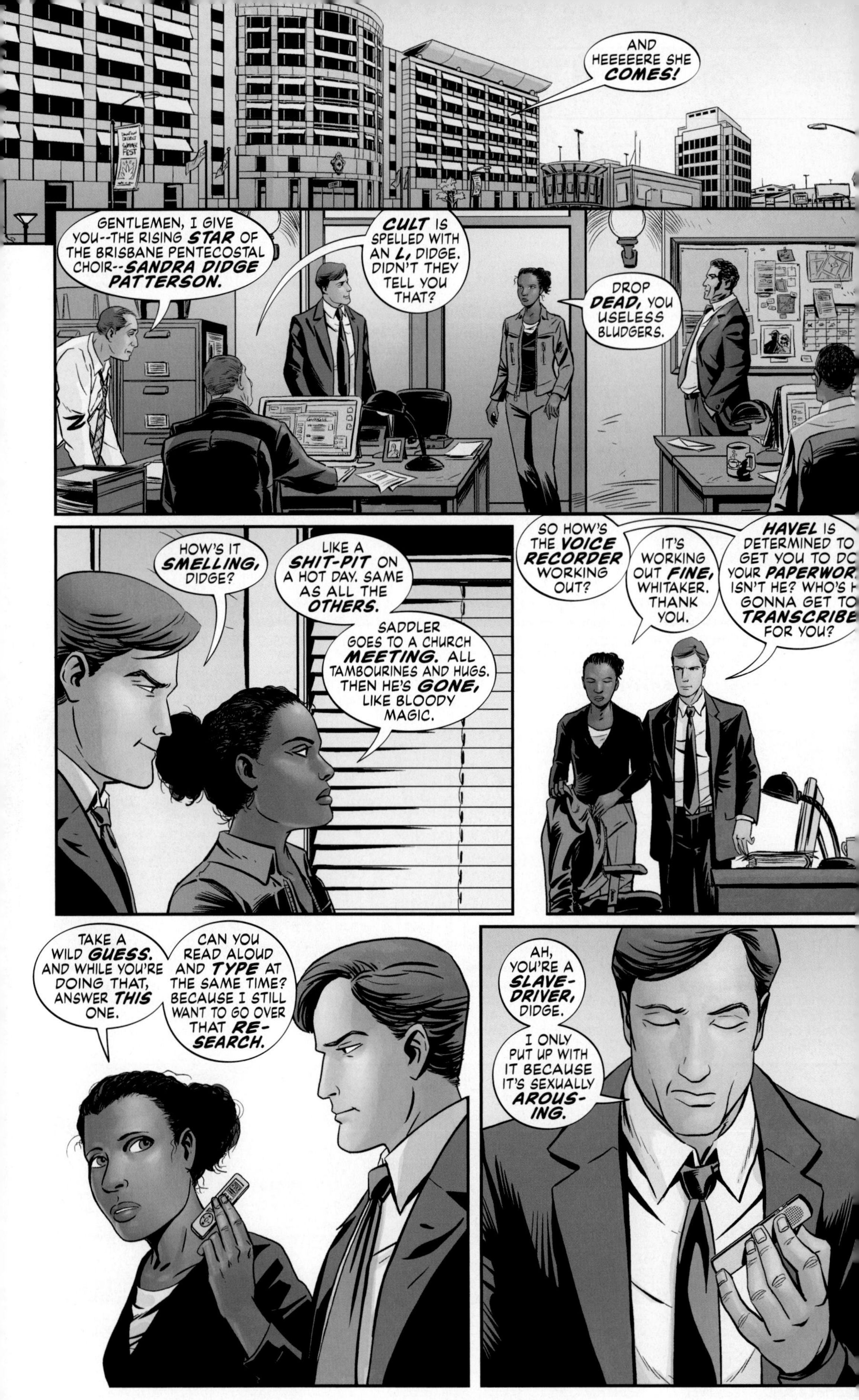

AND HEEEEEERE SHE COMES!
GENTLEMEN, I GIVE YOU--THE RISING STAR OF THE BRISBANE PENTECOSTAL CHOIR--SANDRA DIDGE PATTERSON.
CULT IS SPELLED WITH AN L, DIDGE. DIDN'T THEY TELL YOU THAT?
DROP DEAD, YOU USELESS BLUDGERS.
HOW'S IT SMELLING, DIDGE?
LIKE A SHIT-PIT ON A HOT DAY. SAME AS ALL THE OTHERS.
SADDLER GOES TO A CHURCH MEETING. ALL TAMBOURINES AND HUGS. THEN HE'S GONE, LIKE BLOODY MAGIC.
SO HOW'S THE VOICE RECORDER WORKING OUT?
IT'S WORKING OUT FINE, WHITAKER. THANK YOU.
TAKE A WILD GUESS. AND WHILE YOU'RE DOING THAT, ANSWER THIS ONE.
CAN YOU READ ALOUD AND TYPE AT THE SAME TIME? BECAUSE I STILL WANT TO GO OVER THAT RE-SEARCH.
AH, YOU'RE A SLAVE-DRIVER, DIDGE.
I ONLY PUT UP WITH IT BECAUSE IT'S SEXUALLY AROUS-ING.

Church of Tommy

...s of
...UTH
...onials
...ed Quotes
...gs
...gs
...ers
...s

...d money to
the word!
...ant to help,
...ur
...end!

...dFriend

NO MORE UNHAPPY ENDINGS!!!

The fool has said in his heart, not just that there's no god but that there's no point. No meaning. No sense in anything.

SUICIDE BOMBINGS!
WARS IN THE MIDDLE EAST!
RAPE AND MURDER ON THE INCREASE!
OPRESSION AND TYRANNY FROM OUR FEDERAL MASTERS!

There's plenty of unhappiness in the world, and there are times when it seems like the peopl... who should be putting it right are the ones who are actually RESPONSABLE for it.

You feel powerless, and you feel betrayed.

You feel as if nothing good can ever happen to you again.

But if all this was a story, then the pain and the suffering wouldn't matter.

WILSON TAYLOR saw the real world, and he wrote about it. It's a world where magic works, and where the greatest of all wizards, Tommy Taylor, died and was resurrected to bring us a message of peace and love.

If that sounds familiar, we're not supprised. The story of the god who dies and then is returned to life was so powerful that it created echoes through all the other worlds and all through time and all through the traditions of other religions. The first ever resurrected god long, long before Jesus Christ – was the Sumerian god TAMMUZ. Yeah, that name sounds familiar, too, doesn't it?

TAMMUZ = TOMMY

The real world of Tommy retroactively creates worlds in which Tommy is just a story. But it's OUR world that's fictional, and now the cracks are starting to show. When you stop believing in the fiction, you'll wake into the reality. Tommy is already here, to show you it's possable and to show you the way.

cult checklist

Compare statements with those made by the group you or a loved one are involved in to help determine if this involvement is cause for concern.
If you check any of these as characteristic of the group in question, particularly if you check many, you may well be dealing with a cult.

- The group is focused on a living leader to whom members display excessively zealous, unquestiong commitment.

-The group is preoccupied with bringing in new members.

-The group engages in deceptive recruiting practices.

-The group has a closed social system that makes a special effort to isolate members from family, friends, etc.

-The group offers unconditional affirmation and support initially, but soon makes its continuance contingent on obedience.

-The group has eclectic, often muddled and internally contradictory, set of teachings - usually a magic-laden philosophy that claims to have infallible answers to questions of existence.

-The group has a strict behavior code that governs all aspects of how one should think, feel and act.

-Mind-numbing techniques such as chanting, meditation, denunciation sessions or debilitating work routines are used to supress dissent.

-The group has a polarized us/them mentality that causes conflict with the wider society.

-The group is elitist, claiming a special, exalted status for itself, its leaders and members.

-The group's leadership is not accountable to any authorities.

When all else fails, read everything.

HOME | BREAKING NEWS | POLITICS | BUSINESS | WORLD | MEDIA | TECHNOLOGY | ENTER...
ARTS | LIVING | STYLE | VIDEO | BLOGS | LINKS

NEW RELIGION FOR A DESPERATE AGE, SAYS CONTROVERSIAL CLERIC

Lucas Filby, charismatic leader of the so-called Church of Tommy, came out fighting today after a court appearance in which he was accused of illegal distribution of psychotropic drugs in his religious services.

"When an old order passes," Filby told reporters on the steps of Brisbane's Morningside courthouse, "it doesn't always realize that it's dying. In this case, the entire world system that has persisted since capitalism emerged out of feudalism is crumbling, but it pretends not to be."

Filby's sermon – or as some might say, rant – took in a vast agenda of modern ills including mass suicides, record highs in diagnoses for mental illness, the simultaneous decline in book reading, cinema-going and church attendance, and the growning anomie of the young.

"The world is a bad story," he said. "And in a bad story, spectacular effects are shovelled in to make up for deficiencies...

Rolling Rock

MUSIC | POLITICS | CULTURE | REVIEWS | ARTISTS | BLOGS

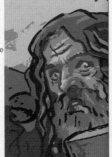

interview

Richie Savoy: The Interview

Page ◂ 4 of 9 ▸

The strangest thing to come out of that period was the suggestion that Tom might be some sort of new messiah--the character from his father's books, brought to life here on earth.
It was a real festival of fuckwits, and Tom was appalled by it. Actually, he was appalled by it twice. First of all, there was the suggestion that he was a fictional character – that in some way he was actually the Tommy of his dad's novels magically come to life. That's hurtful. Even Pinocchio got to be a real boy in the end, but these guys were saying that Tom was just a substantiated rumor.

Then there was the idea that he'd come to save the world. Well, it's nice to have the vote of confidence, of course, but Tom was aware that previous messiahs don't always come too well out of the deal. It's like, once you've got that aura of godliness around you, there's really nowhere to go but down.

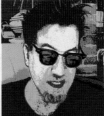

Staying in character as a vampire hasn't exactly hurt your sales, or your sex life, but isn't there also a deeper point about journalism itself? Are we all vampires? Do we believe the story is more important that the truth?
Don't flatter yourself. What I'm doing with the Unwritten is completely different from what you're trying to do here. You're just trying to sell copies. Tom and I are trying to

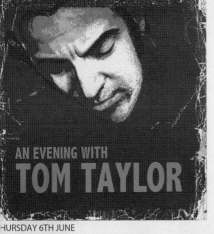

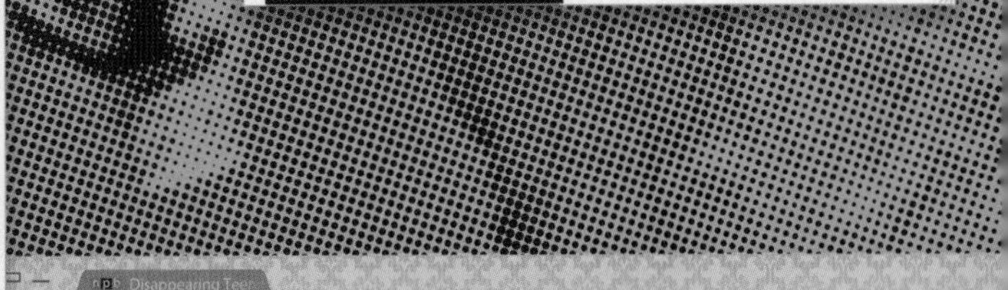

AN EVENING WITH
TOM TAYLOR

...HURSDAY 6TH JUNE
...UEENSLAND PERFORMING ARTS CENTRE

"...Utterly dazzling"
L.A.Times

"...ou won't want to miss this."
The Guardian

"Taylor is actually fun to be with – who knew?"

npb Disappearing Teen...

http://www.npb.org/sections/news/DisappearingTeensBaffleQueenslandOfficials.html

...ional public broadcast

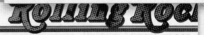

npb news Disappearing Teens Baffle Queensland C...

Berliner Tag - Two...

http://www.BerlinerTag.com/WorldNews/Headlines/TwoMoreQueenslandT...

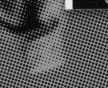

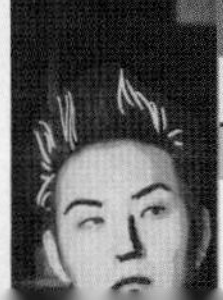

BerlinerTag

WORLD | U.S. | N.Y. / REGION | BUSINESS | TECHNOLOGY | SCIENCE | HEALTH

Two Queensland Tourists Vanish

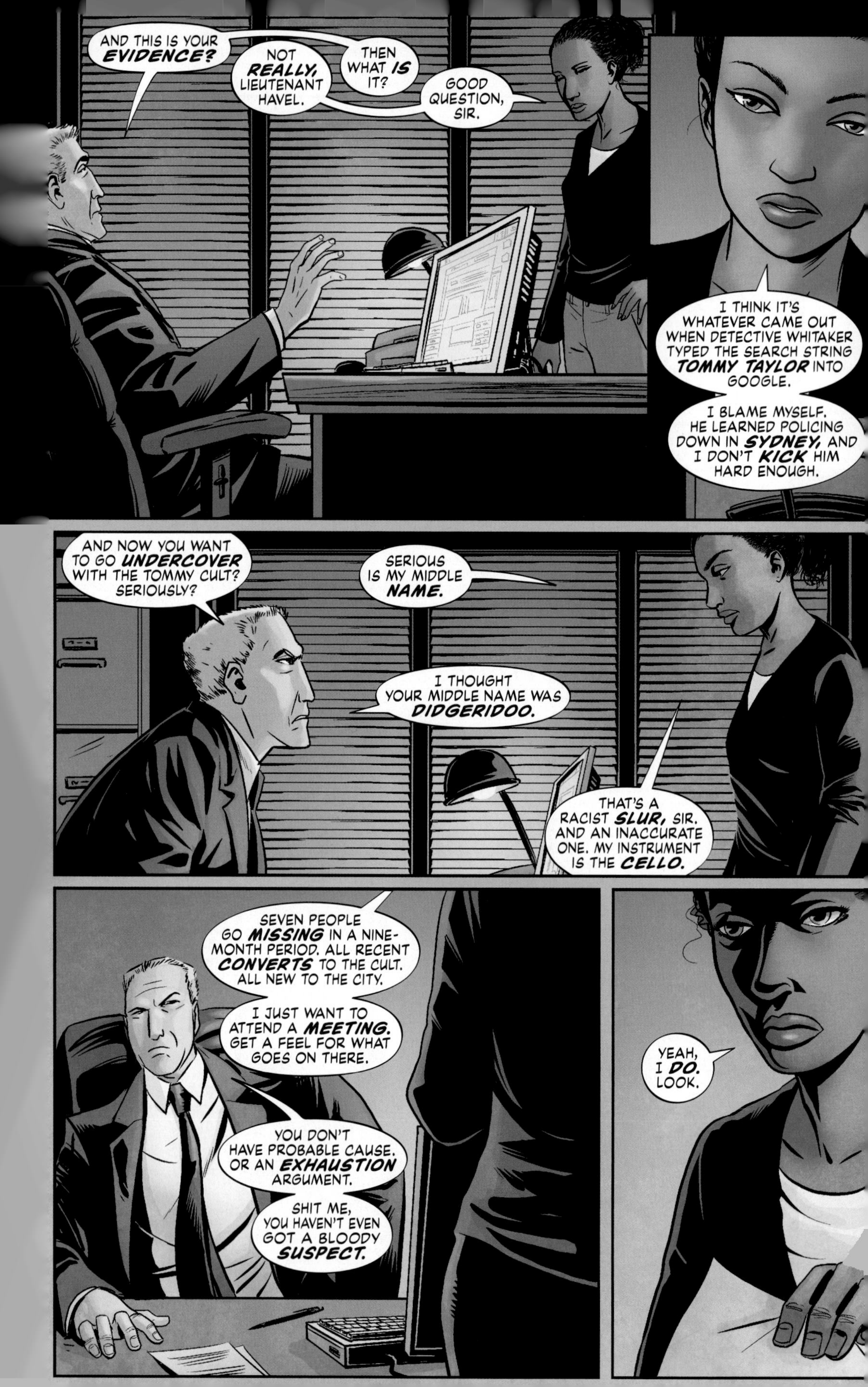
AND THIS IS YOUR EVIDENCE?
NOT REALLY, LIEUTENANT HAVEL.
THEN WHAT IS IT?
GOOD QUESTION, SIR.
I THINK IT'S WHATEVER CAME OUT WHEN DETECTIVE WHITAKER TYPED THE SEARCH STRING TOMMY TAYLOR INTO GOOGLE.
I BLAME MYSELF. HE LEARNED POLICING DOWN IN SYDNEY, AND I DON'T KICK HIM HARD ENOUGH.
AND NOW YOU WANT TO GO UNDERCOVER WITH THE TOMMY CULT? SERIOUSLY?
SERIOUS IS MY MIDDLE NAME.
I THOUGHT YOUR MIDDLE NAME WAS DIDGERIDOO.
THAT'S A RACIST SLUR, SIR. AND AN INACCURATE ONE. MY INSTRUMENT IS THE CELLO.
SEVEN PEOPLE GO MISSING IN A NINE-MONTH PERIOD. ALL RECENT CONVERTS TO THE CULT. ALL NEW TO THE CITY.
I JUST WANT TO ATTEND A MEETING. GET A FEEL FOR WHAT GOES ON THERE.
YOU DON'T HAVE PROBABLE CAUSE. OR AN EXHAUSTION ARGUMENT.
SHIT ME, YOU HAVEN'T EVEN GOT A BLOODY SUSPECT.
YEAH, I DO. LOOK.

Church of Tommy
552 videos
uploaded by: Giabrenna
Church of Tommy

Tom Taylor cult
Subscribe

Australian cult leader, Lucas Filby, claims
Tommy Taylor books are the new Bible.

#ChurchofTommy

Like | Add to | Share | Embed

00:00/7:23   SHARE

887,540

Crazy guy rants about his "new church." At 3:14 you can see where the poor
newslady starts grinding her teeth and wonders when she can wrap up the
interview, but he never lets her get in a word! I love the TT books, but this
guy. is. NUTS. Back away from the Grape-Aid and run, bro.

Tags: crazy, batshit, cult, TommyTaylor, TomTaylor, Kare11News, DNN, interview

All Comments (20,912)
OLZ. Oh he drank the Grape-Aide. He drank ALL the Grape-Aidz!
sted by: PyroIncendiary

st because you don't accept his truth doesn't mean he's wrong. Who's to
r this is any less valid than the story of Jesus?
: by: RimtheSky

l, let's take a look at the EVIDENCE, HMMM? Tom Taylor was DEAD.
A. D. We know this for a FACT. And he's ALIVE now, you think someone
rewed up "DEAD GUY" and this is all COINCIDENCE? You people are
rant. You should try READING the Tommy Taylor books some time.
: DefiantK

ust anyone who's sporting that level of hobobeard. That kind of facial
sn't happen to sane people
inceButler

LUCAS FILBY. FORMER PRESIDENT OF THE AUCKLAND BRANCH OF THE TOMMY TAYLOR FAN CLUB.

CURRENT SPIRITUAL LEADER OF THE **CHURCH OF TOMMY**--WHOSE MEMBERS SCREAM "WHO ARE YOU?" AT **TOM TAYLOR** EVERY TIME HE MAKES A PUBLIC **APPEARANCE.**

CLOSEST THING THEY'VE GOT TO A **PRAYER,** APPARENTLY. UNLESS IT'S MEANT TO BE A **BLESSING.**

Who are ye
ILuvLizzie
314,159 views

BITE ME!!!
Richnesme
2,654 views

Tom Taylor Live
CorrrrgiDan
3,142 views

Cabal Exposed
4thLoneGunman
1,792 views

13:52

Leviathanism
WhaleBOy
994 views

8:07

THIS DAG MET **ALL** OF THEM. EVERYONE WHO WENT MISSING.

HE'S THE COMMON **FACTOR,** SIR. THE ONLY ONE WE'VE BEEN ABLE TO **FIND.**

HE'S ALSO A RELIGIOUS **LEADER.** I'M NOT KEEN TO KICK UP A **BARNEY** WITH A CHURCH. EVEN A CHURCH FULL OF **CRETINS.**

AND I DON'T KNOW IF YOU'RE THE RIGHT PERSON FOR THE **JOB,** DIDGE. NOT WITH YOUR **PROBLEM.**

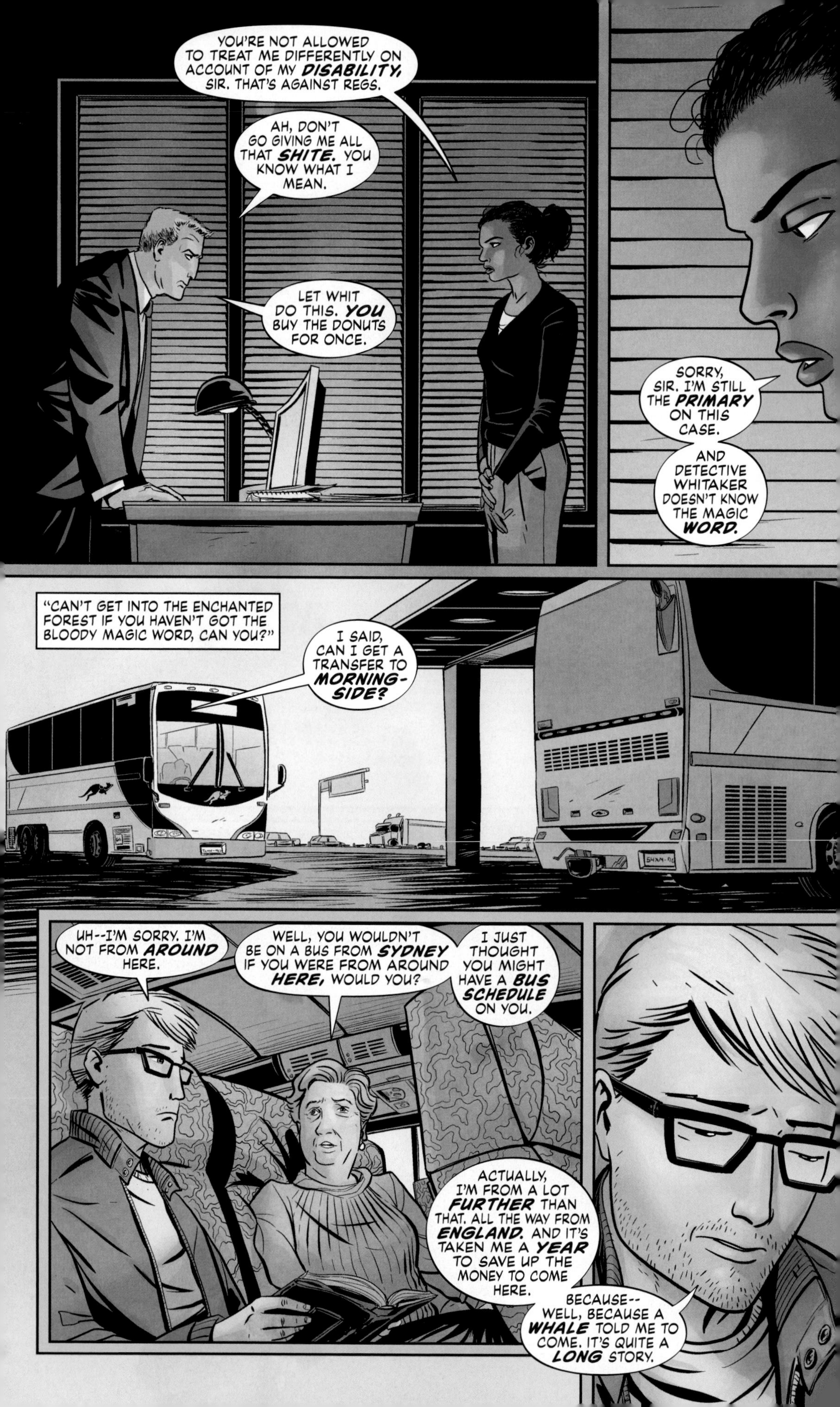
YOU'RE NOT ALLOWED TO TREAT ME DIFFERENTLY ON ACCOUNT OF MY DISABILITY, SIR. THAT'S AGAINST REGS.
AH, DON'T GO GIVING ME ALL THAT SHITE. YOU KNOW WHAT I MEAN.
LET WHIT DO THIS. YOU BUY THE DONUTS FOR ONCE.
SORRY, SIR. I'M STILL THE PRIMARY ON THIS CASE.
AND DETECTIVE WHITAKER DOESN'T KNOW THE MAGIC WORD.
"CAN'T GET INTO THE ENCHANTED FOREST IF YOU HAVEN'T GOT THE BLOODY MAGIC WORD, CAN YOU?"
I SAID, CAN I GET A TRANSFER TO MORNING-SIDE?
UH--I'M SORRY. I'M NOT FROM AROUND HERE.
WELL, YOU WOULDN'T BE ON A BUS FROM SYDNEY IF YOU WERE FROM AROUND HERE, WOULD YOU?
I JUST THOUGHT YOU MIGHT HAVE A BUS SCHEDULE ON YOU.
ACTUALLY, I'M FROM A LOT FURTHER THAN THAT. ALL THE WAY FROM ENGLAND. AND IT'S TAKEN ME A YEAR TO SAVE UP THE MONEY TO COME HERE.
BECAUSE--WELL, BECAUSE A WHALE TOLD ME TO COME. IT'S QUITE A LONG STORY.

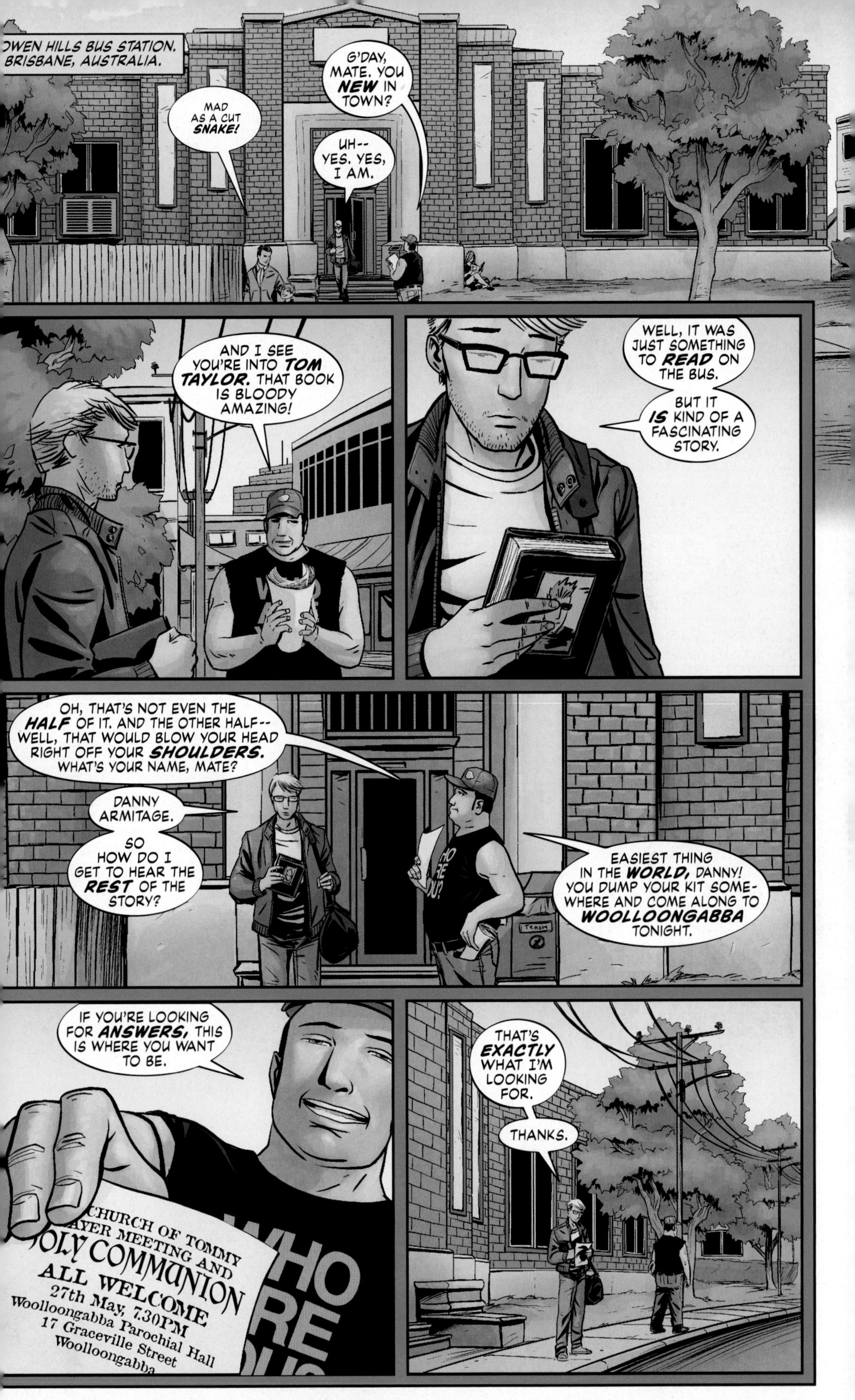
OWEN HILLS BUS STATION. BRISBANE, AUSTRALIA.
G'DAY, MATE. YOU NEW IN TOWN?
MAD AS A CUT SNAKE!
UH-- YES. YES, I AM.
AND I SEE YOU'RE INTO TOM TAYLOR. THAT BOOK IS BLOODY AMAZING!
WELL, IT WAS JUST SOMETHING TO READ ON THE BUS.
BUT IT IS KIND OF A FASCINATING STORY.
OH, THAT'S NOT EVEN THE HALF OF IT. AND THE OTHER HALF-- WELL, THAT WOULD BLOW YOUR HEAD RIGHT OFF YOUR SHOULDERS. WHAT'S YOUR NAME, MATE?
DANNY ARMITAGE.
SO HOW DO I GET TO HEAR THE REST OF THE STORY?
EASIEST THING IN THE WORLD, DANNY! YOU DUMP YOUR KIT SOME-WHERE AND COME ALONG TO WOOLLOONGABBA TONIGHT.
TRASH
IF YOU'RE LOOKING FOR ANSWERS, THIS IS WHERE YOU WANT TO BE.
CHURCH OF TOMMY
AYER MEETING AND
OLY COMMUNION
ALL WELCOME
27th May, 7.30PM
Woolloongabba Parochial Hall
17 Graceville Street
Woolloongabba
THAT'S EXACTLY WHAT I'M LOOKING FOR.
THANKS.

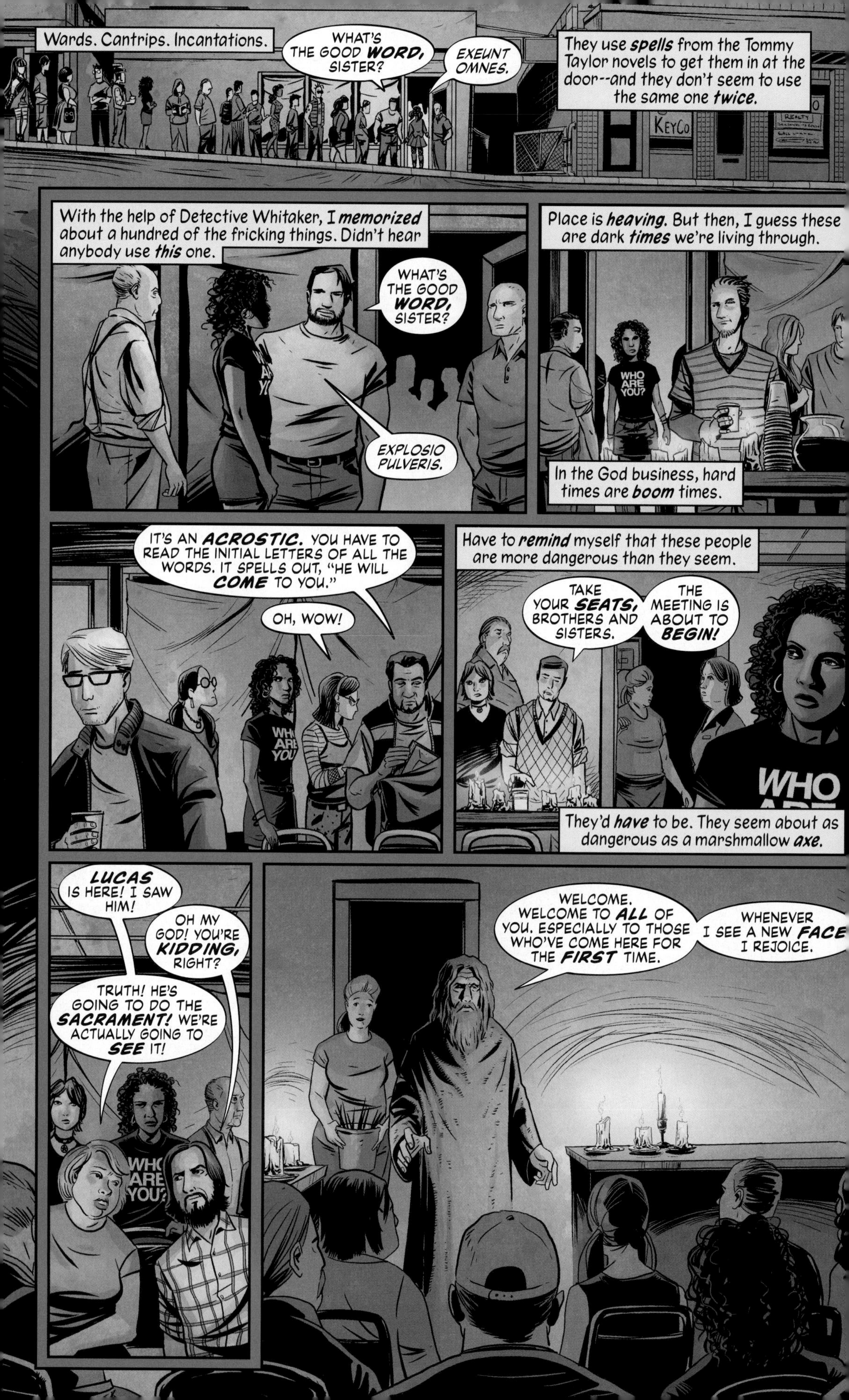
Wards. Cantrips. Incantations.
WHAT'S THE GOOD WORD, SISTER?
EXEUNT OMNES.
They use spells from the Tommy Taylor novels to get them in at the door--and they don't seem to use the same one twice.
KEYCO
REALTY
With the help of Detective Whitaker, I memorized about a hundred of the fricking things. Didn't hear anybody use this one.
WHAT'S THE GOOD WORD, SISTER?
EXPLOSIO PULVERIS.
Place is heaving. But then, I guess these are dark times we're living through.
WHO ARE YOU?
In the God business, hard times are boom times.
IT'S AN ACROSTIC. YOU HAVE TO READ THE INITIAL LETTERS OF ALL THE WORDS. IT SPELLS OUT, "HE WILL COME TO YOU."
OH, WOW!
WHO ARE YOU
Have to remind myself that these people are more dangerous than they seem.
TAKE YOUR SEATS, BROTHERS AND SISTERS.
THE MEETING IS ABOUT TO BEGIN!
WHO
They'd have to be. They seem about as dangerous as a marshmallow axe.
LUCAS IS HERE! I SAW HIM!
OH MY GOD! YOU'RE KIDDING, RIGHT?
TRUTH! HE'S GOING TO DO THE SACRAMENT! WE'RE ACTUALLY GOING TO SEE IT!
WHO ARE YOU?
WELCOME. WELCOME TO ALL OF YOU. ESPECIALLY TO THOSE WHO'VE COME HERE FOR THE FIRST TIME.
WHENEVER I SEE A NEW FACE I REJOICE.

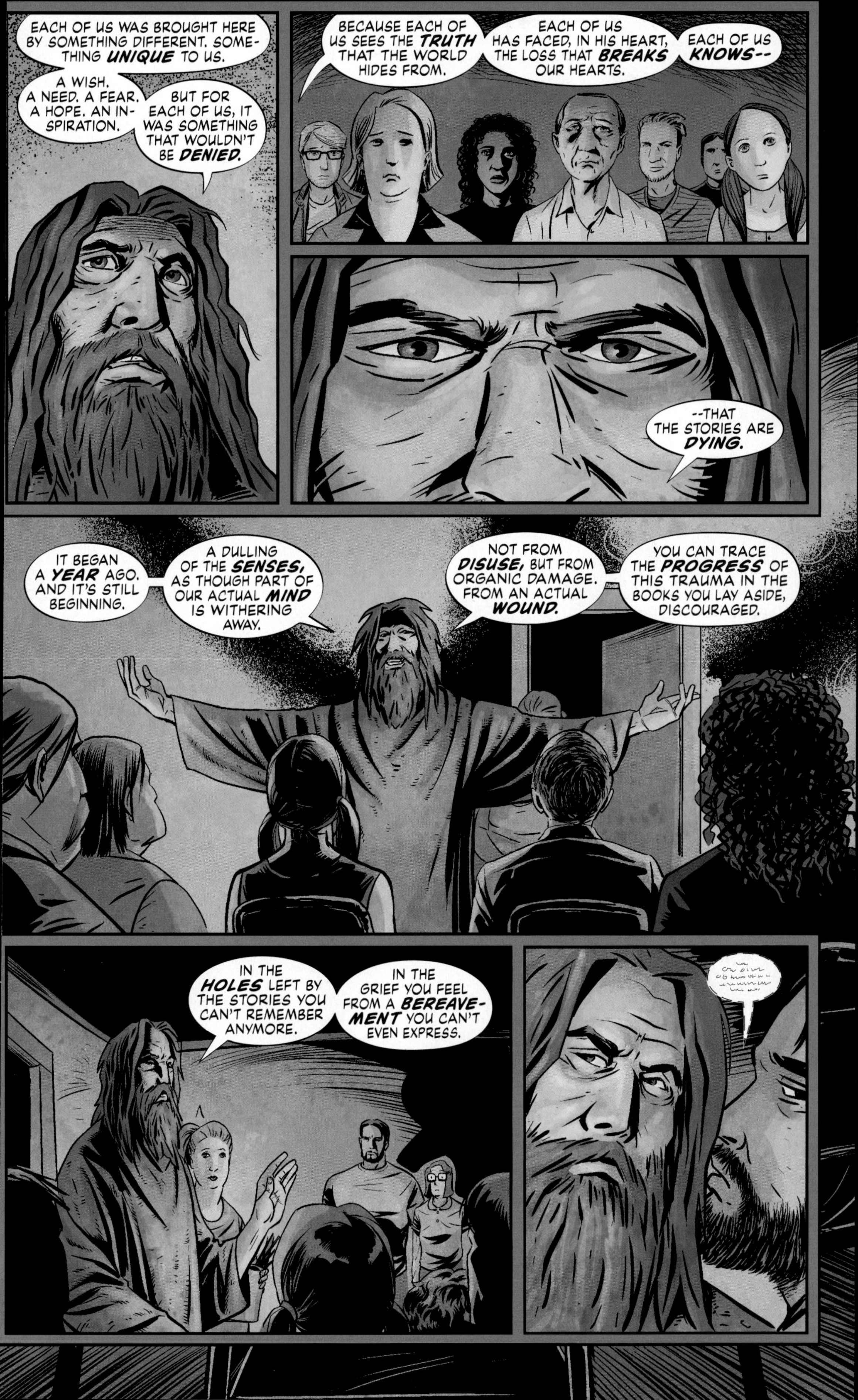
EACH OF US WAS BROUGHT HERE BY SOMETHING DIFFERENT. SOMETHING *UNIQUE* TO US.
A WISH. A NEED. A FEAR. A HOPE. AN INSPIRATION.
BUT FOR EACH OF US, IT WAS SOMETHING THAT WOULDN'T BE *DENIED.*
BECAUSE EACH OF US SEES THE *TRUTH* THAT THE WORLD HIDES FROM.
EACH OF US HAS FACED, IN HIS HEART, THE LOSS THAT *BREAKS* OUR HEARTS.
EACH OF US *KNOWS--*
--THAT THE STORIES ARE *DYING.*
IT BEGAN A *YEAR* AGO. AND IT'S STILL BEGINNING.
A DULLING OF THE *SENSES,* AS THOUGH PART OF OUR ACTUAL *MIND* IS WITHERING AWAY.
NOT FROM *DISUSE,* BUT FROM ORGANIC DAMAGE. FROM AN ACTUAL *WOUND.*
YOU CAN TRACE THE *PROGRESS* OF THIS TRAUMA IN THE BOOKS YOU LAY ASIDE, DISCOURAGED.
IN THE *HOLES* LEFT BY THE STORIES YOU CAN'T REMEMBER ANYMORE.
IN THE GRIEF YOU FEEL FROM A *BEREAVEMENT* YOU CAN'T EVEN EXPRESS.

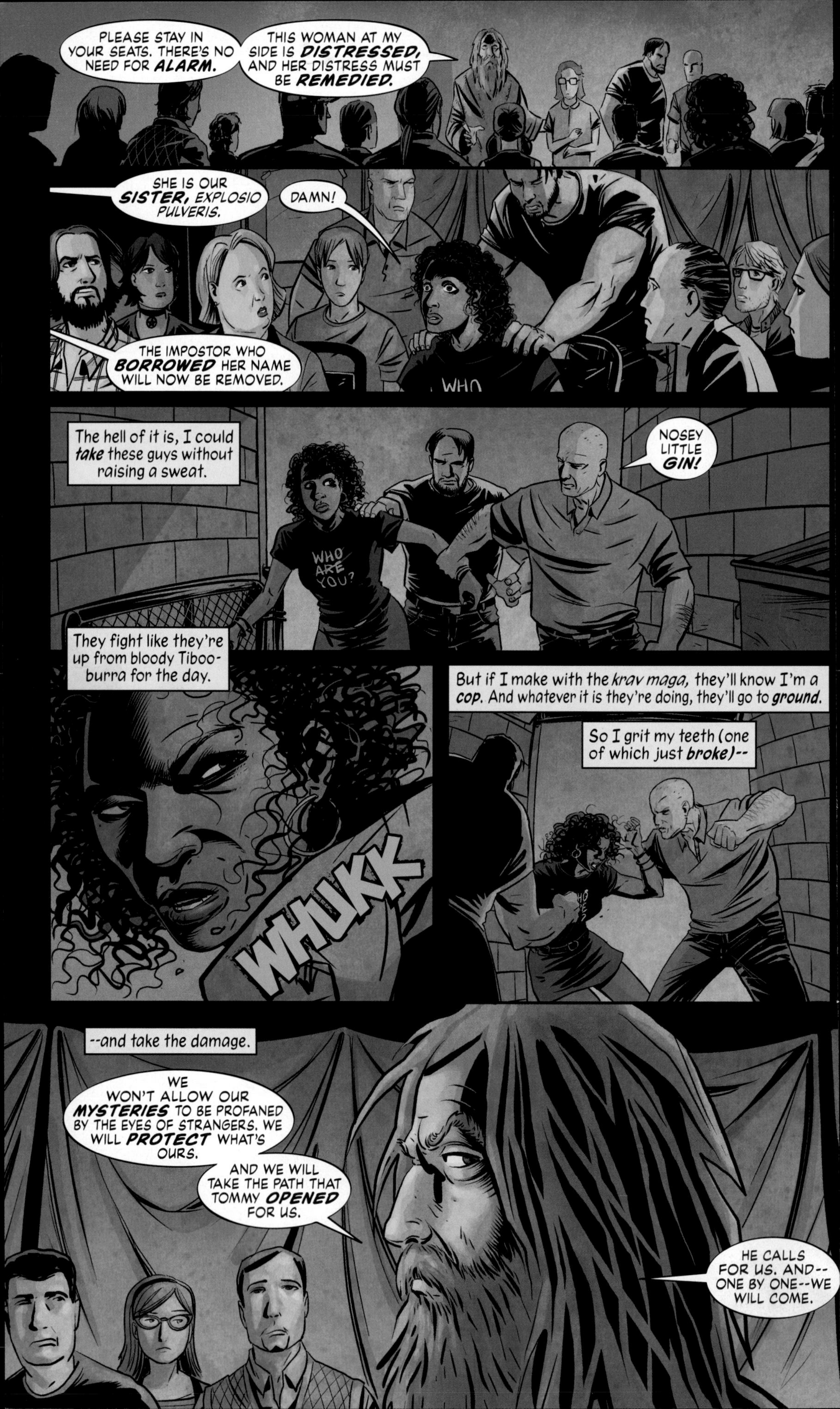

PLEASE STAY IN YOUR SEATS. THERE'S NO NEED FOR ALARM.
THIS WOMAN AT MY SIDE IS DISTRESSED, AND HER DISTRESS MUST BE REMEDIED.
SHE IS OUR SISTER, EXPLOSIO PULVERIS.
DAMN!
THE IMPOSTOR WHO BORROWED HER NAME WILL NOW BE REMOVED.
WHO
The hell of it is, I could take these guys without raising a sweat.
NOSEY LITTLE GIN!
WHO ARE YOU?
They fight like they're up from bloody Tiboo-burra for the day.
WHUKK
But if I make with the krav maga, they'll know I'm a cop. And whatever it is they're doing, they'll go to ground.
So I grit my teeth (one of which just broke)--
--and take the damage.
WE WON'T ALLOW OUR MYSTERIES TO BE PROFANED BY THE EYES OF STRANGERS. WE WILL PROTECT WHAT'S OURS.
AND WE WILL TAKE THE PATH THAT TOMMY OPENED FOR US.
HE CALLS FOR US. AND-- ONE BY ONE--WE WILL COME.

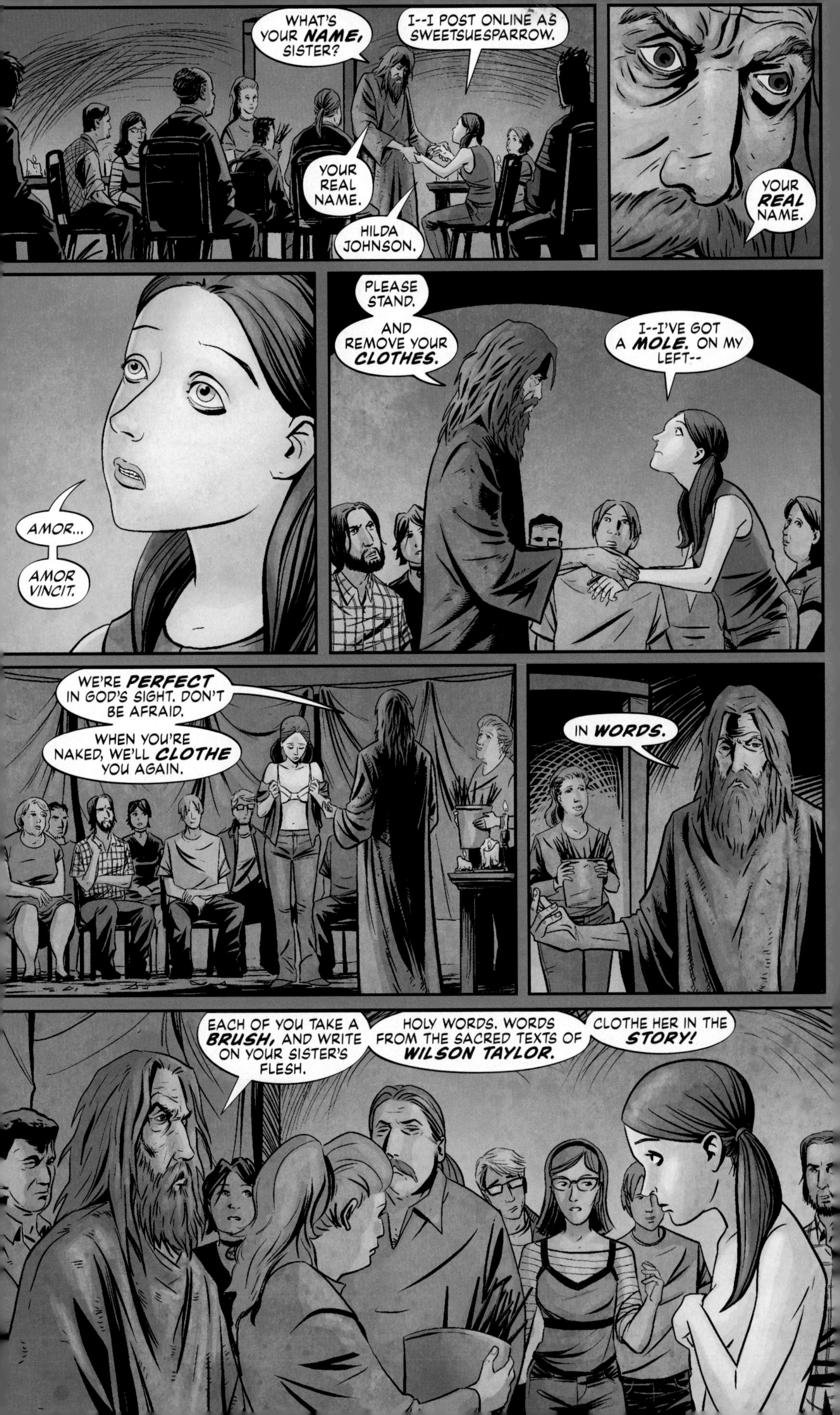
WHAT'S YOUR NAME, SISTER?
I--I POST ONLINE AS SWEETSUESPARROW.
YOUR REAL NAME.
HILDA JOHNSON.
YOUR REAL NAME.
AMOR...
AMOR VINCIT.
PLEASE STAND.
AND REMOVE YOUR CLOTHES.
I--I'VE GOT A MOLE. ON MY LEFT--
WE'RE PERFECT IN GOD'S SIGHT. DON'T BE AFRAID.
WHEN YOU'RE NAKED, WE'LL CLOTHE YOU AGAIN.
IN WORDS.
EACH OF YOU TAKE A BRUSH, AND WRITE ON YOUR SISTER'S FLESH.
HOLY WORDS. WORDS FROM THE SACRED TEXTS OF WILSON TAYLOR.
CLOTHE HER IN THE STORY!

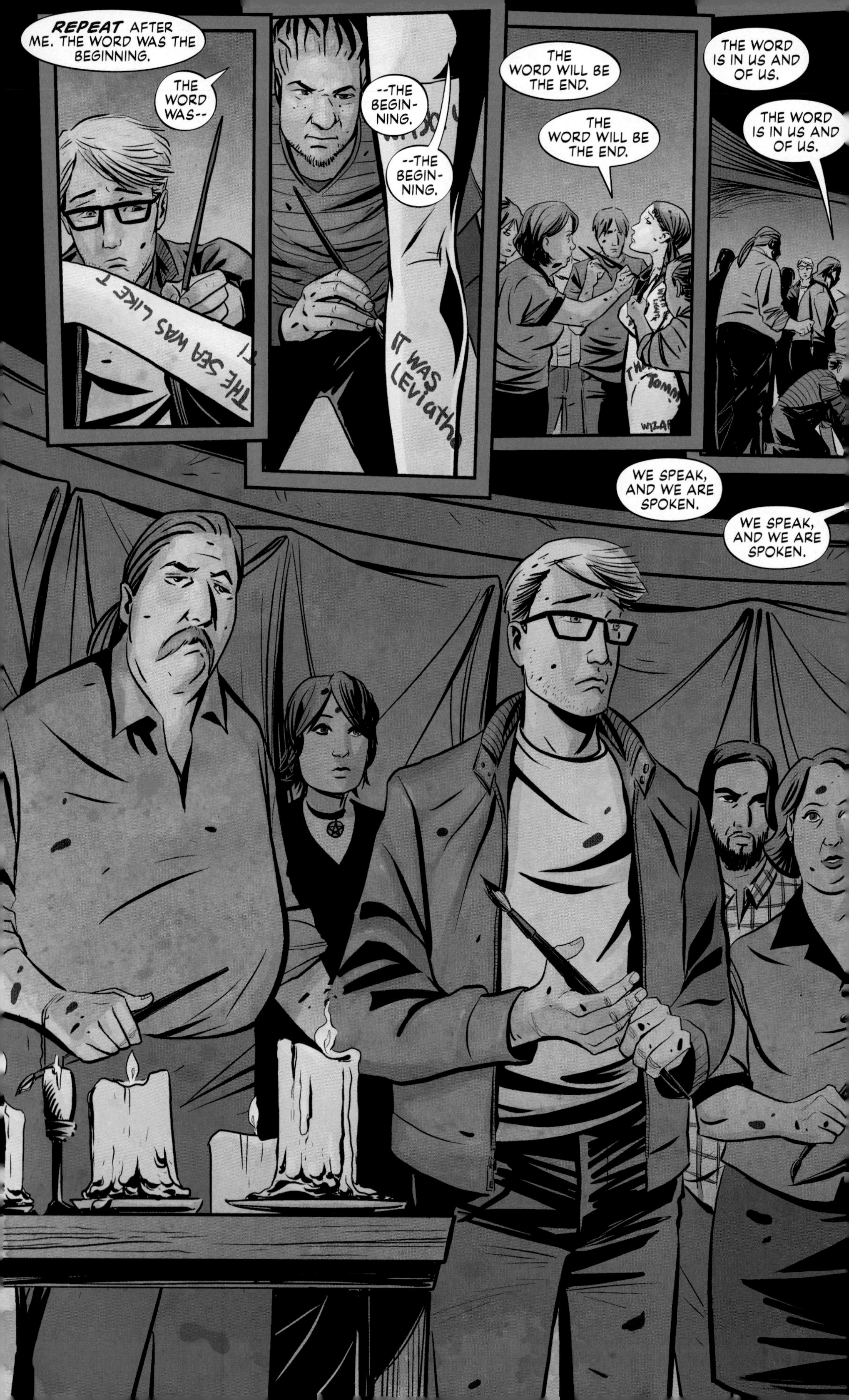

REPEAT AFTER ME. THE WORD WAS THE BEGINNING.
THE WORD WAS--
--THE BEGIN-NING.
--THE BEGIN-NING.
THE WORD WILL BE THE END.
THE WORD WILL BE THE END.
THE WORD IS IN US AND OF US.
THE WORD IS IN US AND OF US.
WE SPEAK, AND WE ARE SPOKEN.
WE SPEAK, AND WE ARE SPOKEN.

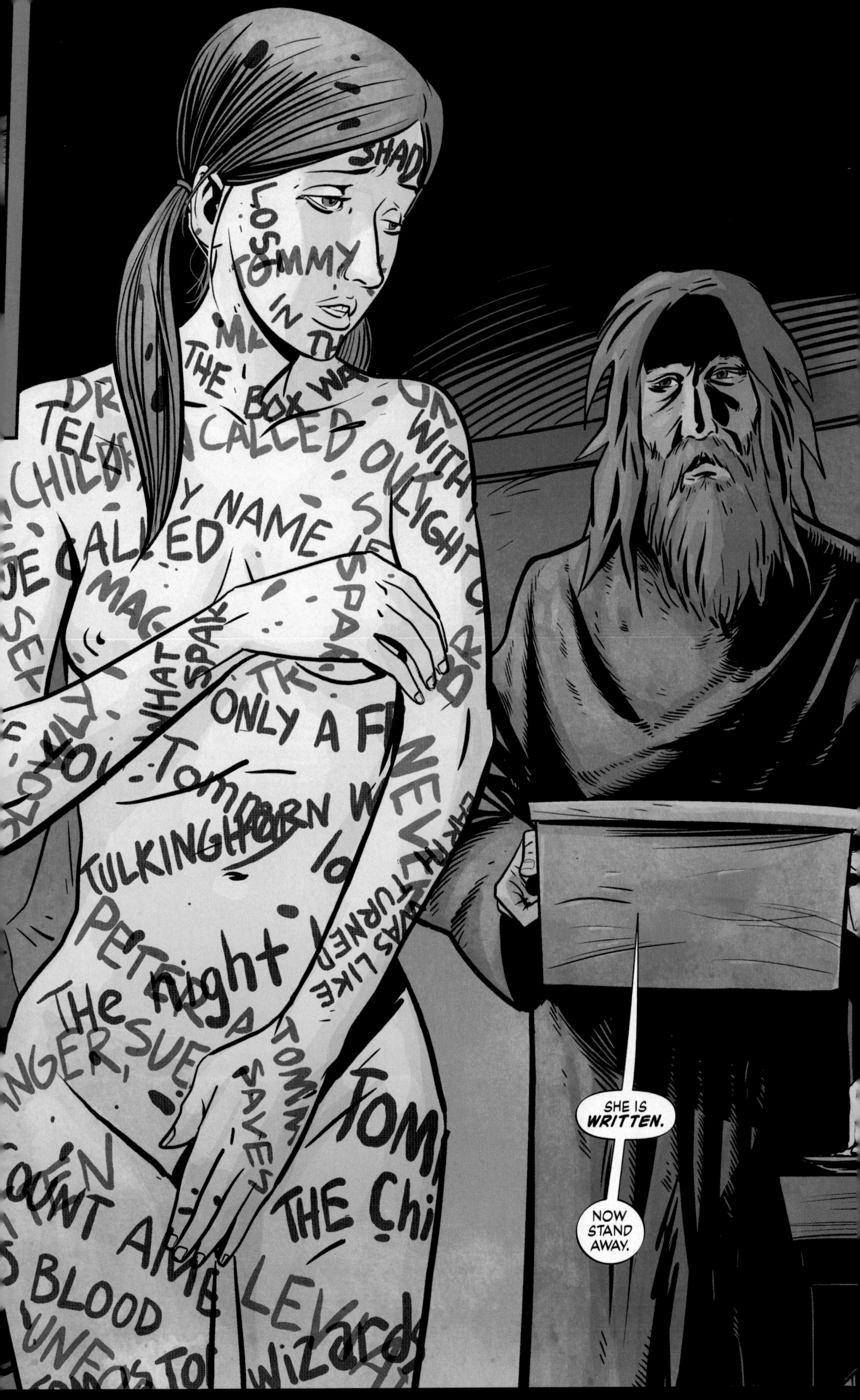
SHE IS WRITTEN.
NOW STAND AWAY.

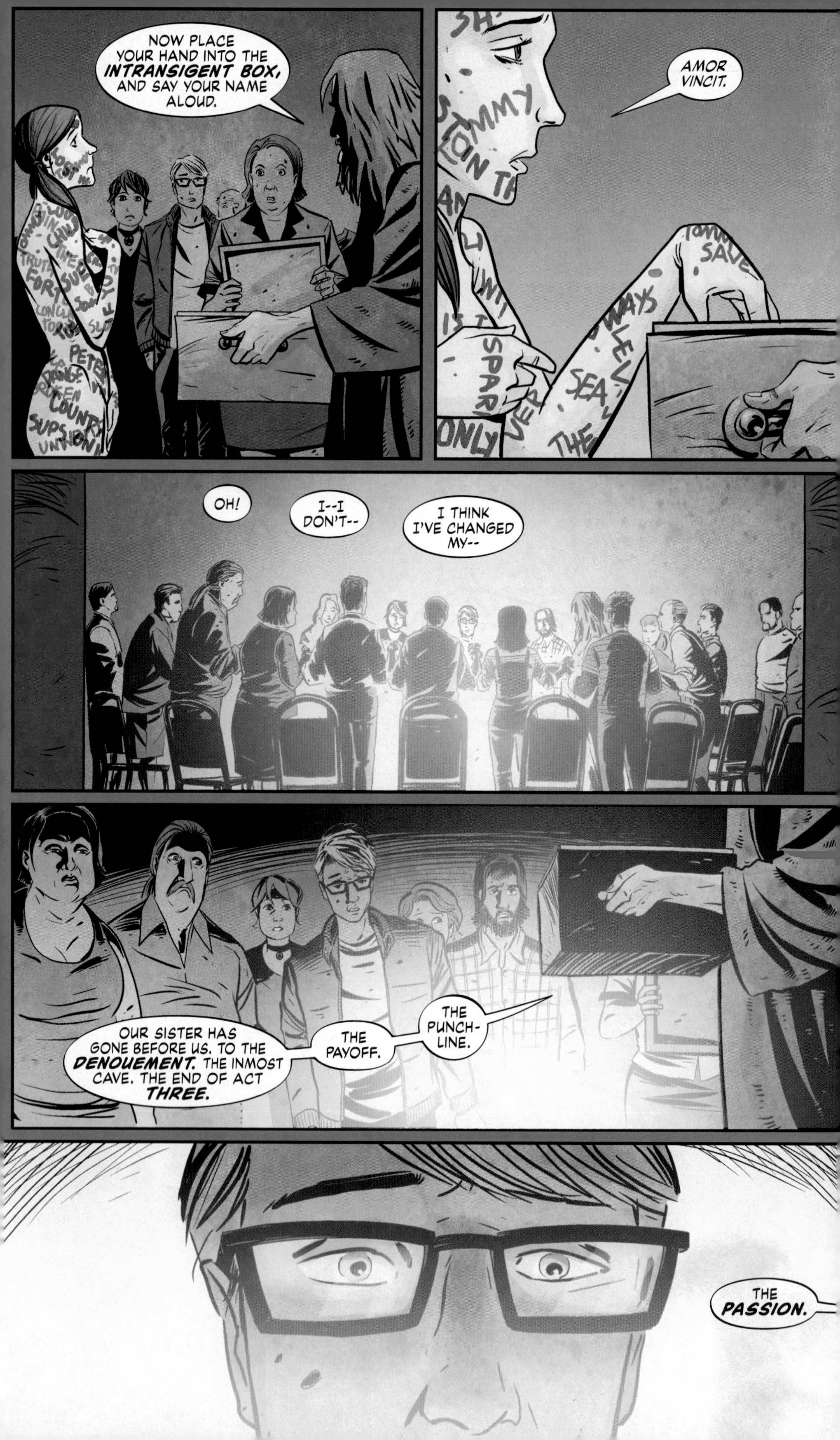
NOW PLACE YOUR HAND INTO THE INTRANSIGENT BOX, AND SAY YOUR NAME ALOUD.
AMOR VINCIT.
OH!
I--I DON'T--
I THINK I'VE CHANGED MY--
OUR SISTER HAS GONE BEFORE US. TO THE DENOUEMENT. THE INMOST CAVE. THE END OF ACT THREE.
THE PAYOFF.
THE PUNCH-LINE.
THE PASSION.

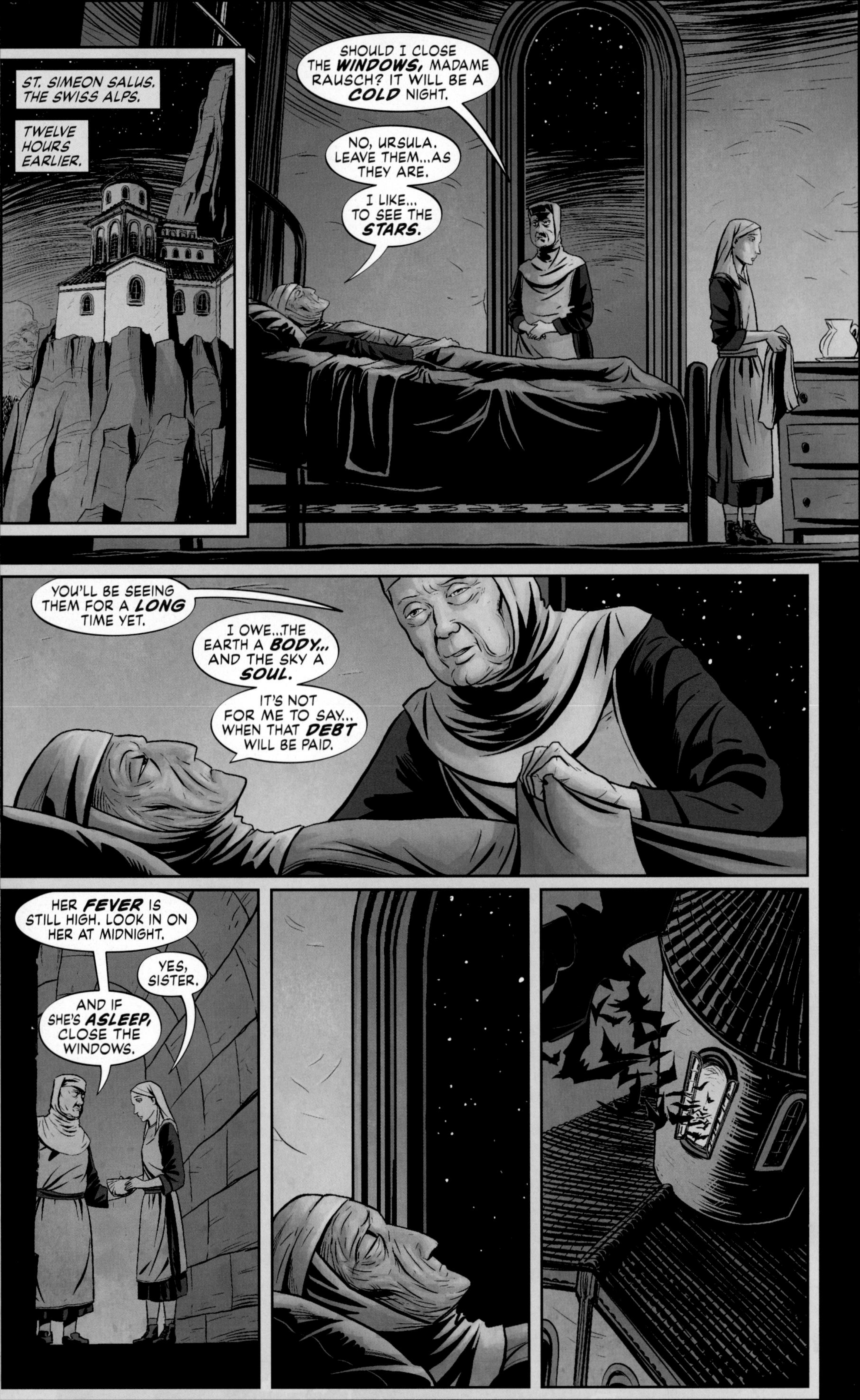
ST. SIMEON SALUS. THE SWISS ALPS.
TWELVE HOURS EARLIER.
SHOULD I CLOSE THE WINDOWS, MADAME RAUSCH? IT WILL BE A COLD NIGHT.
NO, URSULA. LEAVE THEM...AS THEY ARE.
I LIKE... TO SEE THE STARS.
YOU'LL BE SEEING THEM FOR A LONG TIME YET.
I OWE...THE EARTH A BODY... AND THE SKY A SOUL.
IT'S NOT FOR ME TO SAY... WHEN THAT DEBT WILL BE PAID.
HER FEVER IS STILL HIGH. LOOK IN ON HER AT MIDNIGHT.
YES, SISTER.
AND IF SHE'S ASLEEP, CLOSE THE WINDOWS.

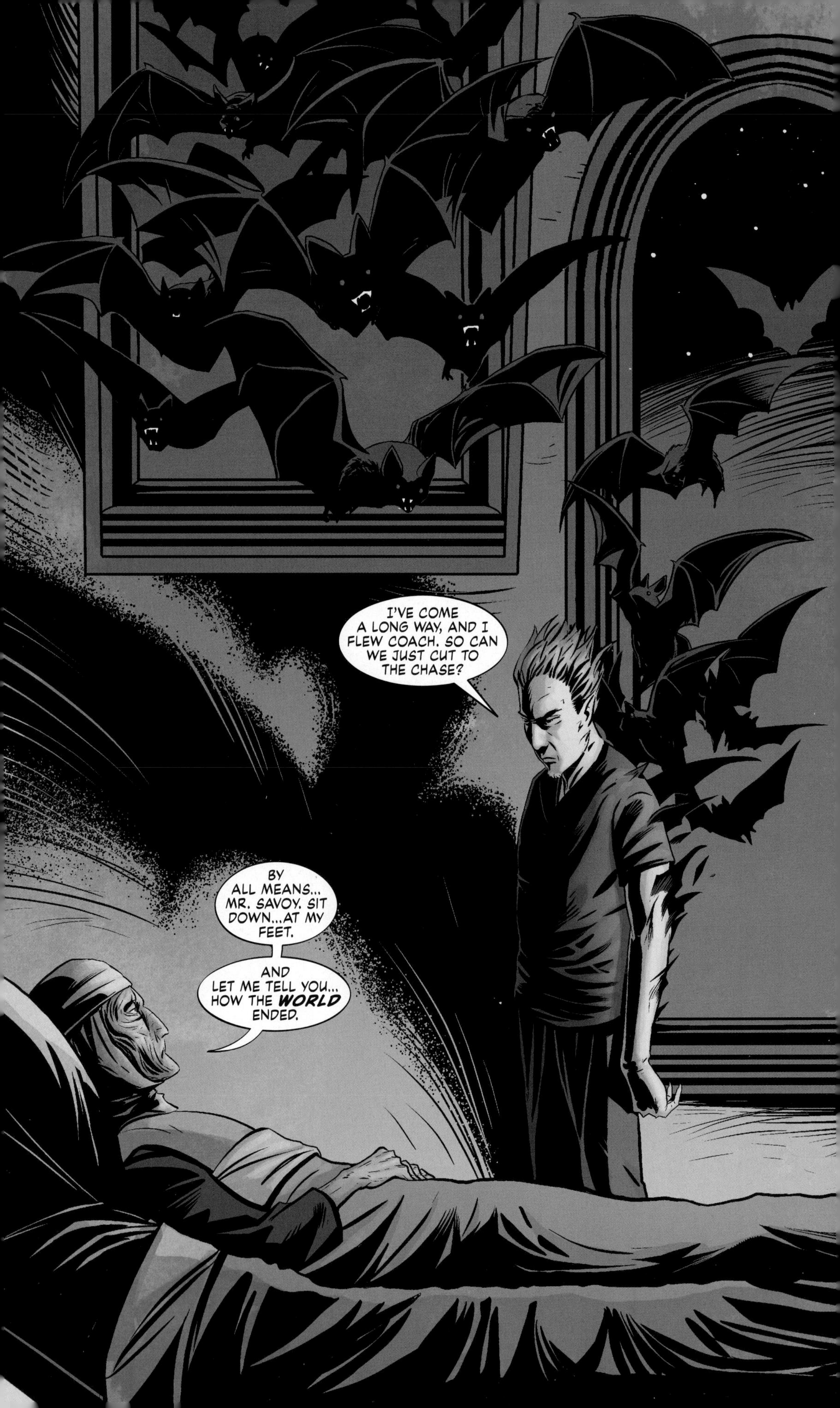
I'VE COME A LONG WAY, AND I FLEW COACH. SO CAN WE JUST CUT TO THE CHASE?
BY ALL MEANS... MR. SAVOY. SIT DOWN...AT MY FEET.
AND LET ME TELL YOU... HOW THE WORLD ENDED.

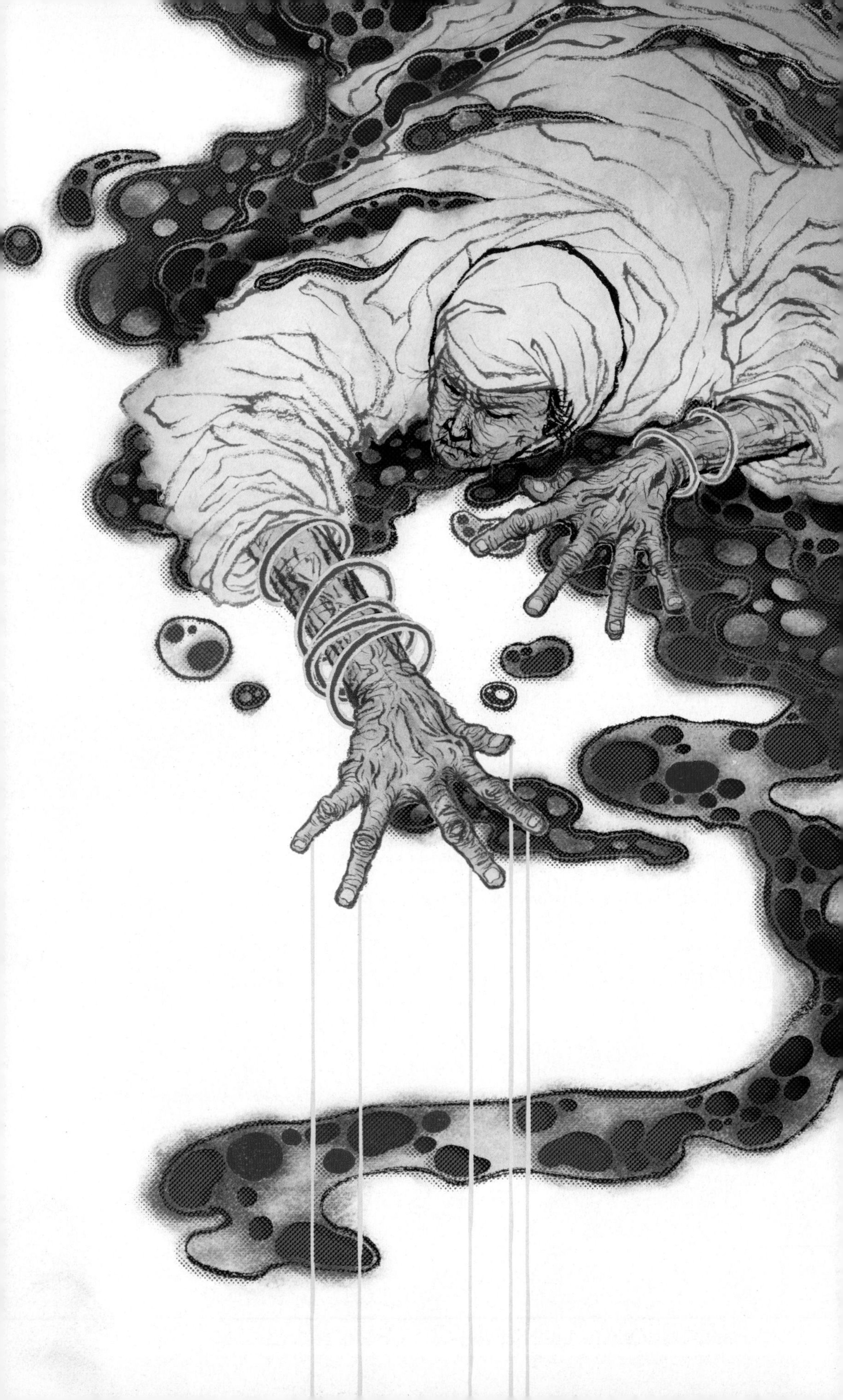

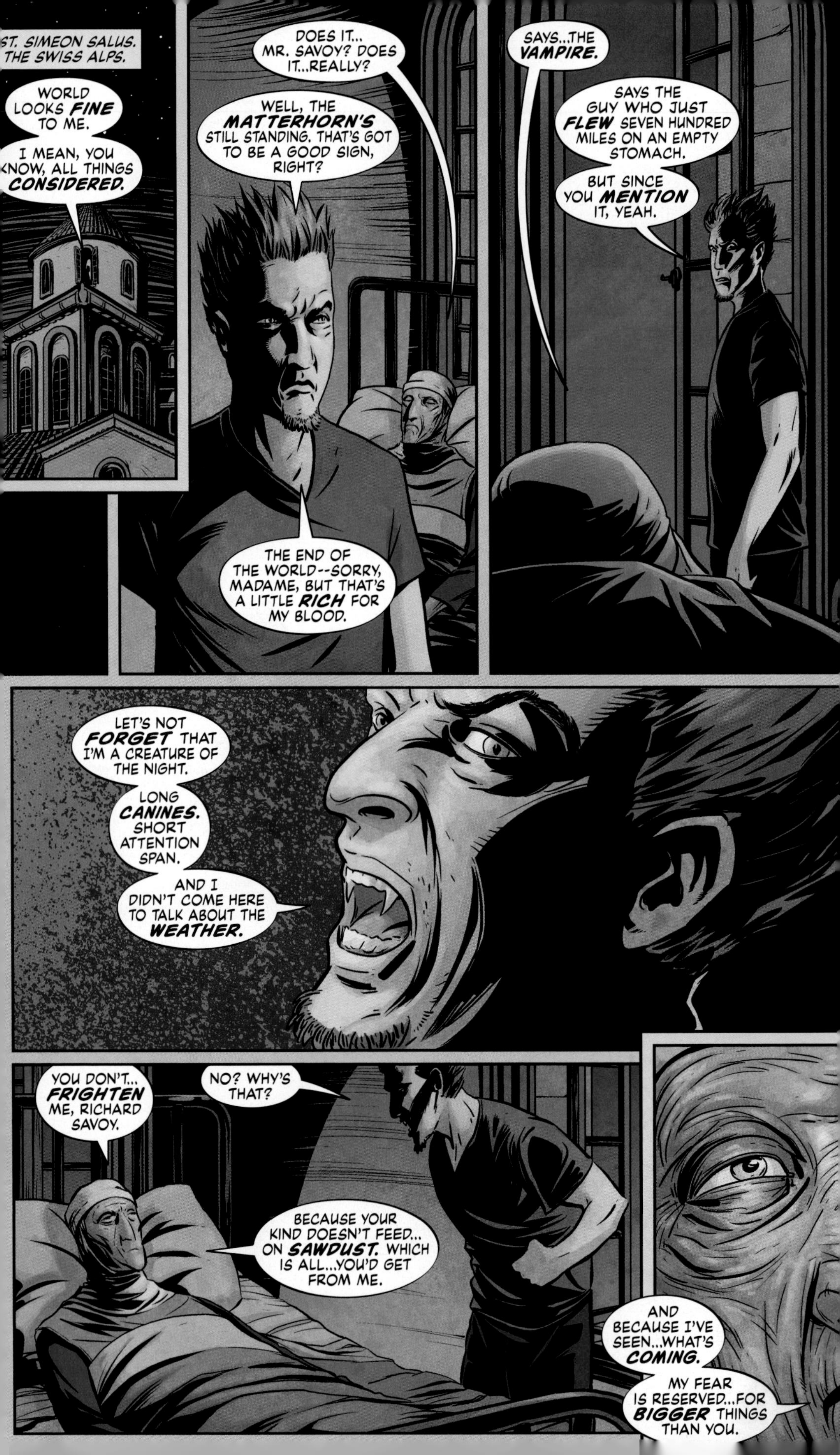
ST. SIMEON SALUS. THE SWISS ALPS.
WORLD LOOKS FINE TO ME.
I MEAN, YOU KNOW, ALL THINGS CONSIDERED.
DOES IT... MR. SAVOY? DOES IT...REALLY?
WELL, THE MATTERHORN'S STILL STANDING. THAT'S GOT TO BE A GOOD SIGN, RIGHT?
THE END OF THE WORLD--SORRY, MADAME, BUT THAT'S A LITTLE RICH FOR MY BLOOD.
SAYS...THE VAMPIRE.
SAYS THE GUY WHO JUST FLEW SEVEN HUNDRED MILES ON AN EMPTY STOMACH.
BUT SINCE YOU MENTION IT, YEAH.
LET'S NOT FORGET THAT I'M A CREATURE OF THE NIGHT.
LONG CANINES. SHORT ATTENTION SPAN.
AND I DIDN'T COME HERE TO TALK ABOUT THE WEATHER.
YOU DON'T... FRIGHTEN ME, RICHARD SAVOY.
NO? WHY'S THAT?
BECAUSE YOUR KIND DOESN'T FEED... ON SAWDUST. WHICH IS ALL...YOU'D GET FROM ME.
AND BECAUSE I'VE SEEN...WHAT'S COMING.
MY FEAR IS RESERVED...FOR BIGGER THINGS THAN YOU.

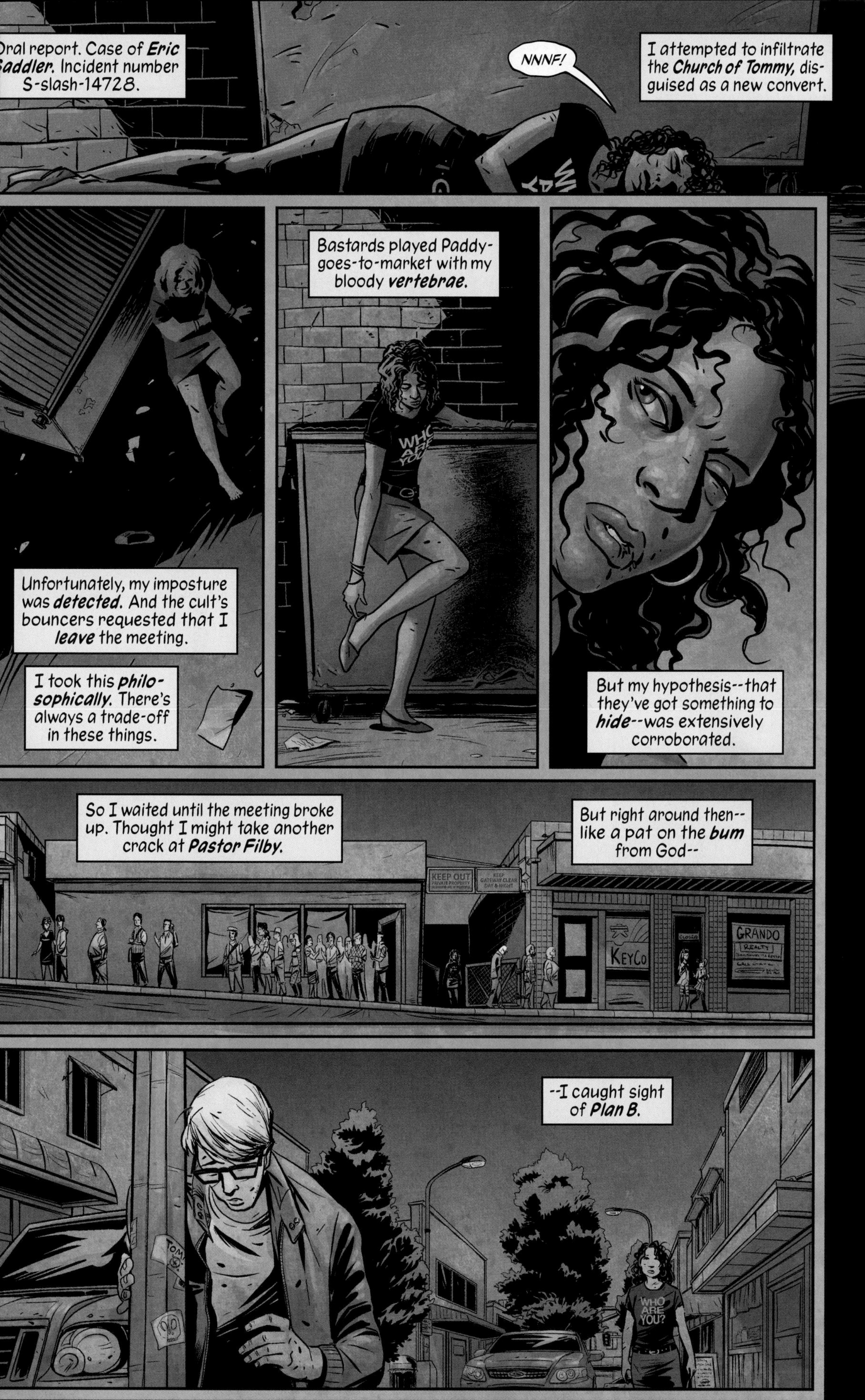
Oral report. Case of Eric Saddler. Incident number S-slash-14728.
NNNF!
I attempted to infiltrate the Church of Tommy, disguised as a new convert.
Bastards played Paddy-goes-to-market with my bloody vertebrae.
Unfortunately, my imposture was detected. And the cult's bouncers requested that I leave the meeting.
I took this philosophically. There's always a trade-off in these things.
But my hypothesis--that they've got something to hide--was extensively corroborated.
So I waited until the meeting broke up. Thought I might take another crack at Pastor Filby.
But right around then--like a pat on the bum from God--
KEEP OUT
KEEP GATEWAY CLEAR DAY & NIGHT
KEYCO
GRANDO REALTY
--I caught sight of Plan B.
WHO ARE YOU?

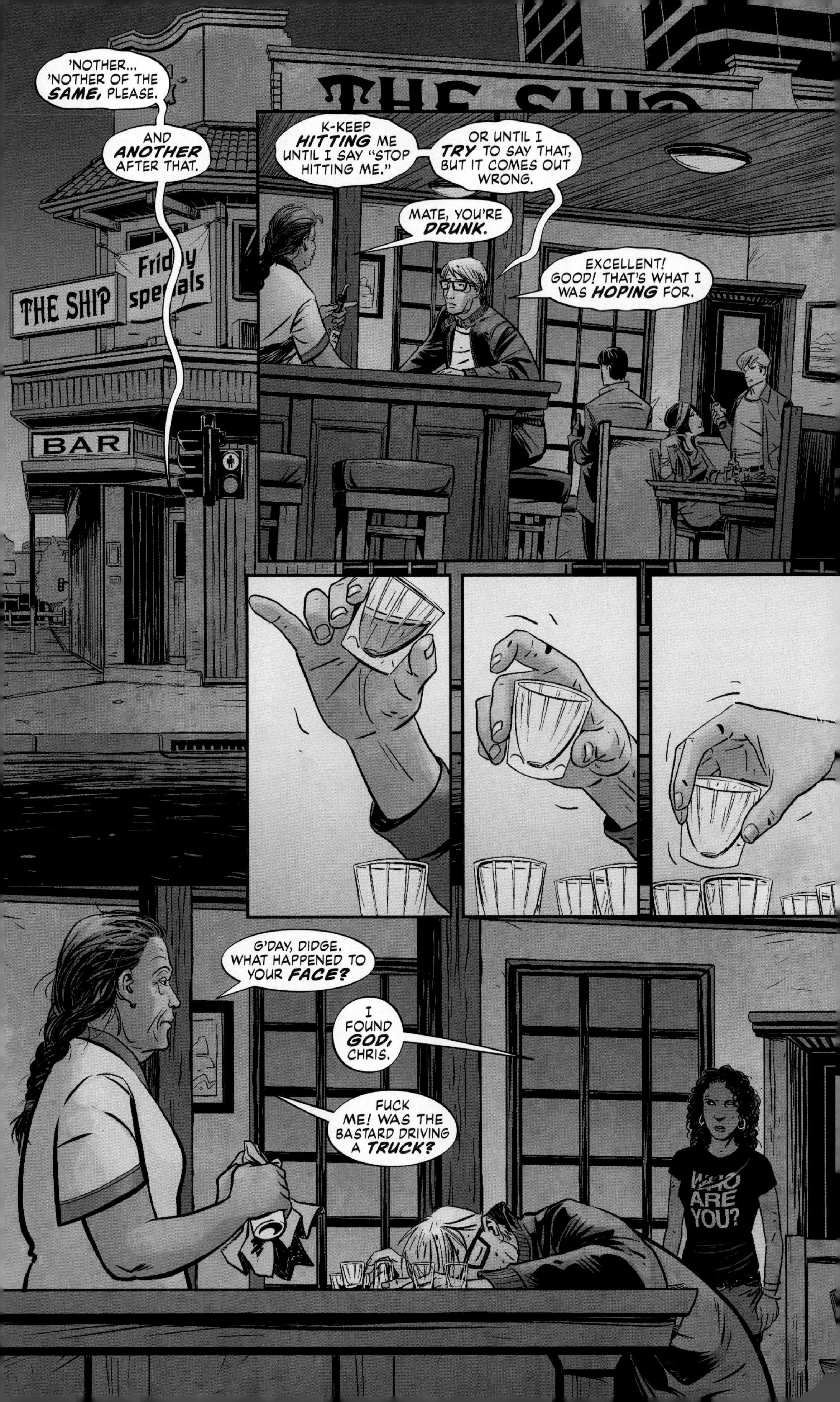
THE SHIP
'NOTHER... 'NOTHER OF THE SAME, PLEASE.
AND ANOTHER AFTER THAT.
THE SHIP
Friday specials
BAR
K-KEEP HITTING ME UNTIL I SAY "STOP HITTING ME."
OR UNTIL I TRY TO SAY THAT, BUT IT COMES OUT WRONG.
MATE, YOU'RE DRUNK.
EXCELLENT! GOOD! THAT'S WHAT I WAS HOPING FOR.
G'DAY, DIDGE. WHAT HAPPENED TO YOUR FACE?
I FOUND GOD, CHRIS.
FUCK ME! WAS THE BASTARD DRIVING A TRUCK?
WHO ARE YOU?

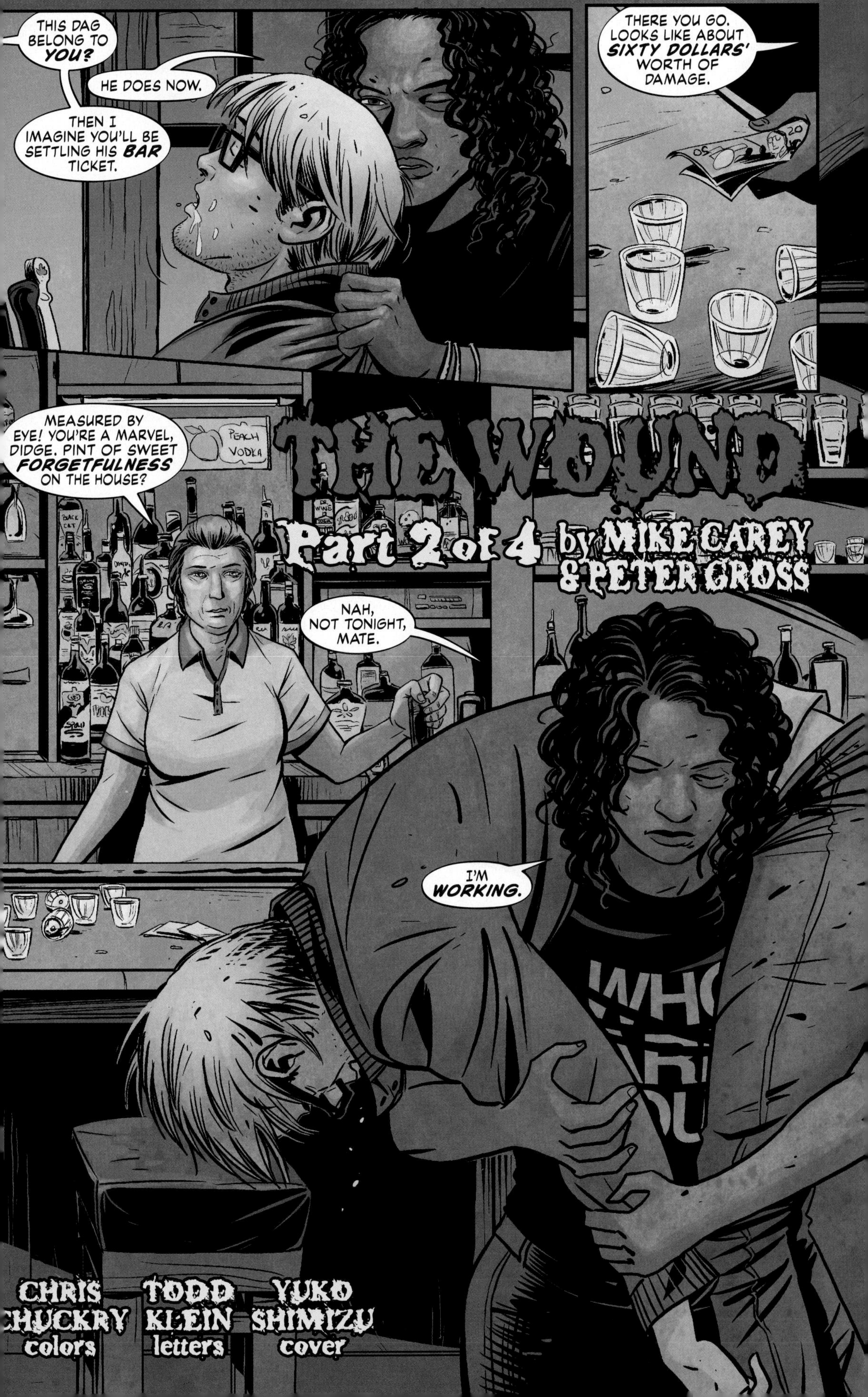
THIS DAG BELONG TO YOU?
HE DOES NOW.
THEN I IMAGINE YOU'LL BE SETTLING HIS BAR TICKET.
THERE YOU GO. LOOKS LIKE ABOUT SIXTY DOLLARS' WORTH OF DAMAGE.
MEASURED BY EYE! YOU'RE A MARVEL, DIDGE. PINT OF SWEET FORGETFULNESS ON THE HOUSE?
PEACH VODKA
THE WOUND
Part 2 of 4 by MIKE CAREY & PETER GROSS
NAH, NOT TONIGHT, MATE.
I'M WORKING.
CHRIS CHUCKRY colors
TODD KLEIN letters
YUKO SHIMIZU cover

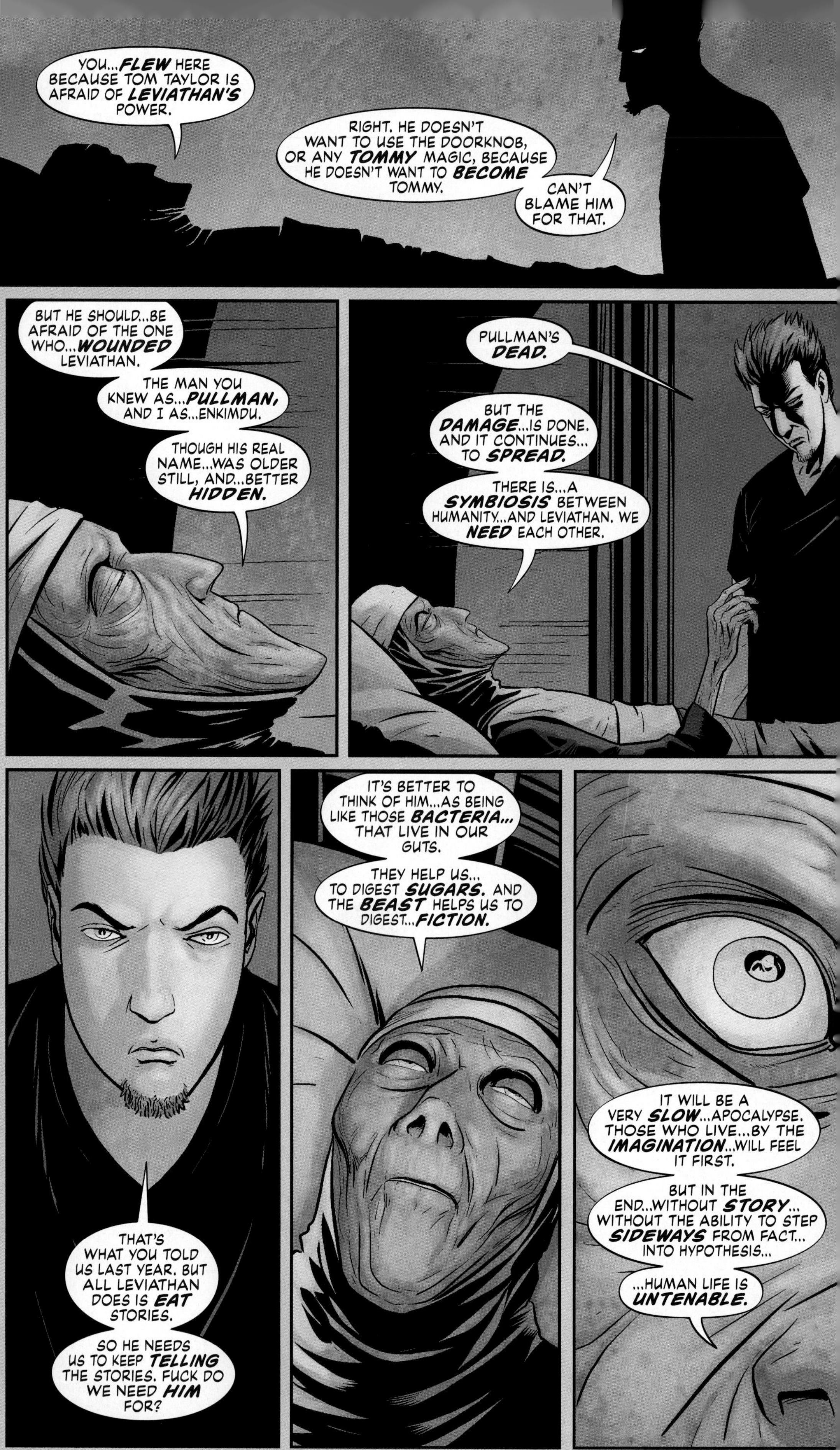
YOU...FLEW HERE BECAUSE TOM TAYLOR IS AFRAID OF LEVIATHAN'S POWER.
RIGHT. HE DOESN'T WANT TO USE THE DOORKNOB, OR ANY TOMMY MAGIC, BECAUSE HE DOESN'T WANT TO BECOME TOMMY.
CAN'T BLAME HIM FOR THAT.
BUT HE SHOULD...BE AFRAID OF THE ONE WHO...WOUNDED LEVIATHAN.
THE MAN YOU KNEW AS...PULLMAN, AND I AS...ENKIMDU.
THOUGH HIS REAL NAME...WAS OLDER STILL, AND...BETTER HIDDEN.
PULLMAN'S DEAD.
BUT THE DAMAGE...IS DONE. AND IT CONTINUES... TO SPREAD.
THERE IS...A SYMBIOSIS BETWEEN HUMANITY...AND LEVIATHAN. WE NEED EACH OTHER.
THAT'S WHAT YOU TOLD US LAST YEAR. BUT ALL LEVIATHAN DOES IS EAT STORIES.
SO HE NEEDS US TO KEEP TELLING THE STORIES. FUCK DO WE NEED HIM FOR?
IT'S BETTER TO THINK OF HIM...AS BEING LIKE THOSE BACTERIA... THAT LIVE IN OUR GUTS.
THEY HELP US... TO DIGEST SUGARS. AND THE BEAST HELPS US TO DIGEST...FICTION.
IT WILL BE A VERY SLOW...APOCALYPSE. THOSE WHO LIVE...BY THE IMAGINATION...WILL FEEL IT FIRST.
BUT IN THE END...WITHOUT STORY... WITHOUT THE ABILITY TO STEP SIDEWAYS FROM FACT... INTO HYPOTHESIS...
...HUMAN LIFE IS UNTENABLE.

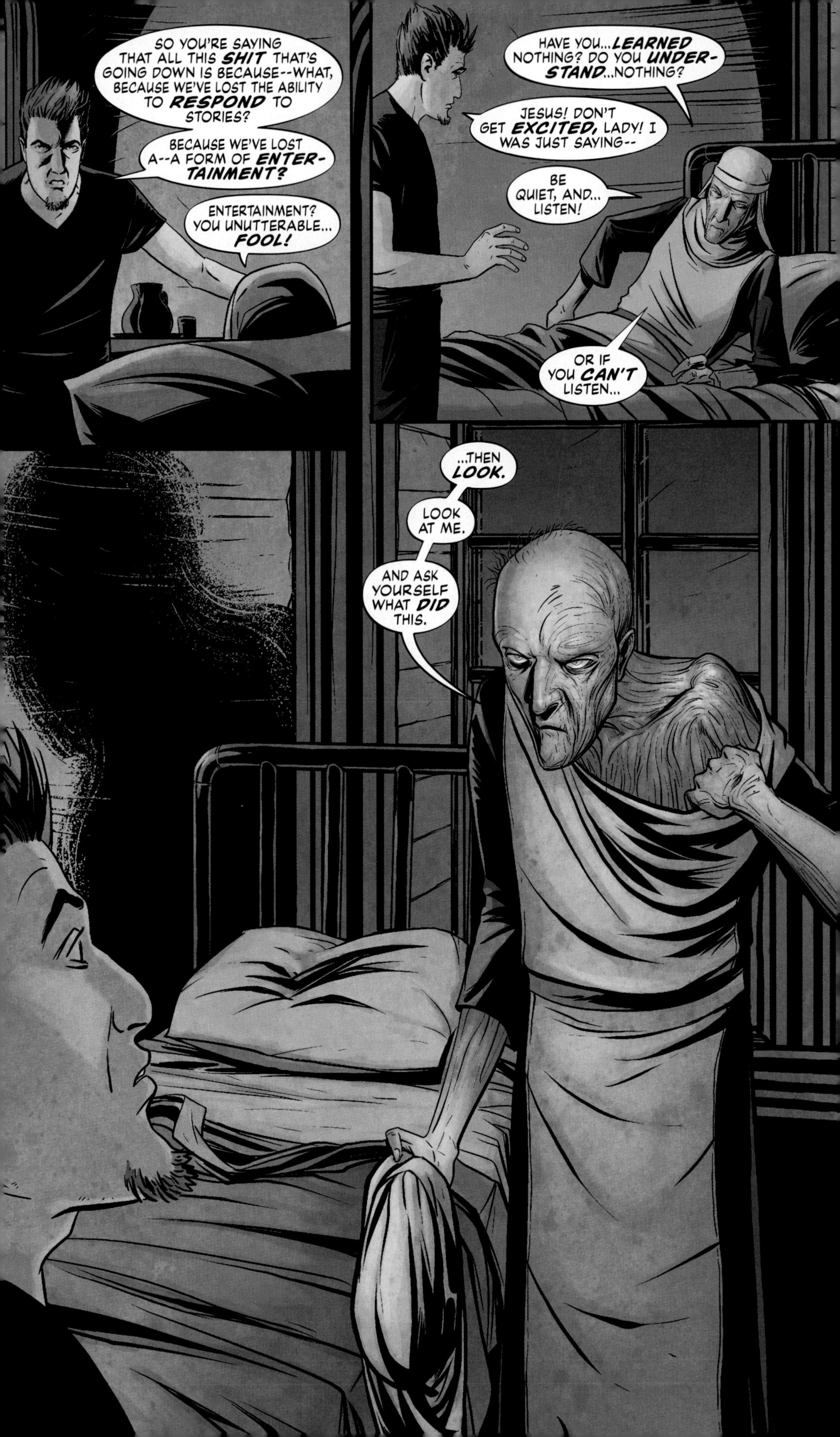
SO YOU'RE SAYING THAT ALL THIS SHIT THAT'S GOING DOWN IS BECAUSE--WHAT, BECAUSE WE'VE LOST THE ABILITY TO RESPOND TO STORIES?
BECAUSE WE'VE LOST A--A FORM OF ENTERTAINMENT?
ENTERTAINMENT? YOU UNUTTERABLE... FOOL!
HAVE YOU...LEARNED NOTHING? DO YOU UNDERSTAND...NOTHING?
JESUS! DON'T GET EXCITED, LADY! I WAS JUST SAYING--
BE QUIET, AND... LISTEN!
OR IF YOU CAN'T LISTEN...
...THEN LOOK.
LOOK AT ME.
AND ASK YOURSELF WHAT DID THIS.

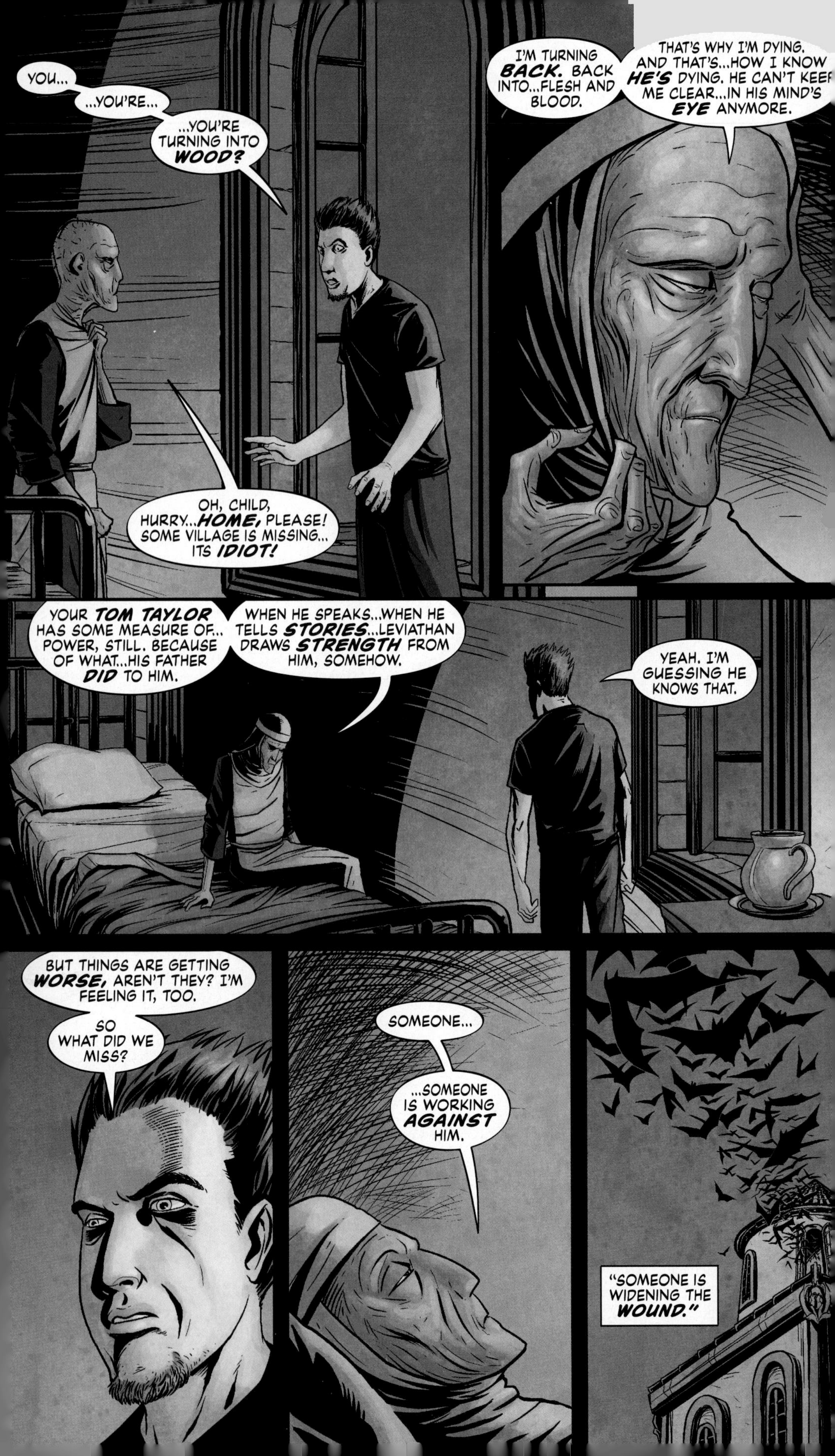
YOU...
...YOU'RE...
...YOU'RE TURNING INTO WOOD?
OH, CHILD, HURRY...HOME, PLEASE! SOME VILLAGE IS MISSING... ITS IDIOT!
I'M TURNING BACK. BACK INTO...FLESH AND BLOOD.
THAT'S WHY I'M DYING. AND THAT'S...HOW I KNOW HE'S DYING. HE CAN'T KEEP ME CLEAR...IN HIS MIND'S EYE ANYMORE.
YOUR TOM TAYLOR HAS SOME MEASURE OF... POWER, STILL. BECAUSE OF WHAT...HIS FATHER DID TO HIM.
WHEN HE SPEAKS...WHEN HE TELLS STORIES...LEVIATHAN DRAWS STRENGTH FROM HIM, SOMEHOW.
YEAH. I'M GUESSING HE KNOWS THAT.
BUT THINGS ARE GETTING WORSE, AREN'T THEY? I'M FEELING IT, TOO.
SO WHAT DID WE MISS?
SOMEONE...
...SOMEONE IS WORKING AGAINST HIM.
"SOMEONE IS WIDENING THE WOUND."

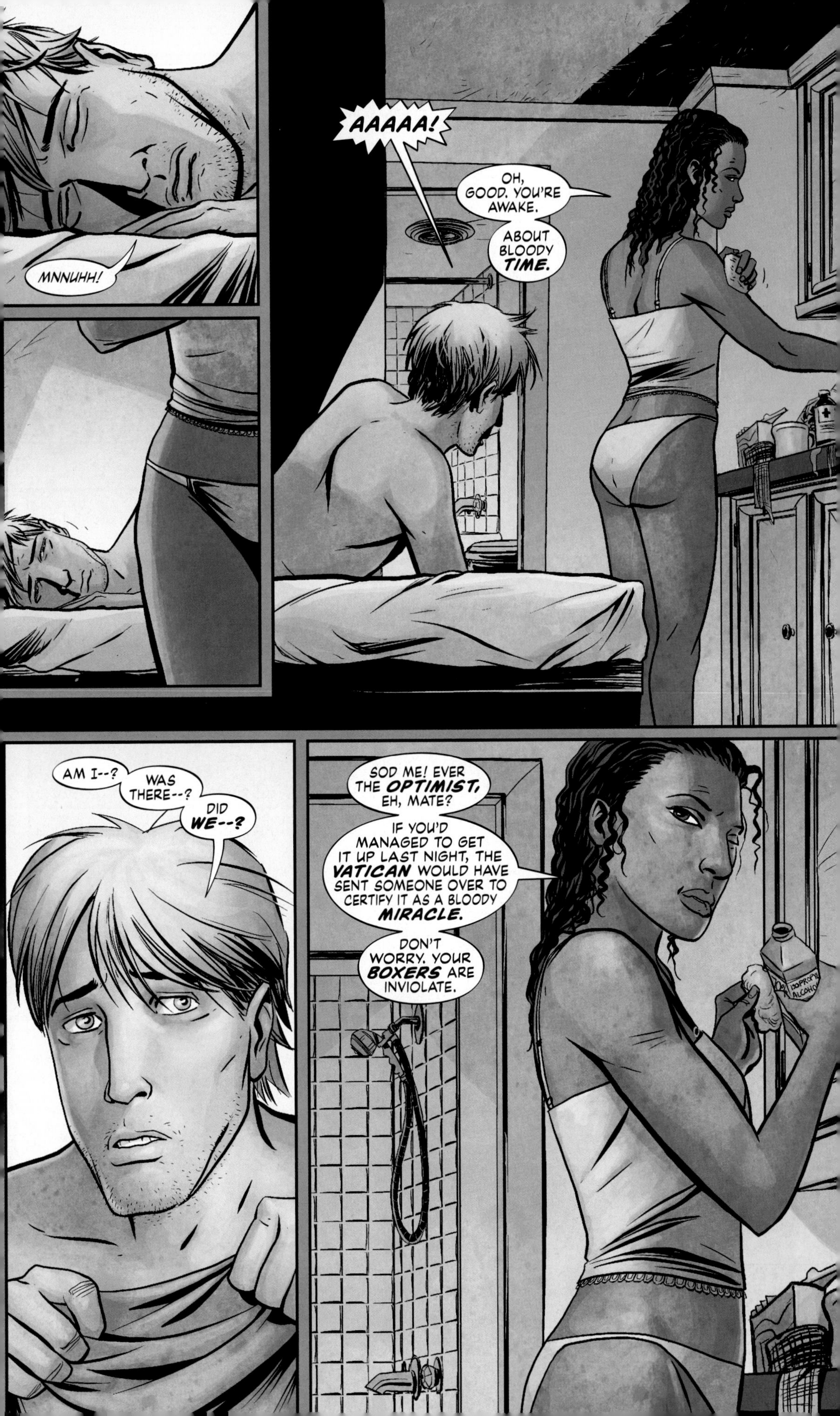
MNNUHH!
AAAAA!
OH, GOOD. YOU'RE AWAKE.
ABOUT BLOODY TIME.
AM I--?
WAS THERE--?
DID WE--?
SOD ME! EVER THE OPTIMIST, EH, MATE?
IF YOU'D MANAGED TO GET IT UP LAST NIGHT, THE VATICAN WOULD HAVE SENT SOMEONE OVER TO CERTIFY IT AS A BLOODY MIRACLE.
DON'T WORRY. YOUR BOXERS ARE INVIOLATE.

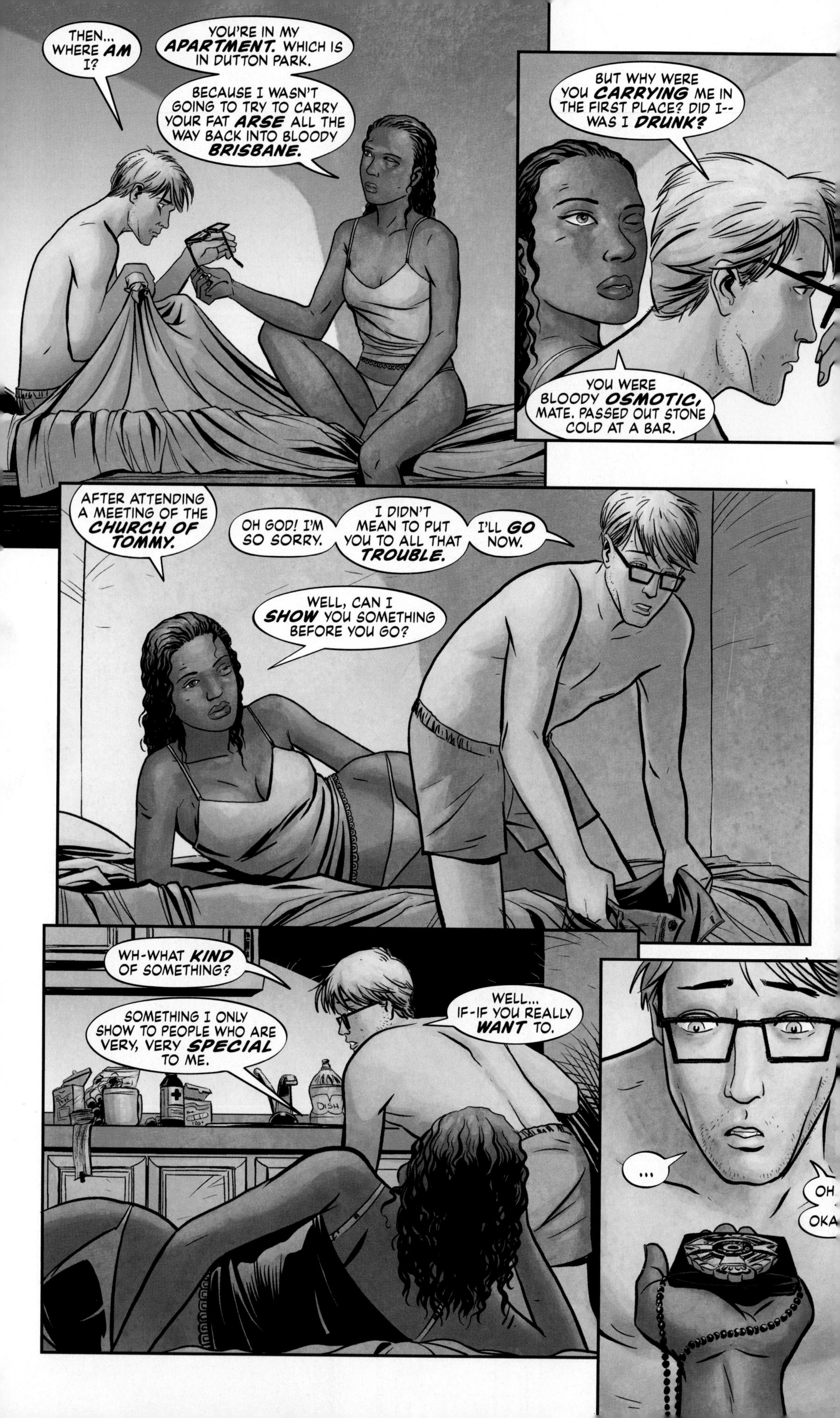
THEN... WHERE AM I?
YOU'RE IN MY APARTMENT. WHICH IS IN DUTTON PARK.
BECAUSE I WASN'T GOING TO TRY TO CARRY YOUR FAT ARSE ALL THE WAY BACK INTO BLOODY BRISBANE.
BUT WHY WERE YOU CARRYING ME IN THE FIRST PLACE? DID I-- WAS I DRUNK?
YOU WERE BLOODY OSMOTIC, MATE. PASSED OUT STONE COLD AT A BAR.
AFTER ATTENDING A MEETING OF THE CHURCH OF TOMMY.
OH GOD! I'M SO SORRY.
I DIDN'T MEAN TO PUT YOU TO ALL THAT TROUBLE.
I'LL GO NOW.
WELL, CAN I SHOW YOU SOMETHING BEFORE YOU GO?
WH-WHAT KIND OF SOMETHING?
SOMETHING I ONLY SHOW TO PEOPLE WHO ARE VERY, VERY SPECIAL TO ME.
WELL... IF-IF YOU REALLY WANT TO.
DISH
...
OH
OKA

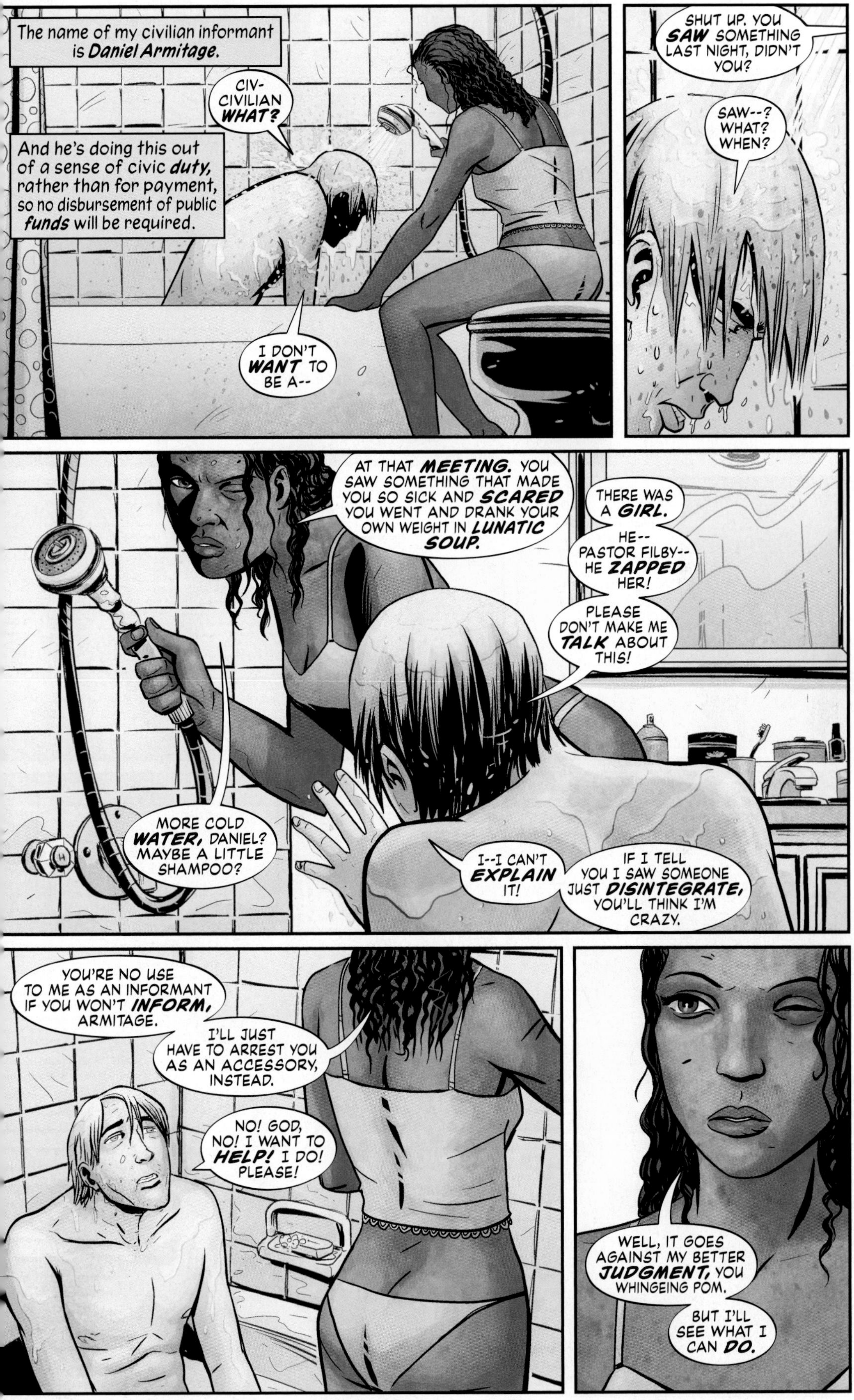
The name of my civilian informant is *Daniel Armitage*.
CIV-CIVILIAN WHAT?
And he's doing this out of a sense of civic *duty*, rather than for payment, so no disbursement of public *funds* will be required.
I DON'T WANT TO BE A--
SHUT UP. YOU SAW SOMETHING LAST NIGHT, DIDN'T YOU?
SAW--? WHAT? WHEN?
AT THAT MEETING. YOU SAW SOMETHING THAT MADE YOU SO SICK AND SCARED YOU WENT AND DRANK YOUR OWN WEIGHT IN LUNATIC SOUP.
THERE WAS A GIRL.
HE-- PASTOR FILBY-- HE ZAPPED HER!
PLEASE DON'T MAKE ME TALK ABOUT THIS!
MORE COLD WATER, DANIEL? MAYBE A LITTLE SHAMPOO?
I--I CAN'T EXPLAIN IT!
IF I TELL YOU I SAW SOMEONE JUST DISINTEGRATE, YOU'LL THINK I'M CRAZY.
YOU'RE NO USE TO ME AS AN INFORMANT IF YOU WON'T INFORM, ARMITAGE.
I'LL JUST HAVE TO ARREST YOU AS AN ACCESSORY, INSTEAD.
NO! GOD, NO! I WANT TO HELP! I DO! PLEASE!
WELL, IT GOES AGAINST MY BETTER JUDGMENT, YOU WHINGEING POM.
BUT I'LL SEE WHAT I CAN DO.

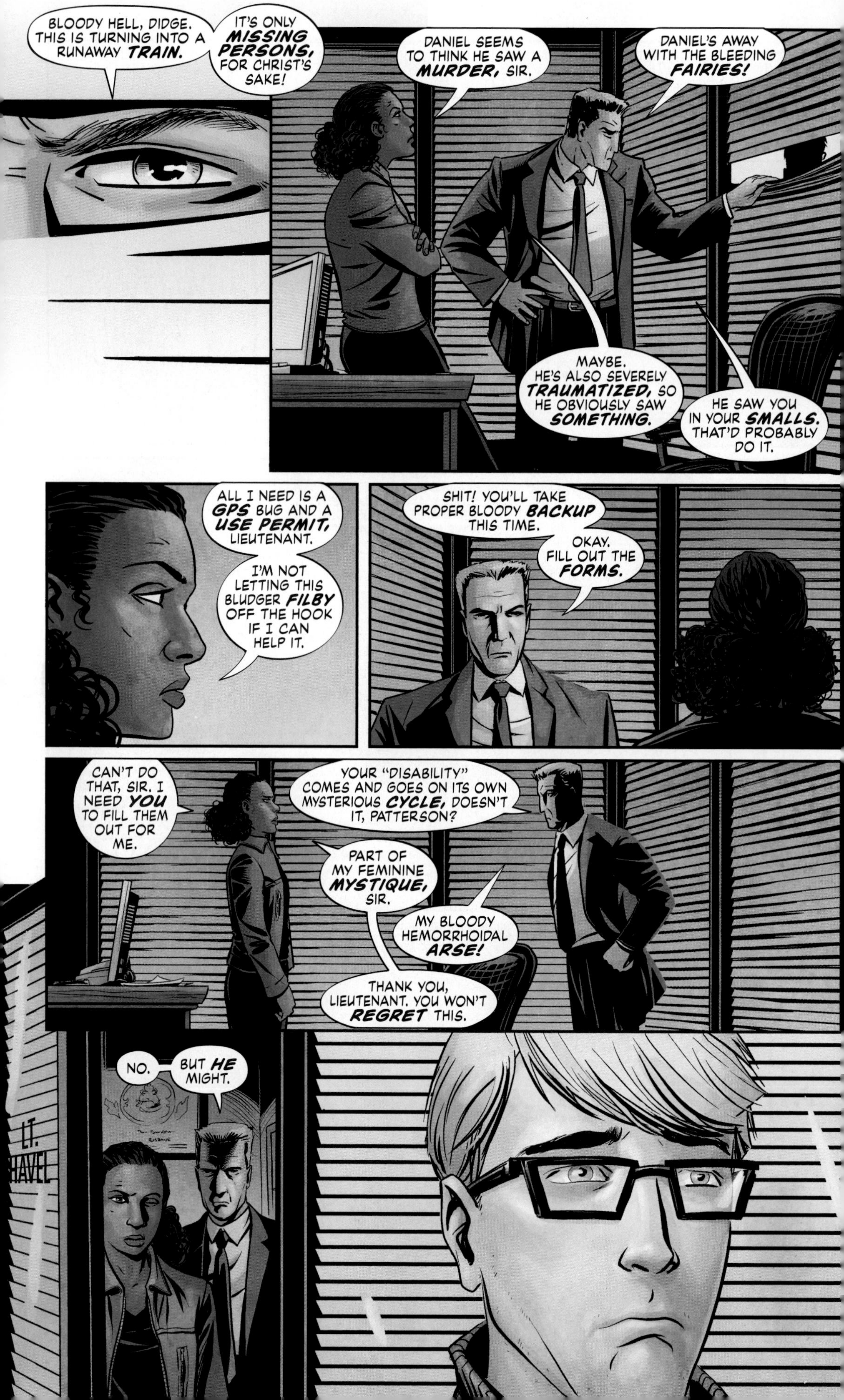
BLOODY HELL, DIDGE. THIS IS TURNING INTO A RUNAWAY TRAIN.
IT'S ONLY MISSING PERSONS, FOR CHRIST'S SAKE!
DANIEL SEEMS TO THINK HE SAW A MURDER, SIR.
DANIEL'S AWAY WITH THE BLEEDING FAIRIES!
MAYBE. HE'S ALSO SEVERELY TRAUMATIZED, SO HE OBVIOUSLY SAW SOMETHING.
HE SAW YOU IN YOUR SMALLS. THAT'D PROBABLY DO IT.
ALL I NEED IS A GPS BUG AND A USE PERMIT, LIEUTENANT.
I'M NOT LETTING THIS BLUDGER FILBY OFF THE HOOK IF I CAN HELP IT.
SHIT! YOU'LL TAKE PROPER BLOODY BACKUP THIS TIME.
OKAY. FILL OUT THE FORMS.
CAN'T DO THAT, SIR. I NEED YOU TO FILL THEM OUT FOR ME.
YOUR "DISABILITY" COMES AND GOES ON ITS OWN MYSTERIOUS CYCLE, DOESN'T IT, PATTERSON?
PART OF MY FEMININE MYSTIQUE, SIR.
MY BLOODY HEMORRHOIDAL ARSE!
THANK YOU, LIEUTENANT. YOU WON'T REGRET THIS.
NO.
BUT HE MIGHT.
LT. HAVEL

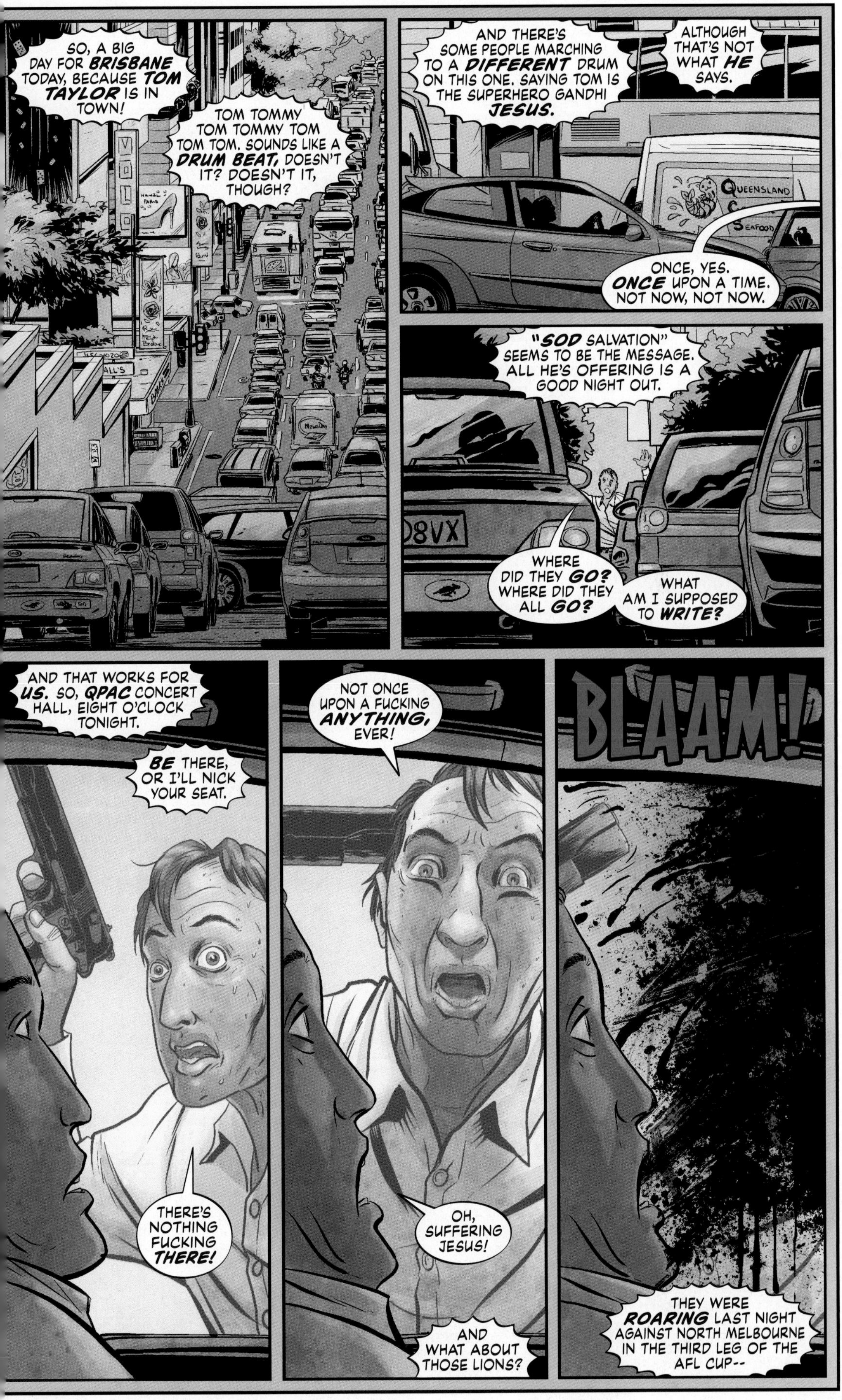

SO, A BIG DAY FOR BRISBANE TODAY, BECAUSE TOM TAYLOR IS IN TOWN!
TOM TOMMY TOM TOMMY TOM TOM TOM. SOUNDS LIKE A DRUM BEAT, DOESN'T IT? DOESN'T IT, THOUGH?
AND THERE'S SOME PEOPLE MARCHING TO A DIFFERENT DRUM ON THIS ONE. SAYING TOM IS THE SUPERHERO GANDHI JESUS.
ALTHOUGH THAT'S NOT WHAT HE SAYS.
QUEENSLAND
SEAFOOD
ONCE, YES. ONCE UPON A TIME. NOT NOW, NOT NOW.
"SOD SALVATION" SEEMS TO BE THE MESSAGE. ALL HE'S OFFERING IS A GOOD NIGHT OUT.
WHERE DID THEY GO? WHERE DID THEY ALL GO?
WHAT AM I SUPPOSED TO WRITE?
AND THAT WORKS FOR US. SO, QPAC CONCERT HALL, EIGHT O'CLOCK TONIGHT.
BE THERE, OR I'LL NICK YOUR SEAT.
THERE'S NOTHING FUCKING THERE!
NOT ONCE UPON A FUCKING ANYTHING, EVER!
OH, SUFFERING JESUS!
AND WHAT ABOUT THOSE LIONS?
BLAAM!
THEY WERE ROARING LAST NIGHT AGAINST NORTH MELBOURNE IN THE THIRD LEG OF THE AFL CUP--

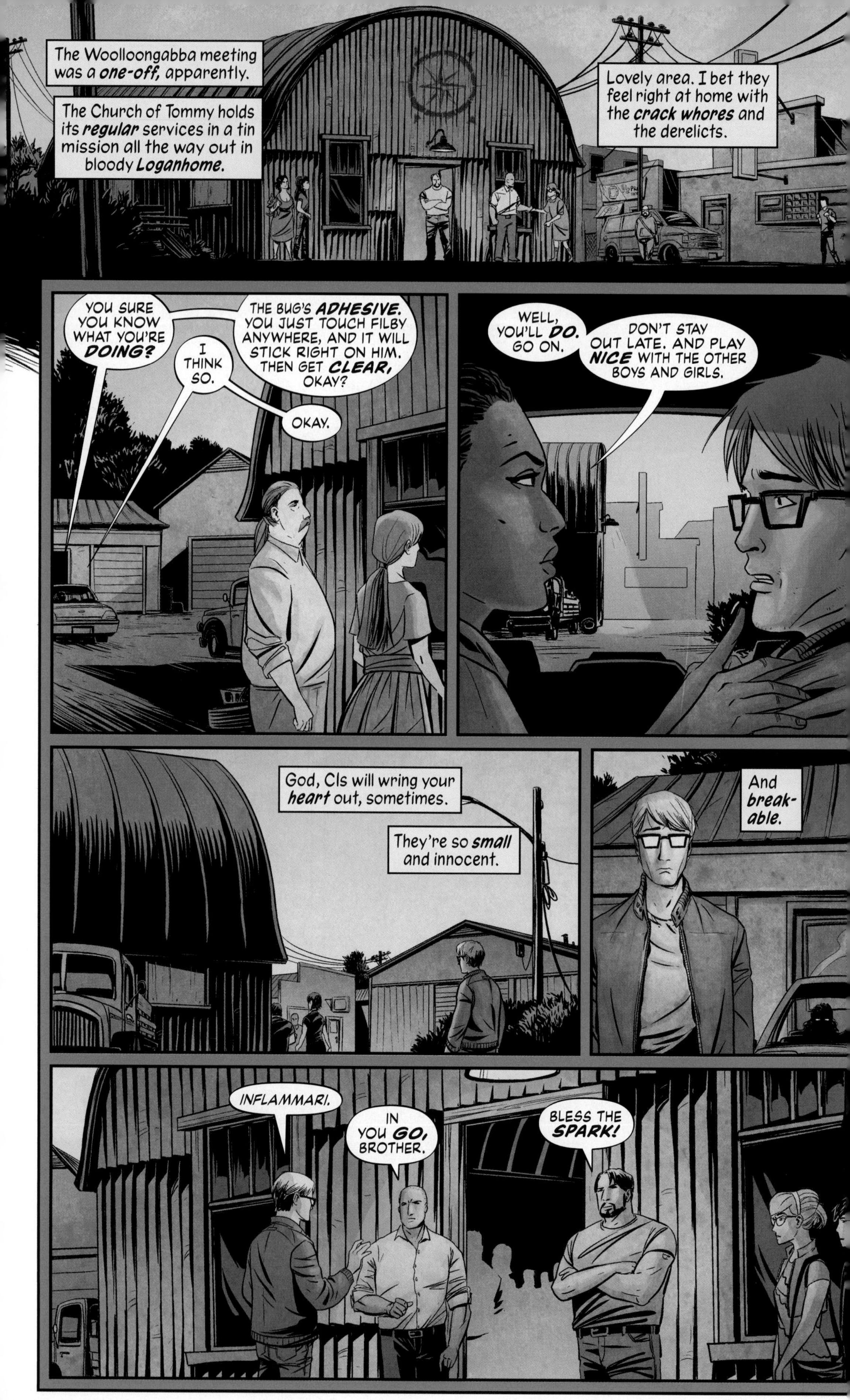
The Woolloongabba meeting was a *one-off,* apparently.
The Church of Tommy holds its *regular* services in a tin mission all the way out in bloody *Loganhome.*
Lovely area. I bet they feel right at home with the *crack whores* and the derelicts.
YOU SURE YOU KNOW WHAT YOU'RE *DOING?*
THE BUG'S *ADHESIVE.* YOU JUST TOUCH FILBY ANYWHERE, AND IT WILL STICK RIGHT ON HIM. THEN GET *CLEAR,* OKAY?
I THINK SO.
OKAY.
WELL, YOU'LL *DO.* GO ON.
DON'T STAY OUT LATE. AND PLAY *NICE* WITH THE OTHER BOYS AND GIRLS.
God, CIs will wring your *heart* out, sometimes.
They're so *small* and innocent.
And *breakable.*
INFLAMMARI.
IN YOU *GO,* BROTHER.
BLESS THE *SPARK!*

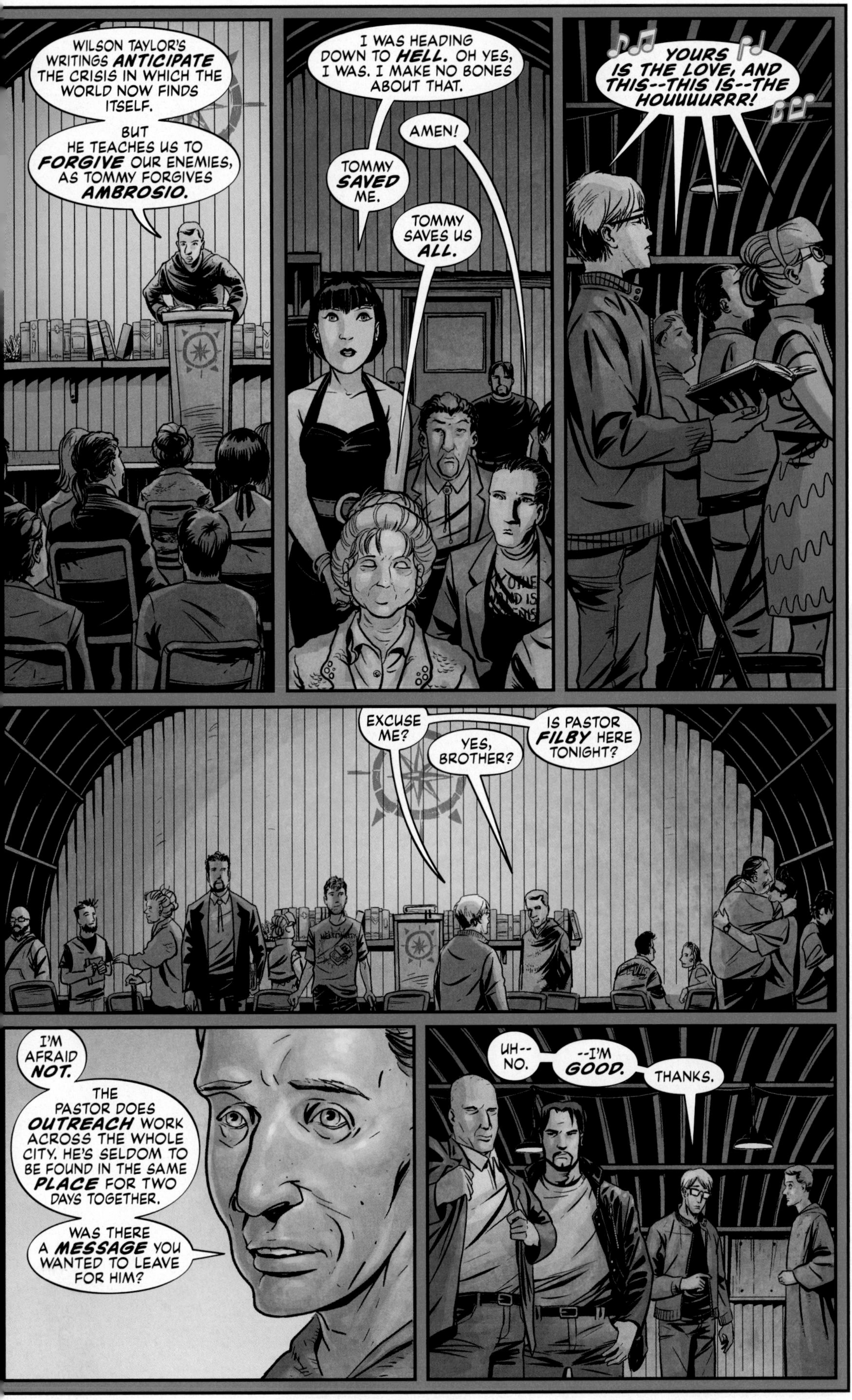
WILSON TAYLOR'S WRITINGS ANTICIPATE THE CRISIS IN WHICH THE WORLD NOW FINDS ITSELF.
BUT HE TEACHES US TO FORGIVE OUR ENEMIES, AS TOMMY FORGIVES AMBROSIO.
I WAS HEADING DOWN TO HELL. OH YES, I WAS. I MAKE NO BONES ABOUT THAT.
AMEN!
TOMMY SAVED ME.
TOMMY SAVES US ALL.
YOURS IS THE LOVE, AND THIS--THIS IS--THE HOUUUURRR!
EXCUSE ME?
YES, BROTHER?
IS PASTOR FILBY HERE TONIGHT?
I'M AFRAID NOT.
THE PASTOR DOES OUTREACH WORK ACROSS THE WHOLE CITY. HE'S SELDOM TO BE FOUND IN THE SAME PLACE FOR TWO DAYS TOGETHER.
WAS THERE A MESSAGE YOU WANTED TO LEAVE FOR HIM?
UH-- NO.
--I'M GOOD.
THANKS.

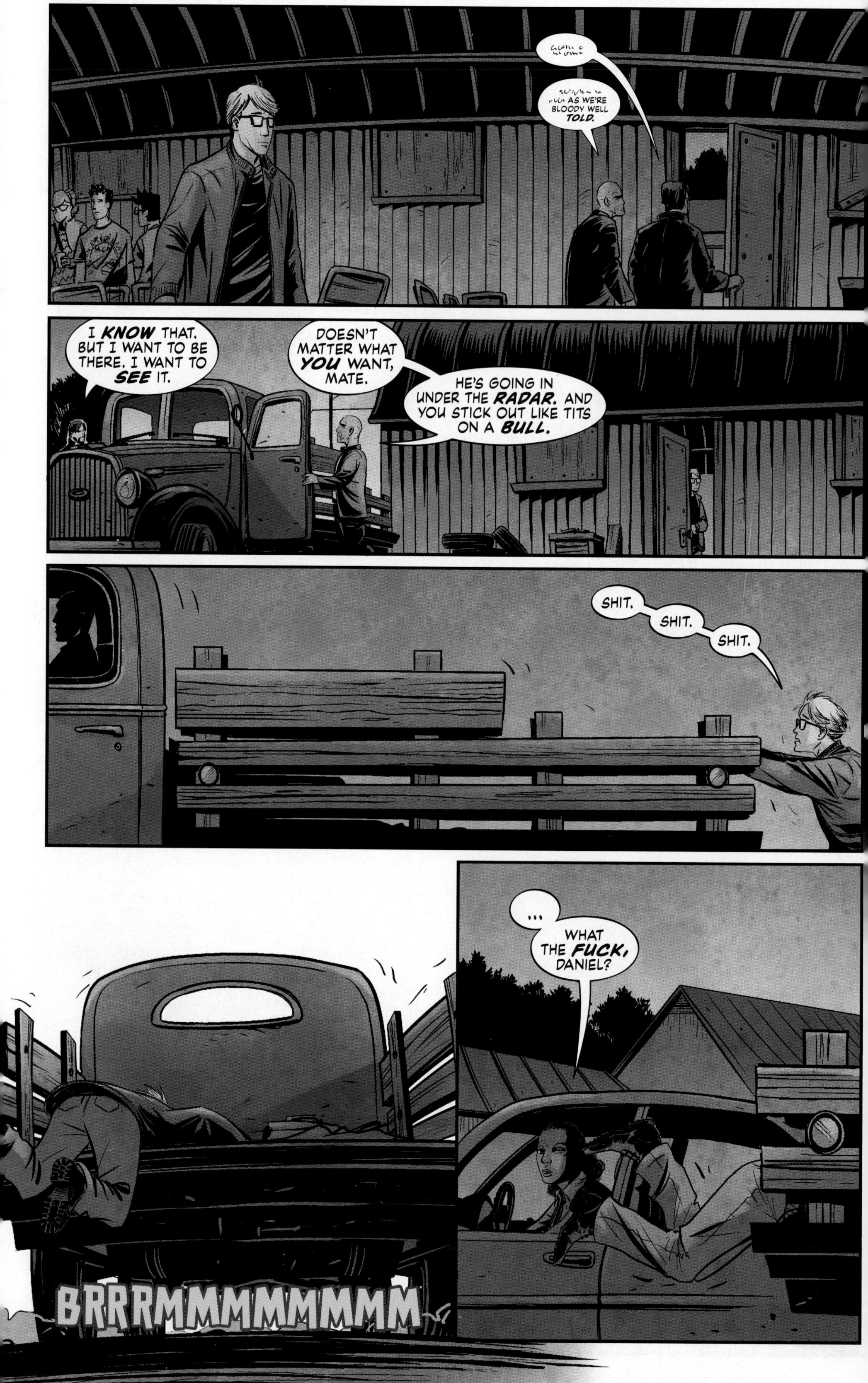

AS WE'RE BLOODY WELL TOLD.
I KNOW THAT. BUT I WANT TO BE THERE. I WANT TO SEE IT.
DOESN'T MATTER WHAT YOU WANT, MATE.
HE'S GOING IN UNDER THE RADAR. AND YOU STICK OUT LIKE TITS ON A BULL.
SHIT.
SHIT.
SHIT.
BRRRMMMMMMMMM
...
WHAT THE FUCK, DANIEL?

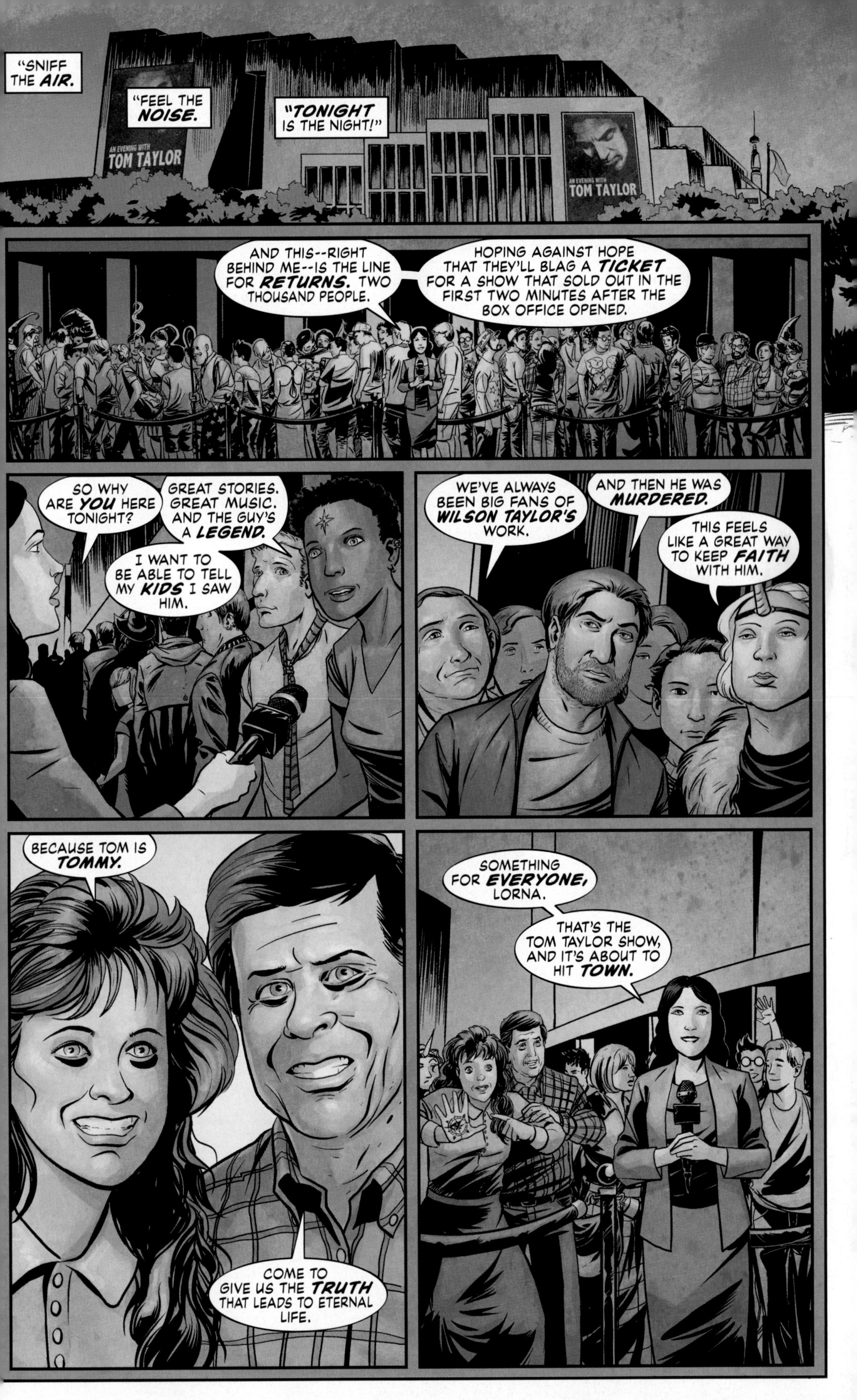
"SNIFF THE AIR.
"FEEL THE NOISE.
"TONIGHT IS THE NIGHT!"
AN EVENING WITH TOM TAYLOR
AN EVENING WITH TOM TAYLOR
AND THIS--RIGHT BEHIND ME--IS THE LINE FOR RETURNS. TWO THOUSAND PEOPLE.
HOPING AGAINST HOPE THAT THEY'LL BLAG A TICKET FOR A SHOW THAT SOLD OUT IN THE FIRST TWO MINUTES AFTER THE BOX OFFICE OPENED.
SO WHY ARE YOU HERE TONIGHT?
GREAT STORIES. GREAT MUSIC. AND THE GUY'S A LEGEND.
I WANT TO BE ABLE TO TELL MY KIDS I SAW HIM.
WE'VE ALWAYS BEEN BIG FANS OF WILSON TAYLOR'S WORK.
AND THEN HE WAS MURDERED.
THIS FEELS LIKE A GREAT WAY TO KEEP FAITH WITH HIM.
BECAUSE TOM IS TOMMY.
COME TO GIVE US THE TRUTH THAT LEADS TO ETERNAL LIFE.
SOMETHING FOR EVERYONE, LORNA.
THAT'S THE TOM TAYLOR SHOW, AND IT'S ABOUT TO HIT TOWN.

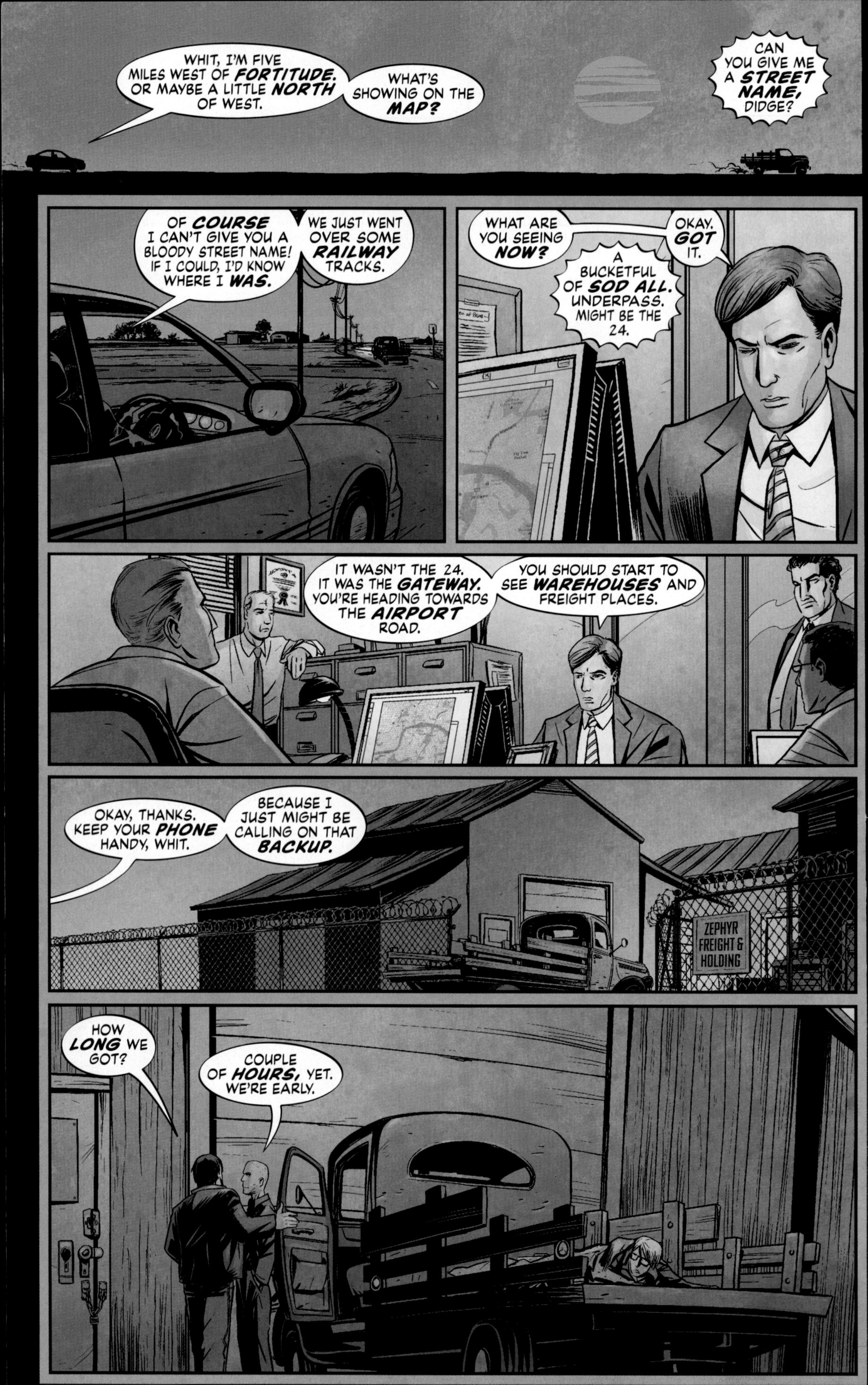
WHIT, I'M FIVE MILES WEST OF FORTITUDE. OR MAYBE A LITTLE NORTH OF WEST.
WHAT'S SHOWING ON THE MAP?
CAN YOU GIVE ME A STREET NAME, DIDGE?
OF COURSE I CAN'T GIVE YOU A BLOODY STREET NAME! IF I COULD, I'D KNOW WHERE I WAS.
WE JUST WENT OVER SOME RAILWAY TRACKS.
WHAT ARE YOU SEEING NOW?
OKAY. GOT IT.
A BUCKETFUL OF SOD ALL. UNDERPASS. MIGHT BE THE 24.
IT WASN'T THE 24. IT WAS THE GATEWAY. YOU'RE HEADING TOWARDS THE AIRPORT ROAD.
YOU SHOULD START TO SEE WAREHOUSES AND FREIGHT PLACES.
OKAY, THANKS. KEEP YOUR PHONE HANDY, WHIT.
BECAUSE I JUST MIGHT BE CALLING ON THAT BACKUP.
ZEPHYR FREIGHT & HOLDING
HOW LONG WE GOT?
COUPLE OF HOURS, YET. WE'RE EARLY.

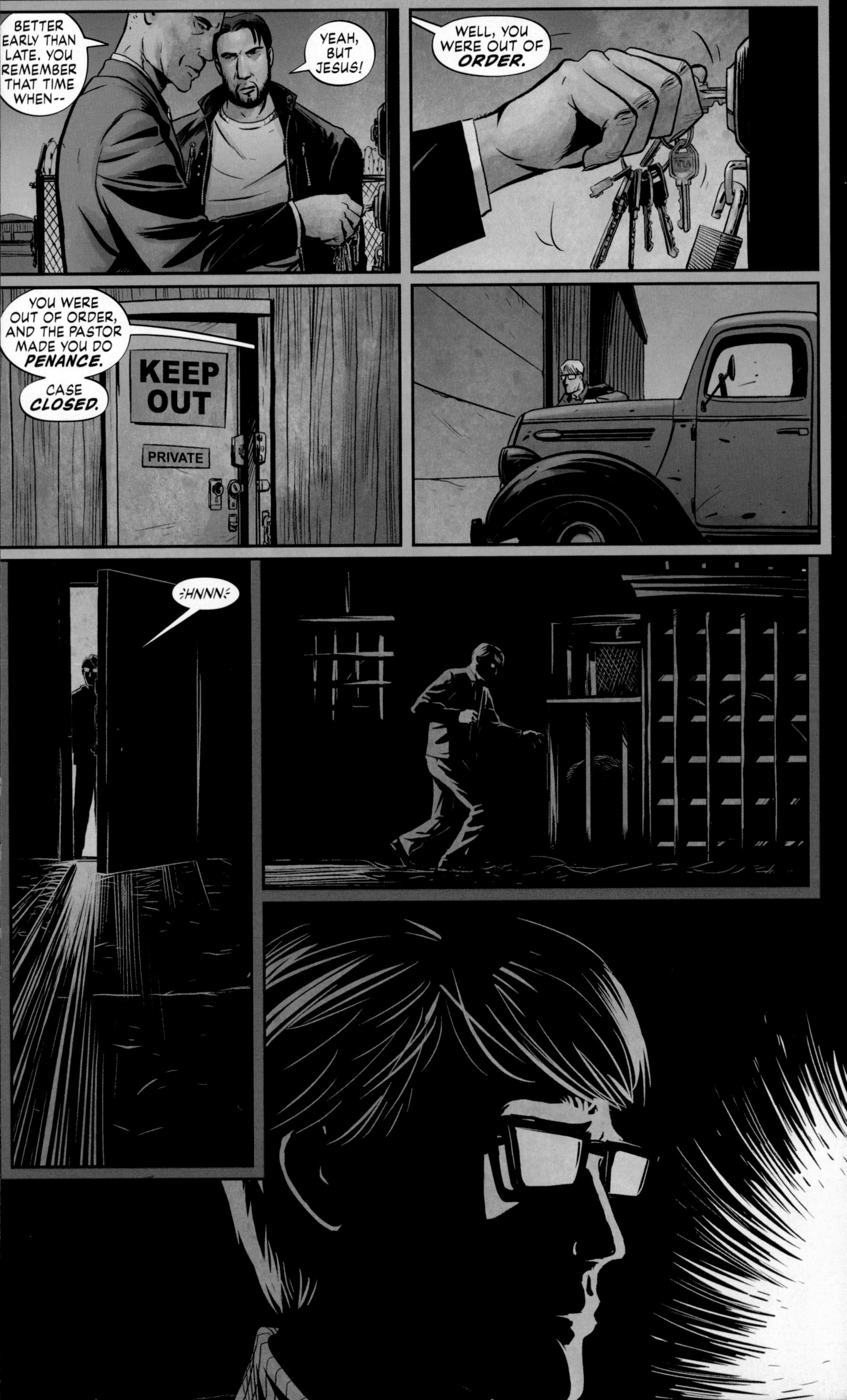

BETTER EARLY THAN LATE. YOU REMEMBER THAT TIME WHEN--
YEAH, BUT JESUS!
WELL, YOU WERE OUT OF ORDER.
YOU WERE OUT OF ORDER, AND THE PASTOR MADE YOU DO PENANCE.
CASE CLOSED.
KEEP OUT
PRIVATE
HNNN

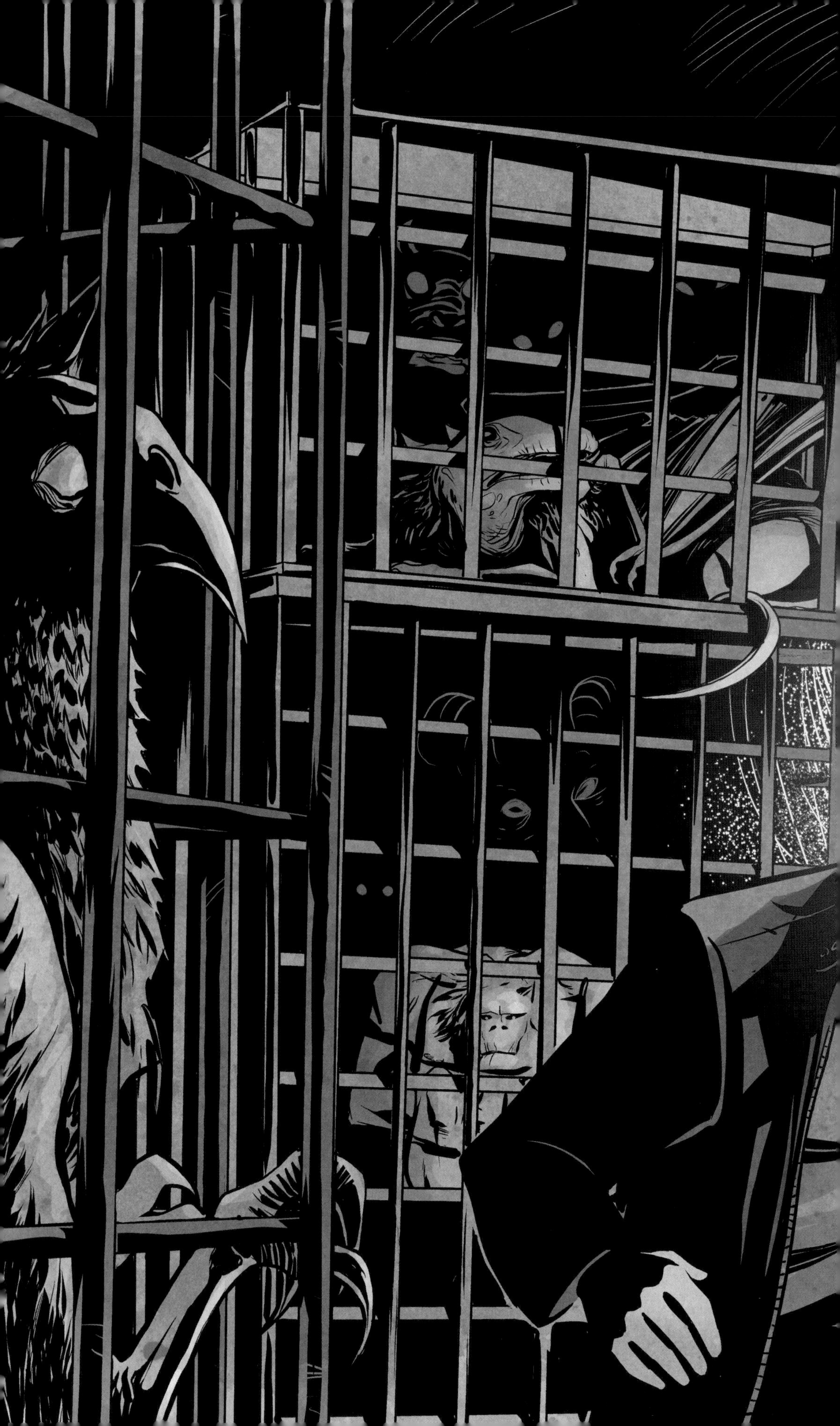

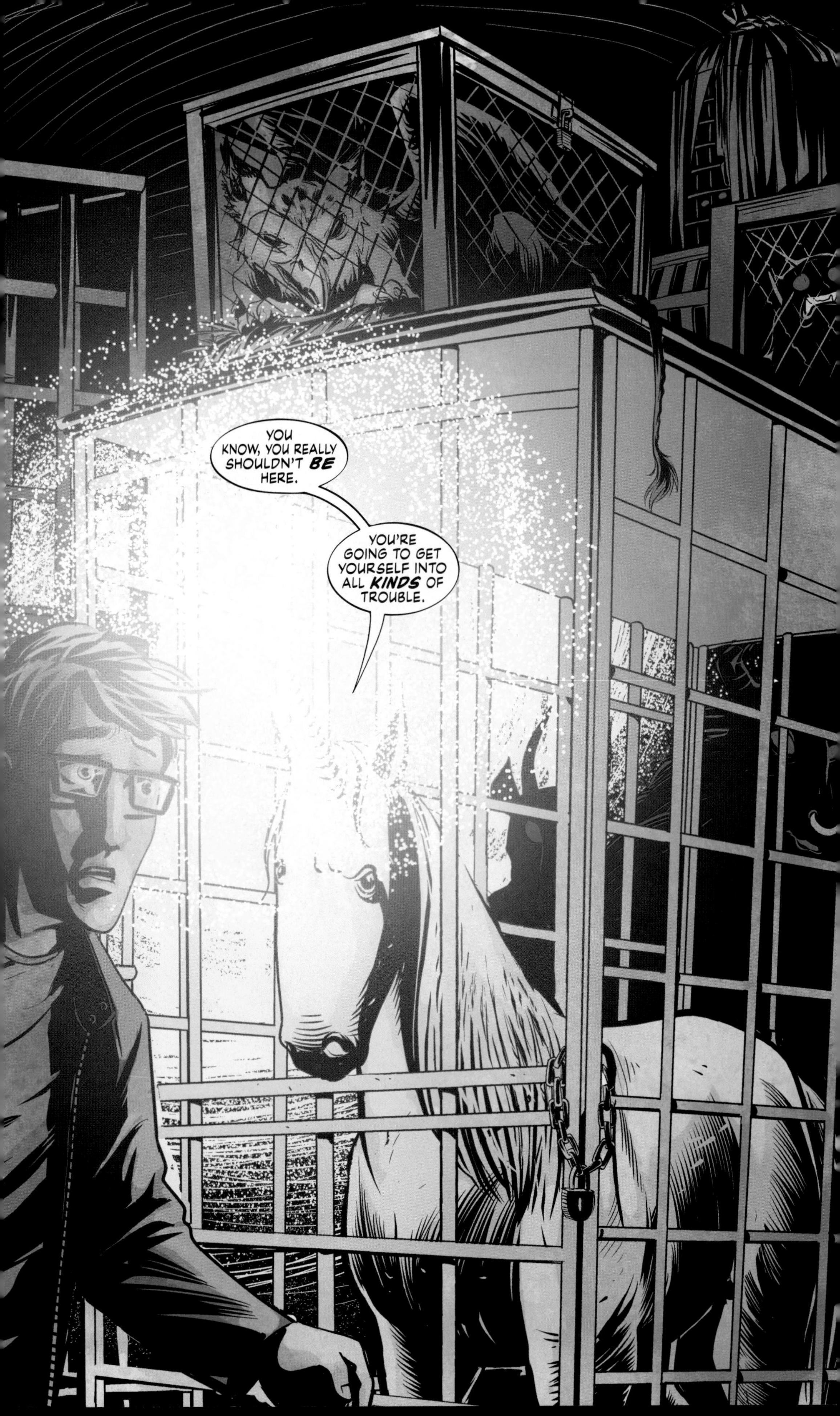
YOU KNOW, YOU REALLY SHOULDN'T BE HERE.
YOU'RE GOING TO GET YOURSELF INTO ALL KINDS OF TROUBLE.

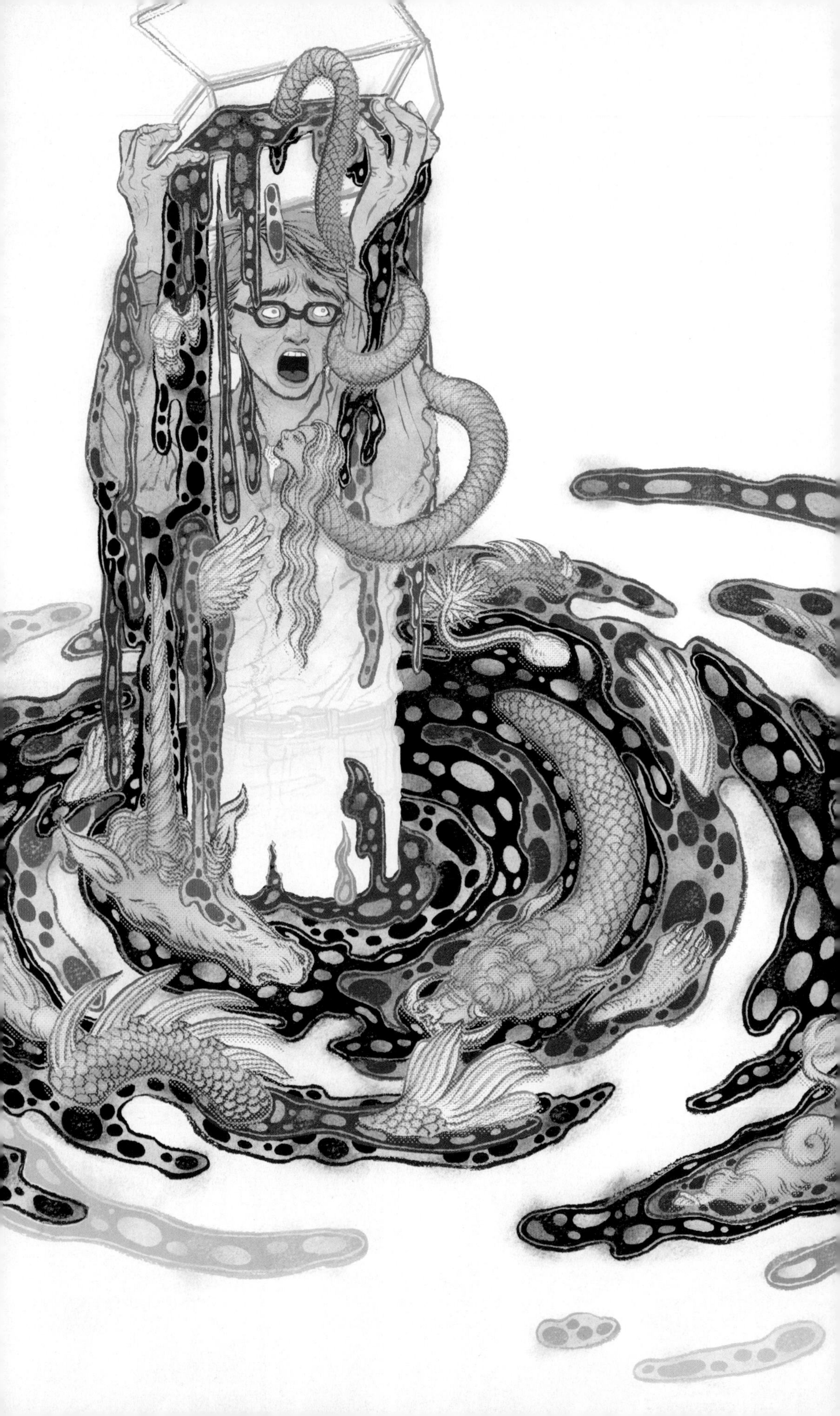

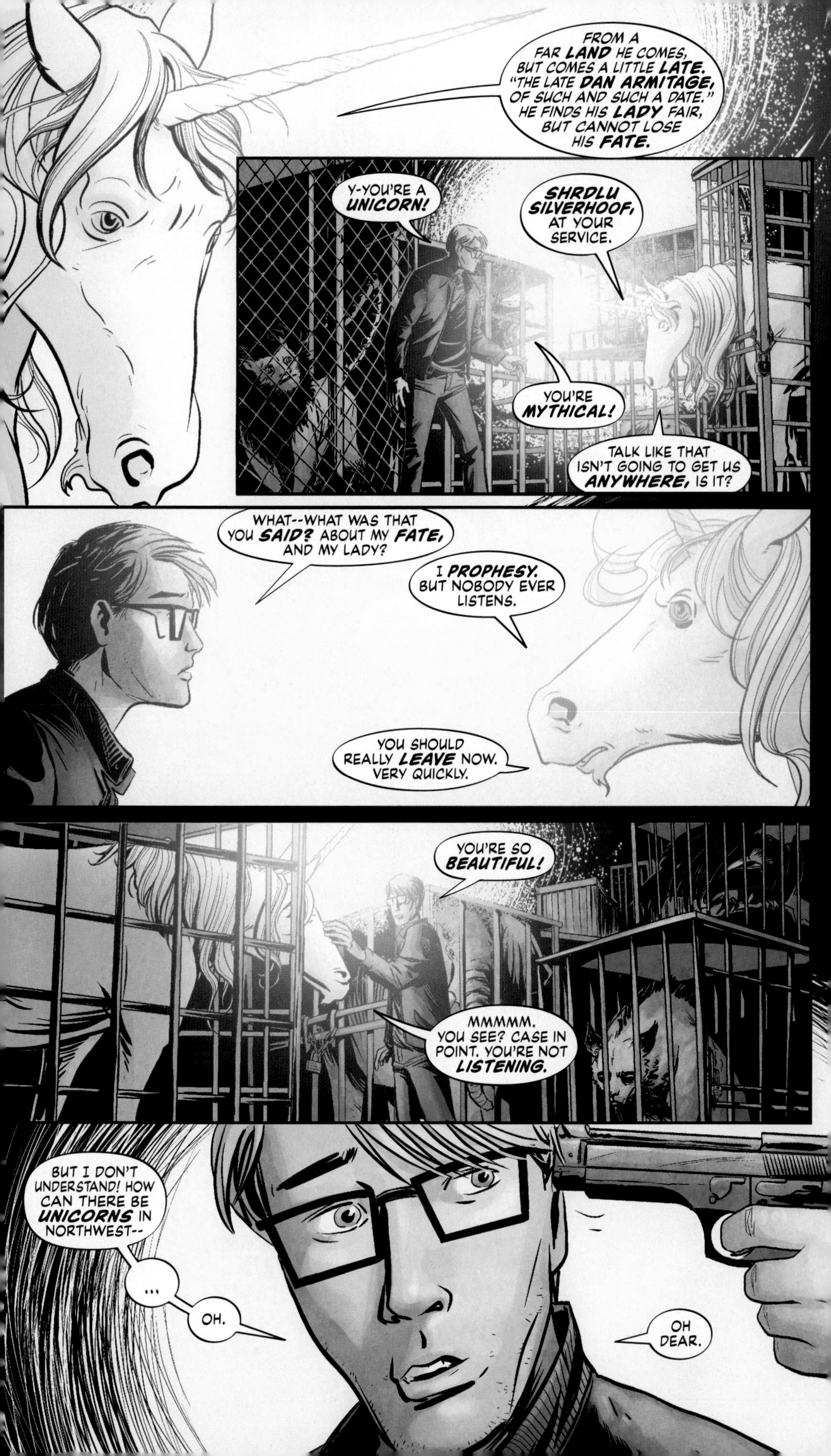
FROM A FAR LAND HE COMES, BUT COMES A LITTLE LATE. "THE LATE DAN ARMITAGE, OF SUCH AND SUCH A DATE." HE FINDS HIS LADY FAIR, BUT CANNOT LOSE HIS FATE.
Y-YOU'RE A UNICORN!
SHRDLU SILVERHOOF, AT YOUR SERVICE.
YOU'RE MYTHICAL!
TALK LIKE THAT ISN'T GOING TO GET US ANYWHERE, IS IT?
WHAT--WHAT WAS THAT YOU SAID? ABOUT MY FATE, AND MY LADY?
I PROPHESY. BUT NOBODY EVER LISTENS.
YOU SHOULD REALLY LEAVE NOW. VERY QUICKLY.
YOU'RE SO BEAUTIFUL!
MMMMM. YOU SEE? CASE IN POINT. YOU'RE NOT LISTENING.
BUT I DON'T UNDERSTAND! HOW CAN THERE BE UNICORNS IN NORTHWEST--
...
OH.
OH DEAR.

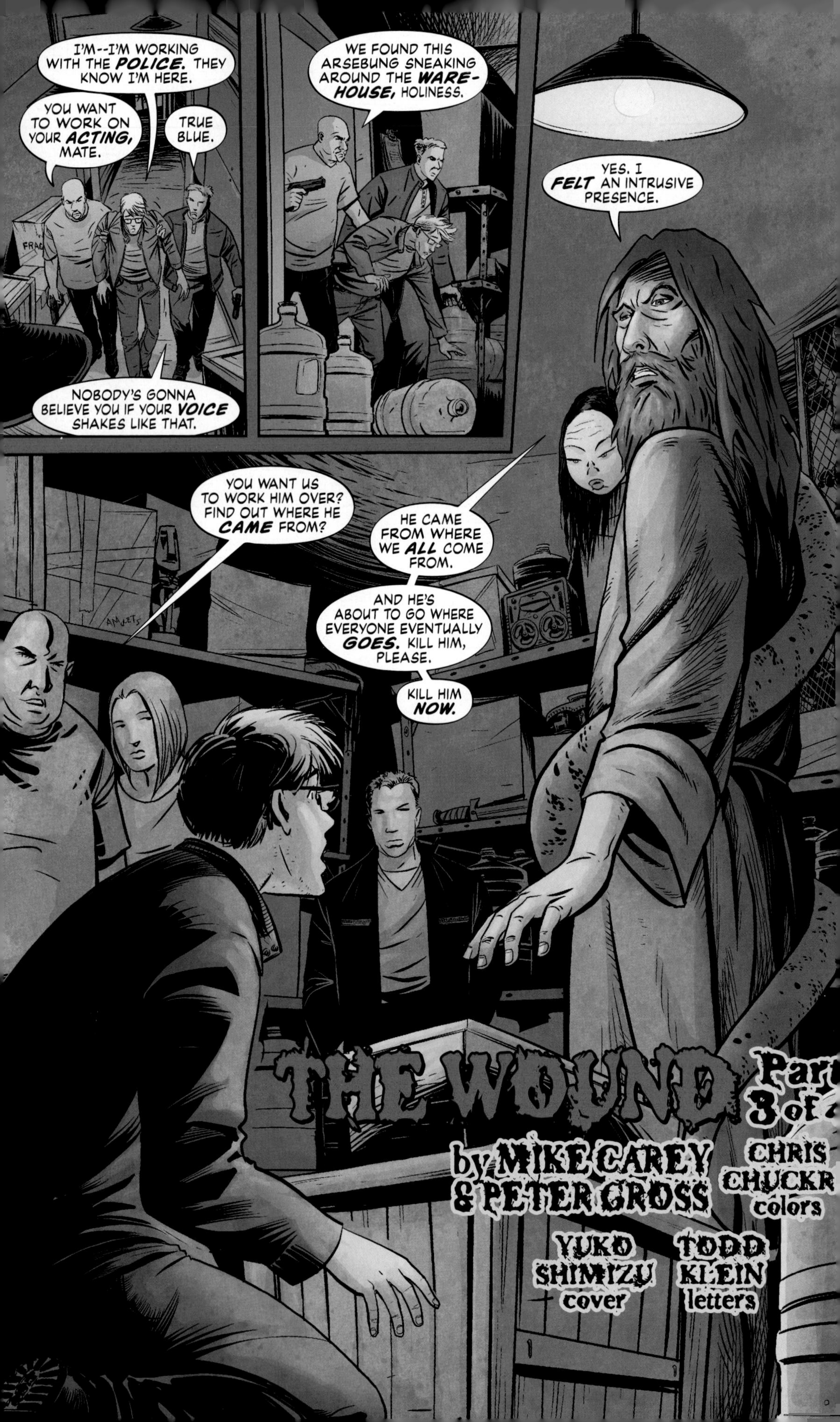
I'M--I'M WORKING WITH THE POLICE. THEY KNOW I'M HERE.
YOU WANT TO WORK ON YOUR ACTING, MATE.
TRUE BLUE.
NOBODY'S GONNA BELIEVE YOU IF YOUR VOICE SHAKES LIKE THAT.
WE FOUND THIS ARSEBUNG SNEAKING AROUND THE WARE-HOUSE, HOLINESS.
YES. I FELT AN INTRUSIVE PRESENCE.
YOU WANT US TO WORK HIM OVER? FIND OUT WHERE HE CAME FROM?
HE CAME FROM WHERE WE ALL COME FROM.
AND HE'S ABOUT TO GO WHERE EVERYONE EVENTUALLY GOES. KILL HIM, PLEASE.
KILL HIM NOW.
THE WOUND
Part 3 of
by MIKE CAREY & PETER GROSS
CHRIS CHUCKR colors
YUKO SHIMIZU cover
TODD KLEIN letters

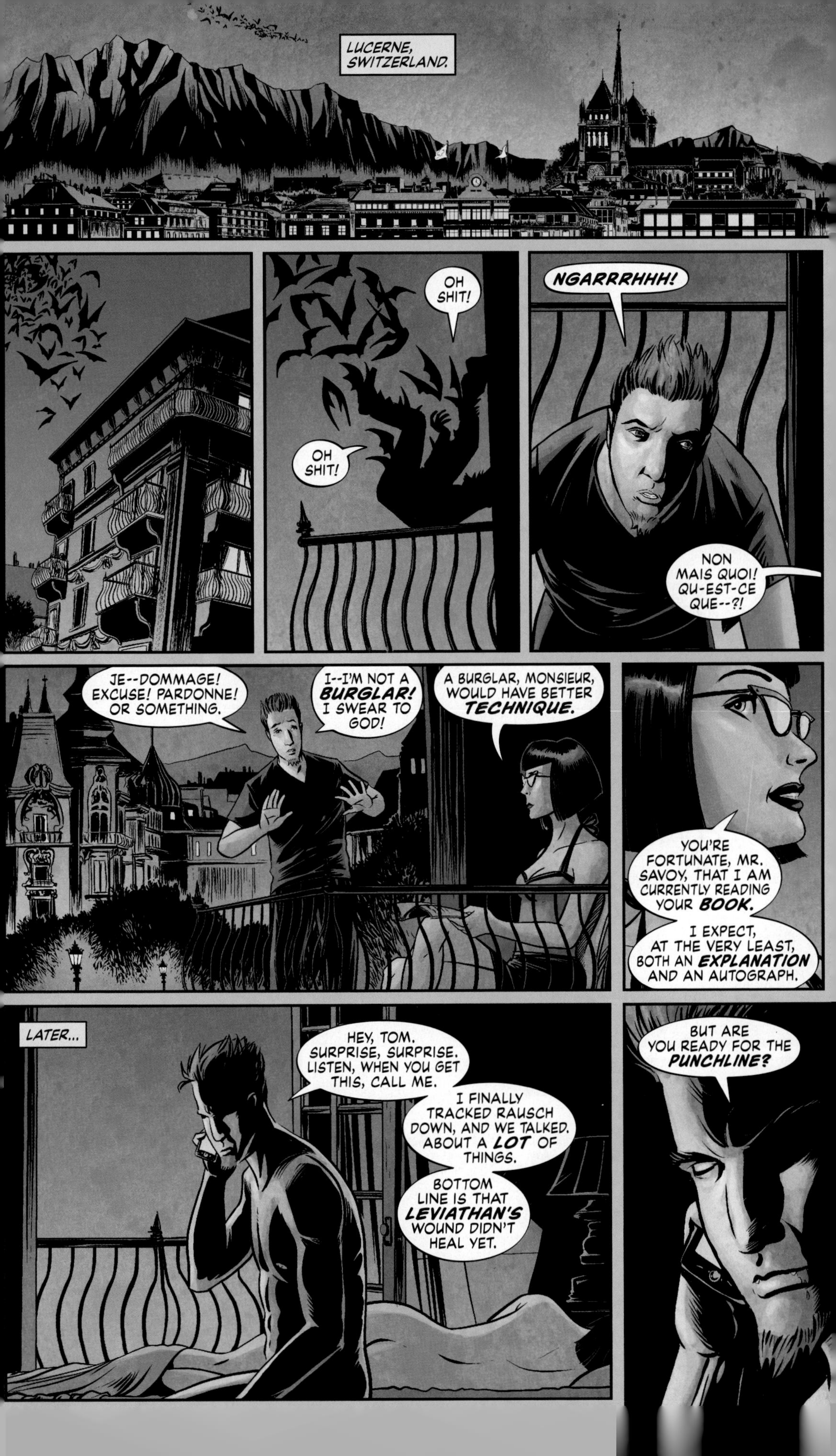

LUCERNE, SWITZERLAND.
OH SHIT!
OH SHIT!
NGARRRHHH!
NON MAIS QUOI! QU-EST-CE QUE--?!
JE--DOMMAGE! EXCUSE! PARDONNE! OR SOMETHING.
I--I'M NOT A BURGLAR! I SWEAR TO GOD!
A BURGLAR, MONSIEUR, WOULD HAVE BETTER TECHNIQUE.
YOU'RE FORTUNATE, MR. SAVOY, THAT I AM CURRENTLY READING YOUR BOOK.
I EXPECT, AT THE VERY LEAST, BOTH AN EXPLANATION AND AN AUTOGRAPH.
LATER...
HEY, TOM. SURPRISE, SURPRISE. LISTEN, WHEN YOU GET THIS, CALL ME.
I FINALLY TRACKED RAUSCH DOWN, AND WE TALKED. ABOUT A LOT OF THINGS.
BOTTOM LINE IS THAT LEVIATHAN'S WOUND DIDN'T HEAL YET.
BUT ARE YOU READY FOR THE PUNCHLINE?

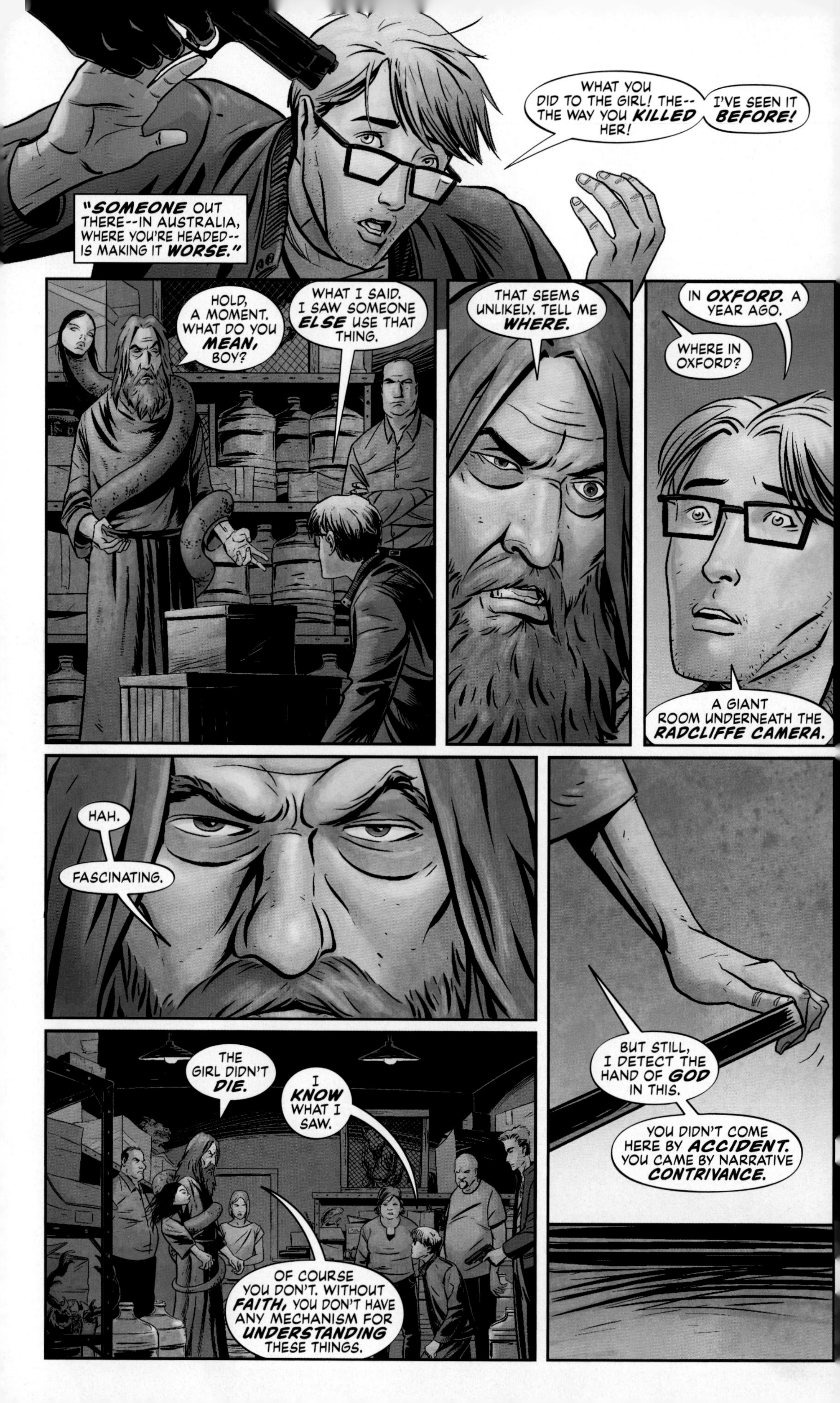

"SOMEONE OUT THERE--IN AUSTRALIA, WHERE YOU'RE HEADED-- IS MAKING IT WORSE."
WHAT YOU DID TO THE GIRL! THE-- THE WAY YOU KILLED HER!
I'VE SEEN IT BEFORE!
HOLD, A MOMENT. WHAT DO YOU MEAN, BOY?
WHAT I SAID. I SAW SOMEONE ELSE USE THAT THING.
THAT SEEMS UNLIKELY. TELL ME WHERE.
IN OXFORD. A YEAR AGO.
WHERE IN OXFORD?
A GIANT ROOM UNDERNEATH THE RADCLIFFE CAMERA.
HAH.
FASCINATING.
THE GIRL DIDN'T DIE.
I KNOW WHAT I SAW.
OF COURSE YOU DON'T. WITHOUT FAITH, YOU DON'T HAVE ANY MECHANISM FOR UNDERSTANDING THESE THINGS.
BUT STILL, I DETECT THE HAND OF GOD IN THIS.
YOU DIDN'T COME HERE BY ACCIDENT. YOU CAME BY NARRATIVE CONTRIVANCE.

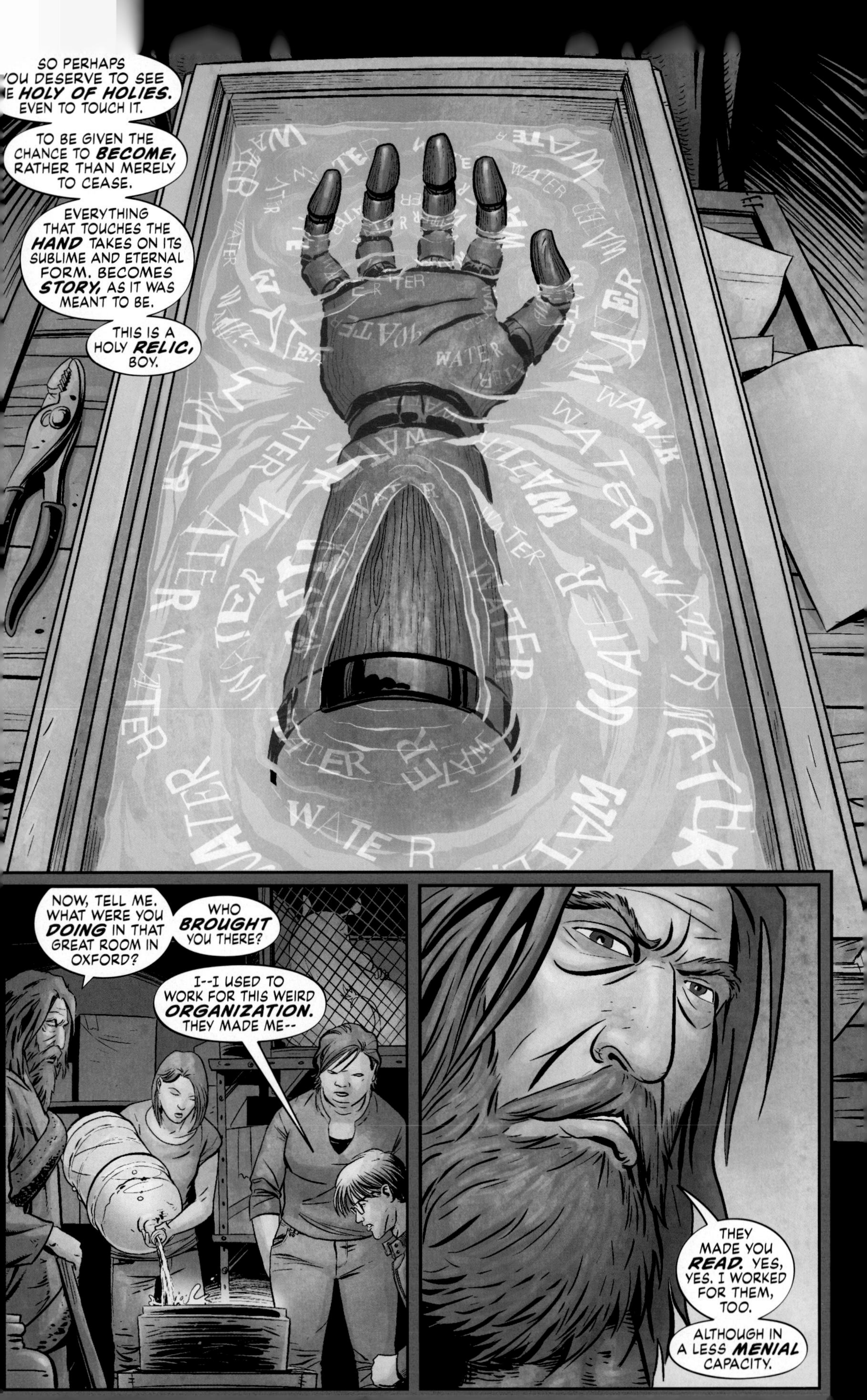
SO PERHAPS OU DESERVE TO SEE E HOLY OF HOLIES. EVEN TO TOUCH IT.
TO BE GIVEN THE CHANCE TO BECOME, RATHER THAN MERELY TO CEASE.
EVERYTHING THAT TOUCHES THE HAND TAKES ON ITS SUBLIME AND ETERNAL FORM. BECOMES STORY, AS IT WAS MEANT TO BE.
THIS IS A HOLY RELIC, BOY.
NOW, TELL ME. WHAT WERE YOU DOING IN THAT GREAT ROOM IN OXFORD?
WHO BROUGHT YOU THERE?
I--I USED TO WORK FOR THIS WEIRD ORGANIZATION. THEY MADE ME--
THEY MADE YOU READ. YES, YES. I WORKED FOR THEM, TOO.
ALTHOUGH IN A LESS MENIAL CAPACITY.

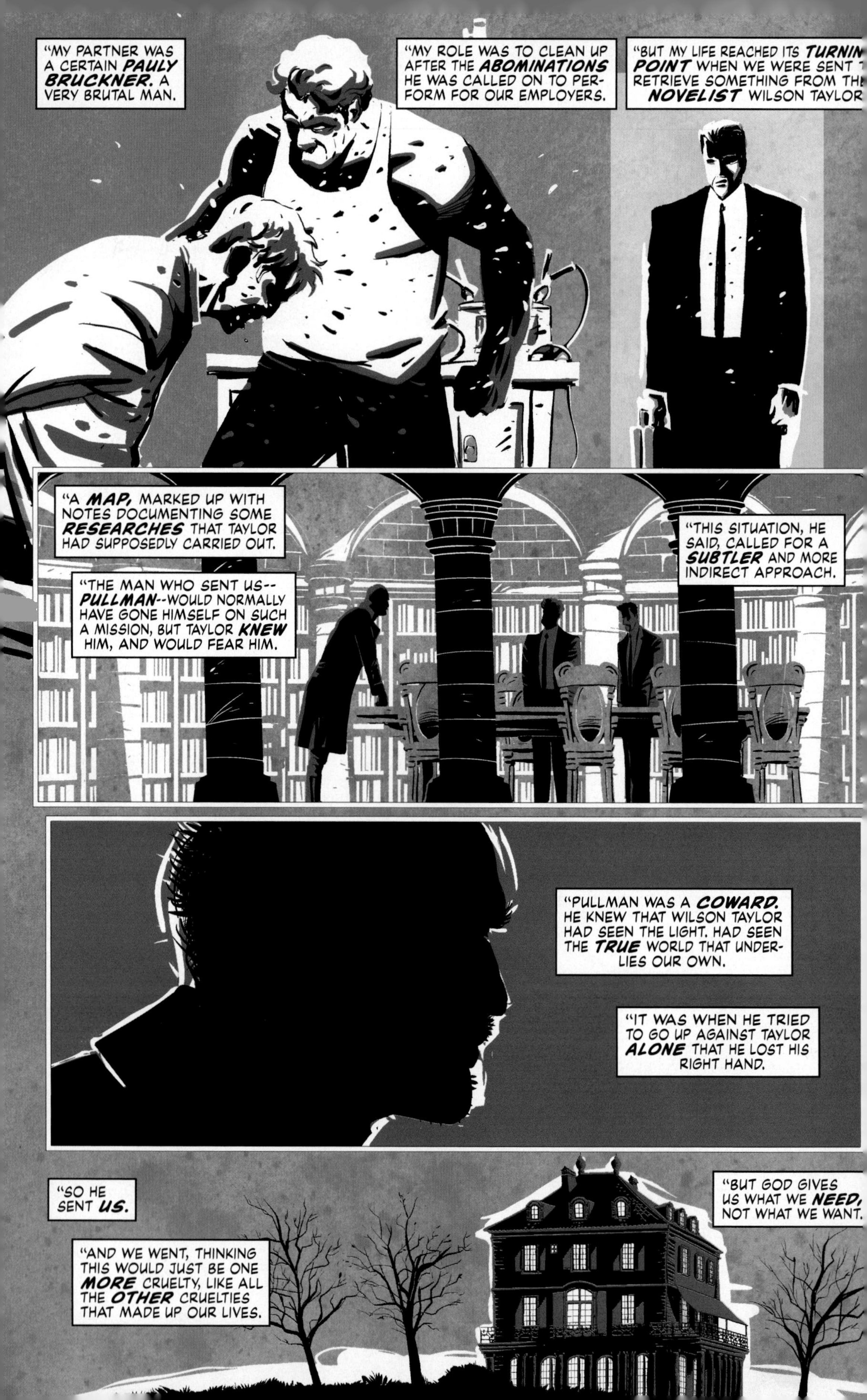
"MY PARTNER WAS A CERTAIN PAULY BRUCKNER. A VERY BRUTAL MAN.
"MY ROLE WAS TO CLEAN UP AFTER THE ABOMINATIONS HE WAS CALLED ON TO PERFORM FOR OUR EMPLOYERS.
"BUT MY LIFE REACHED ITS TURNING POINT WHEN WE WERE SENT TO RETRIEVE SOMETHING FROM THE NOVELIST WILSON TAYLOR.
"A MAP, MARKED UP WITH NOTES DOCUMENTING SOME RESEARCHES THAT TAYLOR HAD SUPPOSEDLY CARRIED OUT.
"THE MAN WHO SENT US--PULLMAN--WOULD NORMALLY HAVE GONE HIMSELF ON SUCH A MISSION, BUT TAYLOR KNEW HIM, AND WOULD FEAR HIM.
"THIS SITUATION, HE SAID, CALLED FOR A SUBTLER AND MORE INDIRECT APPROACH.
"PULLMAN WAS A COWARD. HE KNEW THAT WILSON TAYLOR HAD SEEN THE LIGHT. HAD SEEN THE TRUE WORLD THAT UNDERLIES OUR OWN.
"IT WAS WHEN HE TRIED TO GO UP AGAINST TAYLOR ALONE THAT HE LOST HIS RIGHT HAND.
"SO HE SENT US.
"AND WE WENT, THINKING THIS WOULD JUST BE ONE MORE CRUELTY, LIKE ALL THE OTHER CRUELTIES THAT MADE UP OUR LIVES.
"BUT GOD GIVES US WHAT WE NEED, NOT WHAT WE WANT.

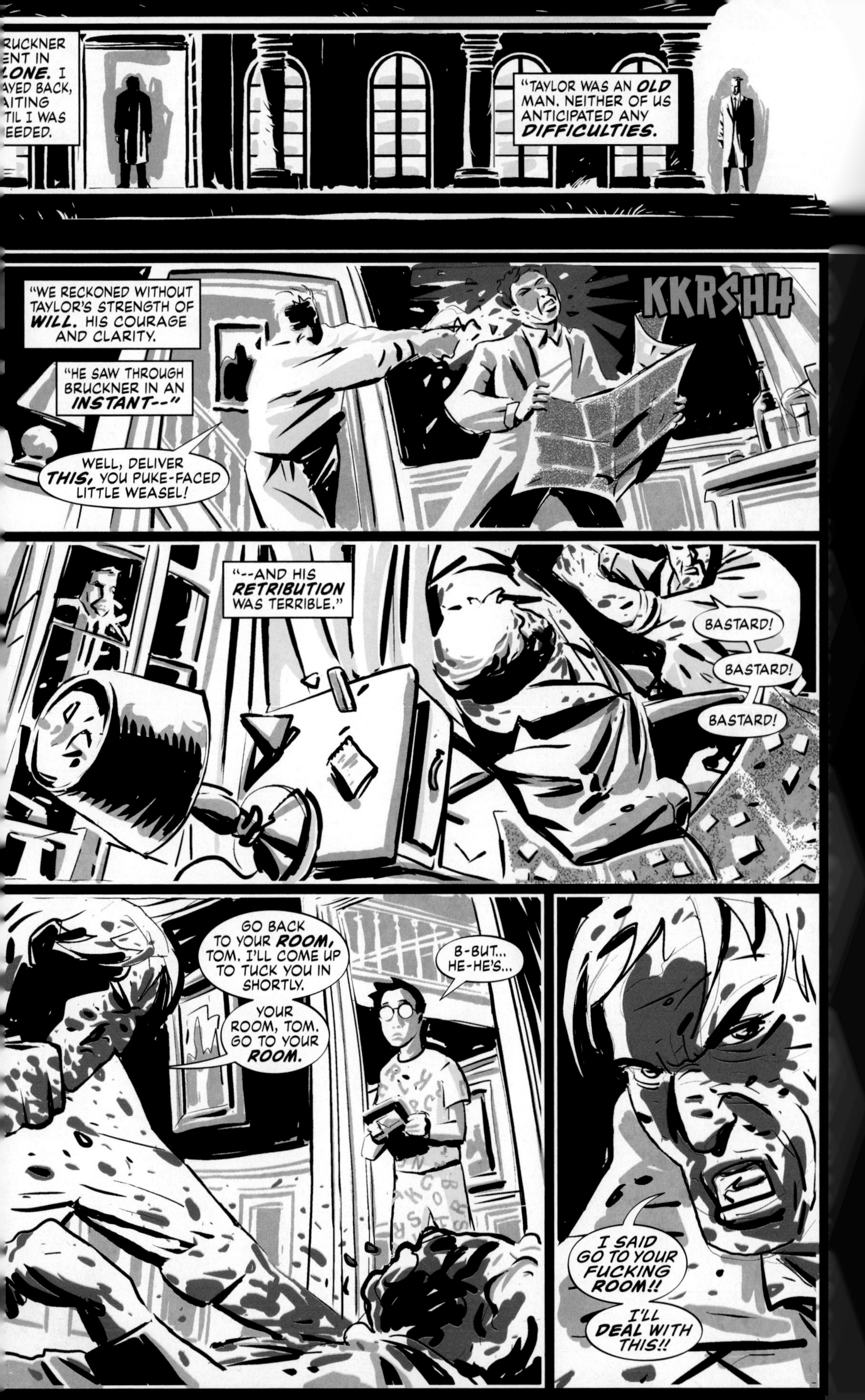

RUCKNER
ENT IN
LONE. I
AYED BACK,
AITING
TIL I WAS
EEDED.
"TAYLOR WAS AN OLD MAN. NEITHER OF US ANTICIPATED ANY DIFFICULTIES.
"WE RECKONED WITHOUT TAYLOR'S STRENGTH OF WILL. HIS COURAGE AND CLARITY.
"HE SAW THROUGH BRUCKNER IN AN INSTANT--"
WELL, DELIVER THIS, YOU PUKE-FACED LITTLE WEASEL!
KKRSHH
"--AND HIS RETRIBUTION WAS TERRIBLE."
BASTARD!
BASTARD!
BASTARD!
GO BACK TO YOUR ROOM, TOM. I'LL COME UP TO TUCK YOU IN SHORTLY.
YOUR ROOM, TOM. GO TO YOUR ROOM.
B-BUT... HE-HE'S...
I SAID GO TO YOUR FUCKING ROOM!!
I'LL DEAL WITH THIS!!

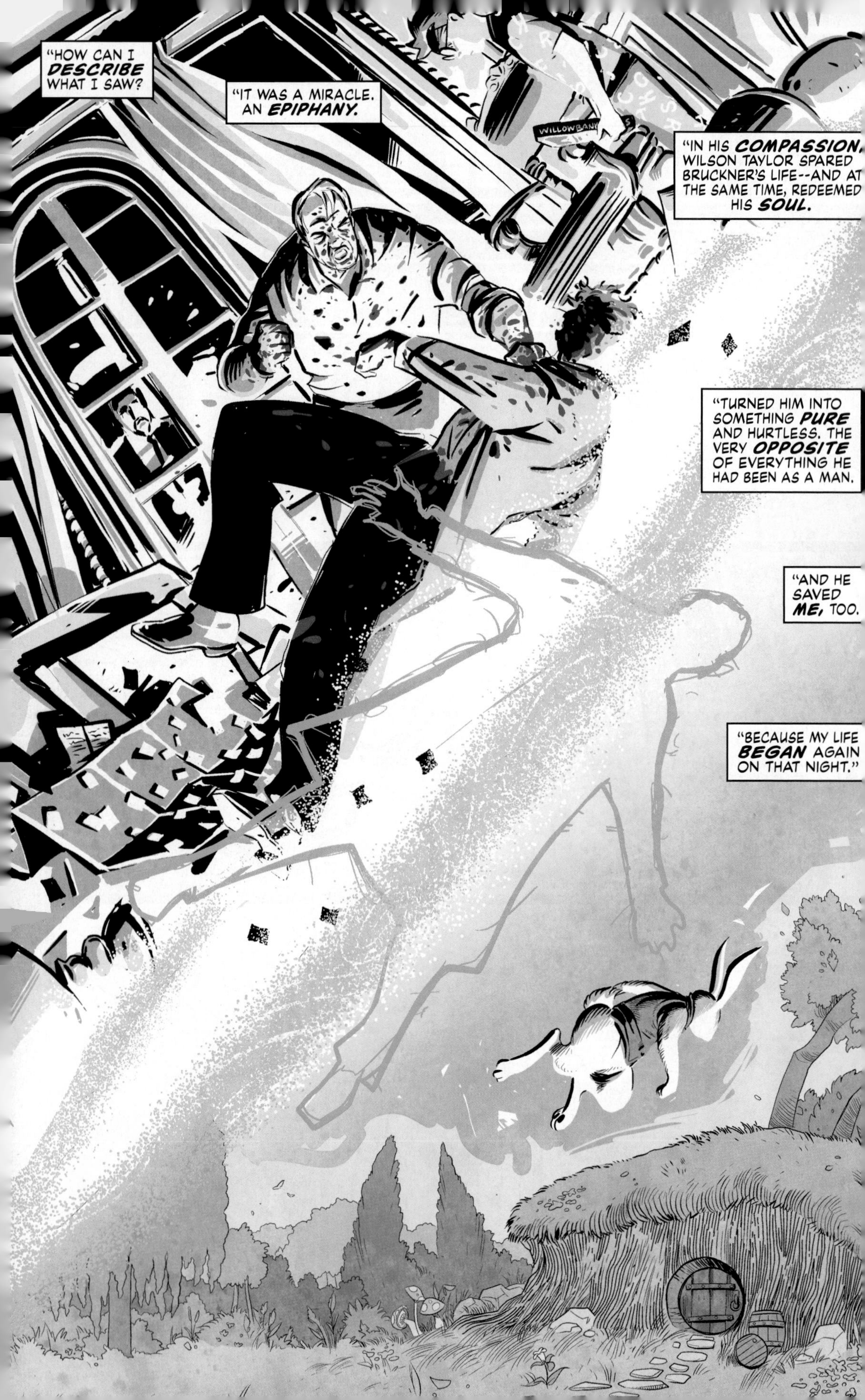
"HOW CAN I DESCRIBE WHAT I SAW?
"IT WAS A MIRACLE. AN EPIPHANY.
"IN HIS COMPASSION, WILSON TAYLOR SPARED BRUCKNER'S LIFE--AND AT THE SAME TIME, REDEEMED HIS SOUL.
"TURNED HIM INTO SOMETHING PURE AND HURTLESS. THE VERY OPPOSITE OF EVERYTHING HE HAD BEEN AS A MAN.
"AND HE SAVED ME, TOO.
"BECAUSE MY LIFE BEGAN AGAIN ON THAT NIGHT."

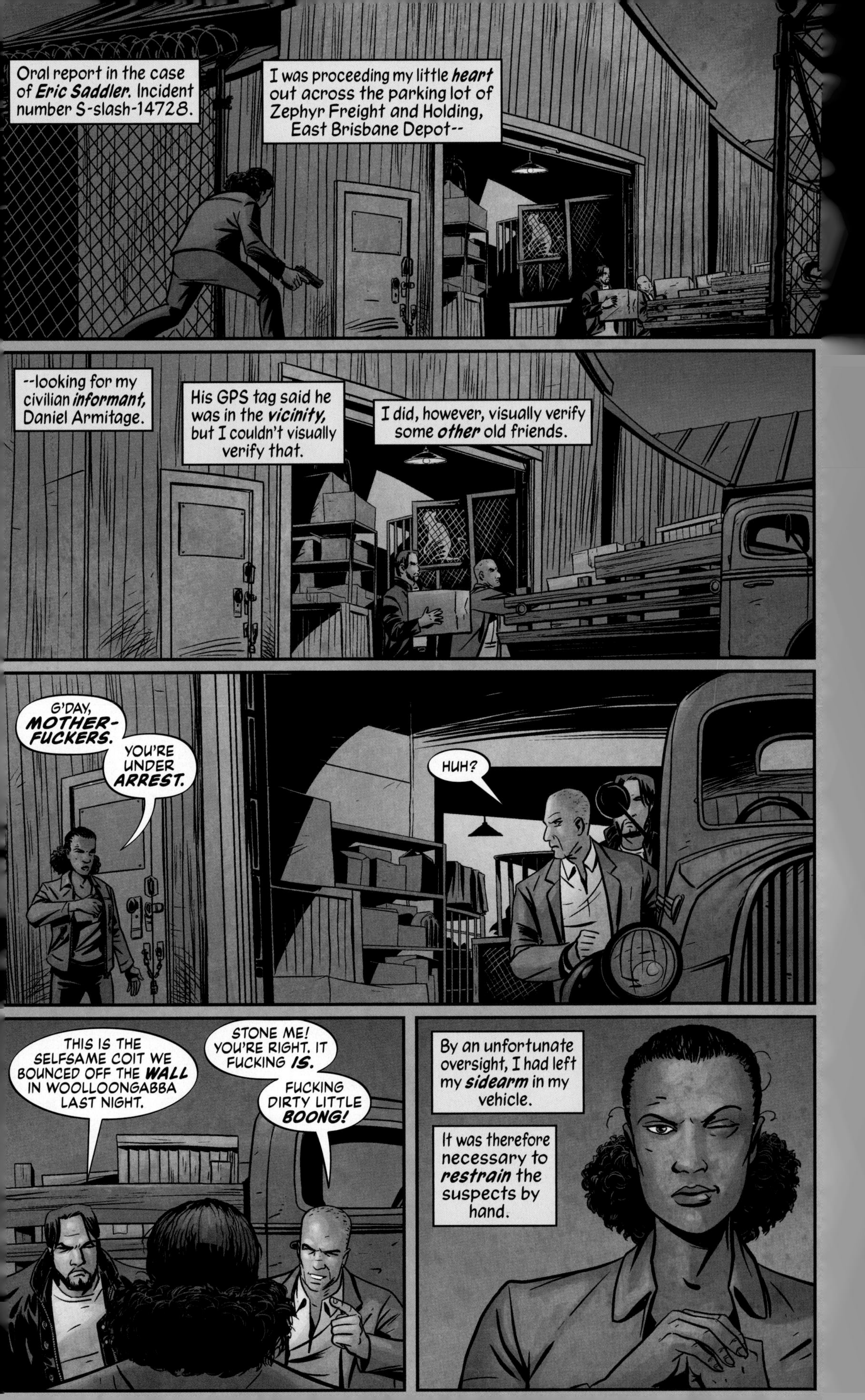
Oral report in the case of Eric Saddler. Incident number S-slash-14728.
I was proceeding my little heart out across the parking lot of Zephyr Freight and Holding, East Brisbane Depot--
--looking for my civilian informant, Daniel Armitage.
His GPS tag said he was in the vicinity, but I couldn't visually verify that.
I did, however, visually verify some other old friends.
G'DAY, MOTHER-FUCKERS.
YOU'RE UNDER ARREST.
HUH?
THIS IS THE SELFSAME COIT WE BOUNCED OFF THE WALL IN WOOLLOONGABBA LAST NIGHT.
STONE ME! YOU'RE RIGHT. IT FUCKING IS.
FUCKING DIRTY LITTLE BOONG!
By an unfortunate oversight, I had left my sidearm in my vehicle.
It was therefore necessary to restrain the suspects by hand.

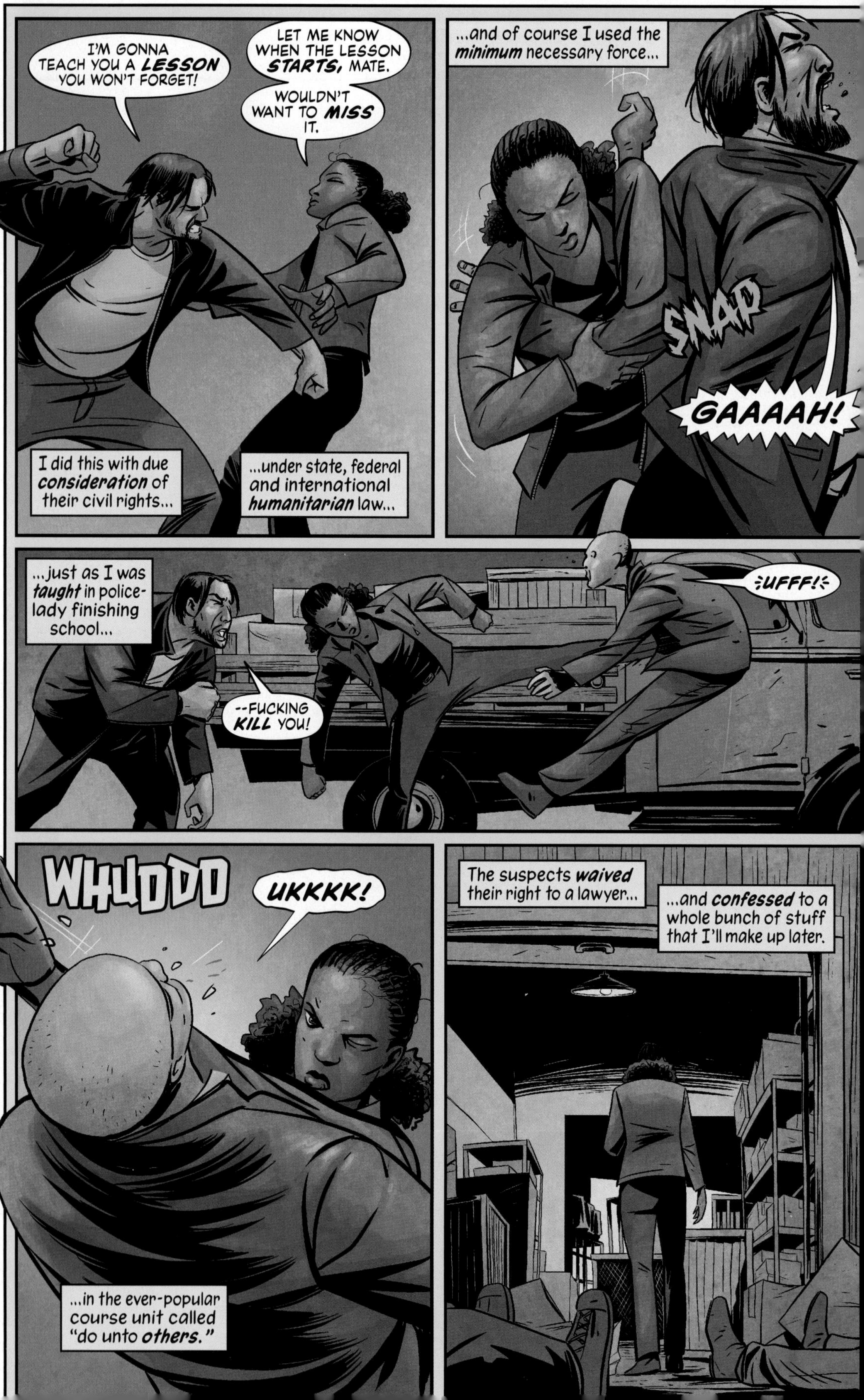
I'M GONNA TEACH YOU A LESSON YOU WON'T FORGET!
LET ME KNOW WHEN THE LESSON STARTS, MATE.
WOULDN'T WANT TO MISS IT.
I did this with due consideration of their civil rights...
...under state, federal and international humanitarian law...
...and of course I used the minimum necessary force...
SNAP
GAAAAH!
...just as I was taught in police-lady finishing school...
--FUCKING KILL YOU!
UFFF!
WHUDDD
UKKKK!
...in the ever-popular course unit called "do unto others."
The suspects waived their right to a lawyer...
...and confessed to a whole bunch of stuff that I'll make up later.

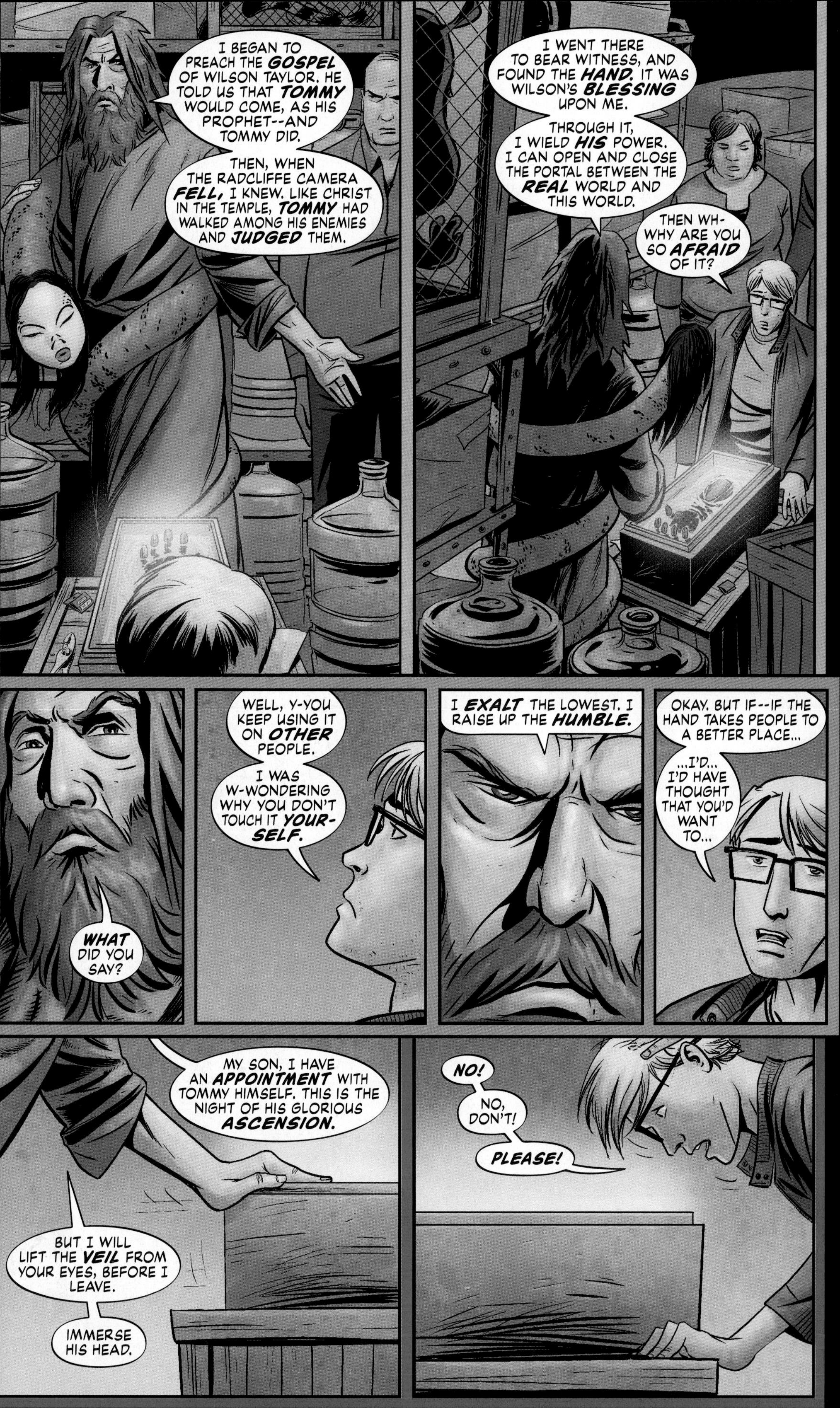
I BEGAN TO PREACH THE GOSPEL OF WILSON TAYLOR. HE TOLD US THAT TOMMY WOULD COME, AS HIS PROPHET--AND TOMMY DID.
THEN, WHEN THE RADCLIFFE CAMERA FELL, I KNEW. LIKE CHRIST IN THE TEMPLE, TOMMY HAD WALKED AMONG HIS ENEMIES AND JUDGED THEM.
I WENT THERE TO BEAR WITNESS, AND FOUND THE HAND. IT WAS WILSON'S BLESSING UPON ME.
THROUGH IT, I WIELD HIS POWER. I CAN OPEN AND CLOSE THE PORTAL BETWEEN THE REAL WORLD AND THIS WORLD.
THEN WH- WHY ARE YOU SO AFRAID OF IT?
WHAT DID YOU SAY?
WELL, Y-YOU KEEP USING IT ON OTHER PEOPLE.
I WAS W-WONDERING WHY YOU DON'T TOUCH IT YOURSELF.
I EXALT THE LOWEST. I RAISE UP THE HUMBLE.
OKAY. BUT IF--IF THE HAND TAKES PEOPLE TO A BETTER PLACE...
...I'D... I'D HAVE THOUGHT THAT YOU'D WANT TO...
MY SON, I HAVE AN APPOINTMENT WITH TOMMY HIMSELF. THIS IS THE NIGHT OF HIS GLORIOUS ASCENSION.
BUT I WILL LIFT THE VEIL FROM YOUR EYES, BEFORE I LEAVE.
IMMERSE HIS HEAD.
NO!
NO, DON'T!
PLEASE!

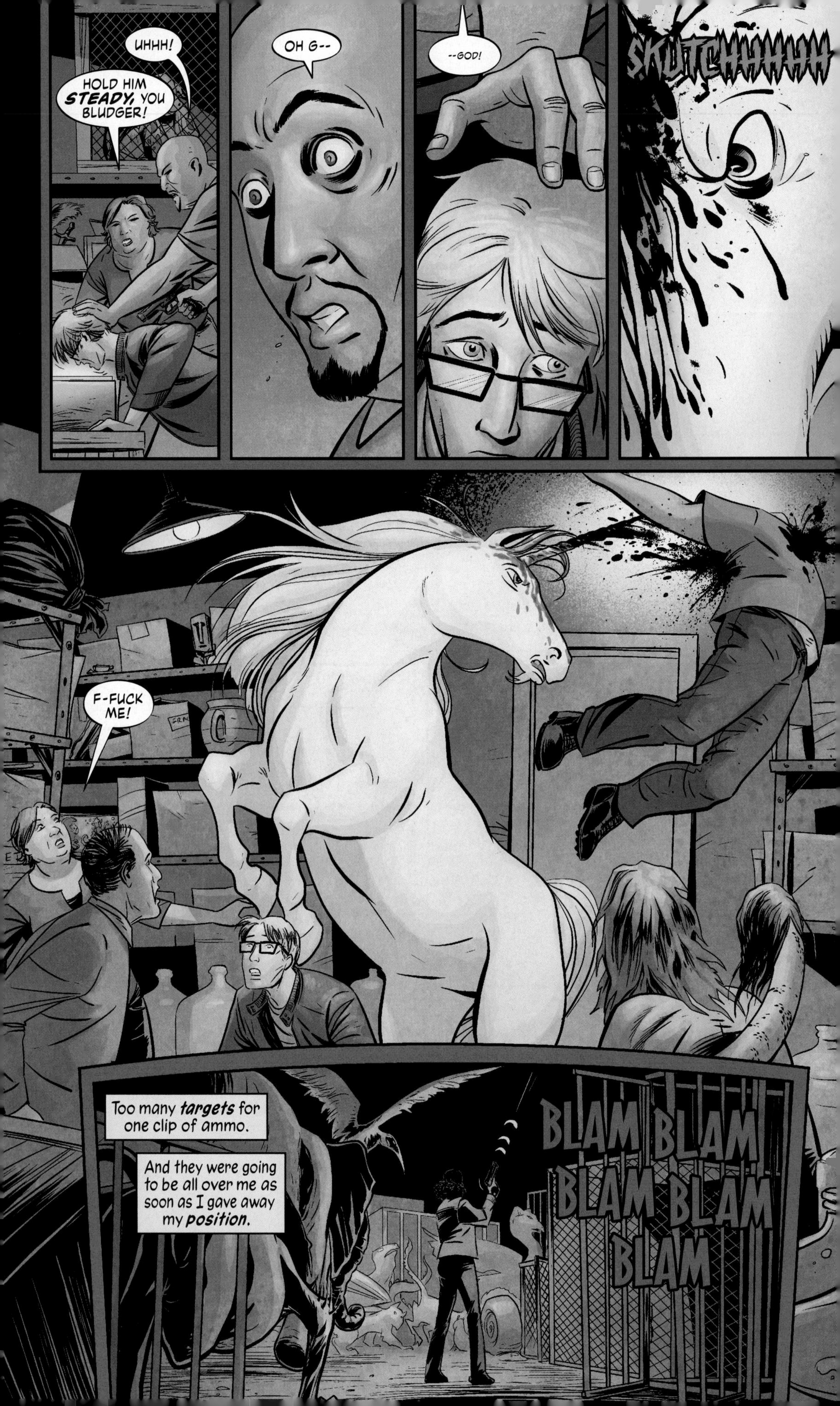
UHHH!
HOLD HIM STEADY, YOU BLUDGER!
OH G--
--GOD!
SKUTCHHHHHH
F-FUCK ME!
Too many targets for one clip of ammo.
And they were going to be all over me as soon as I gave away my position.
BLAM BLAM BLAM BLAM BLAM

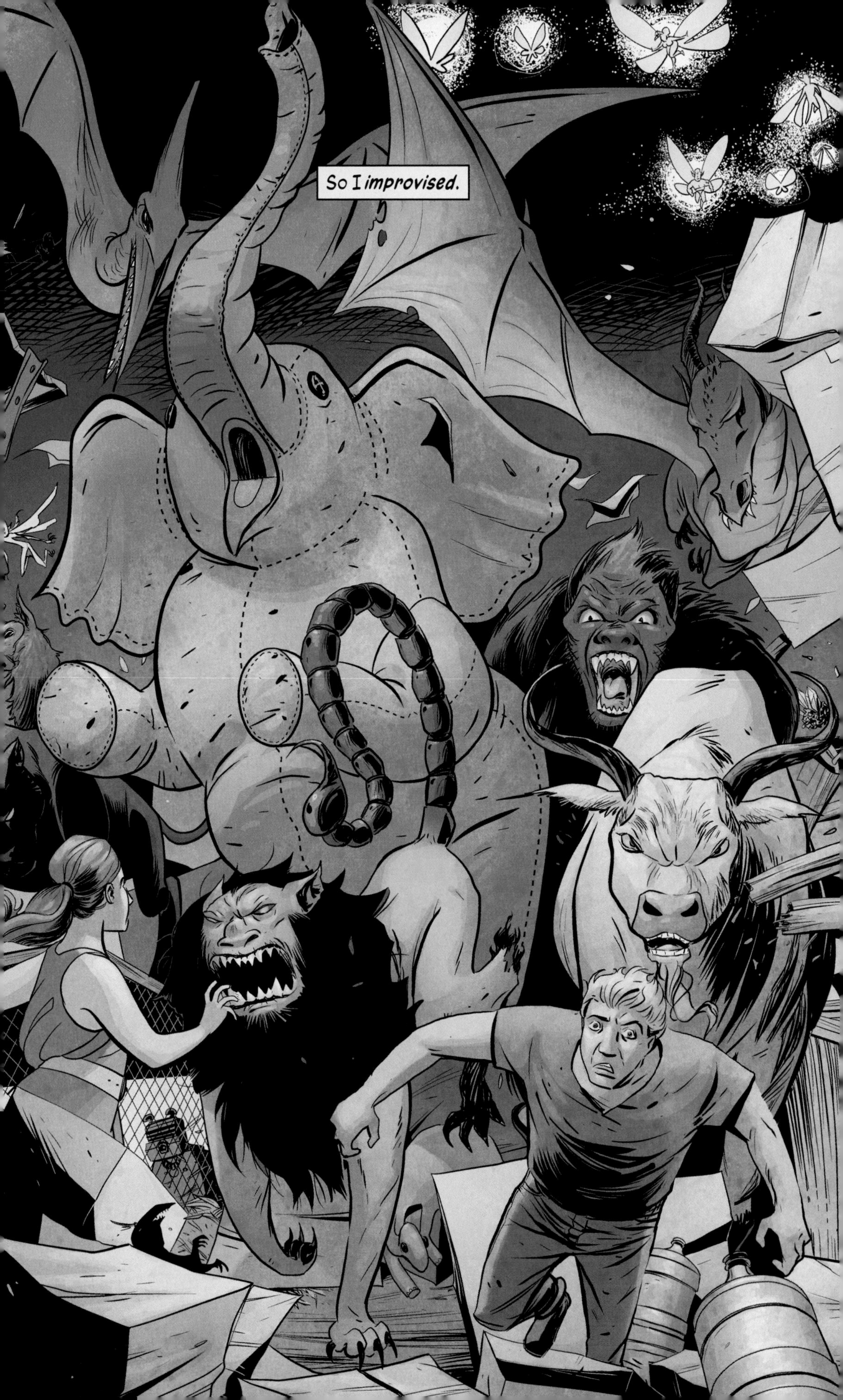
So I *improvised.*

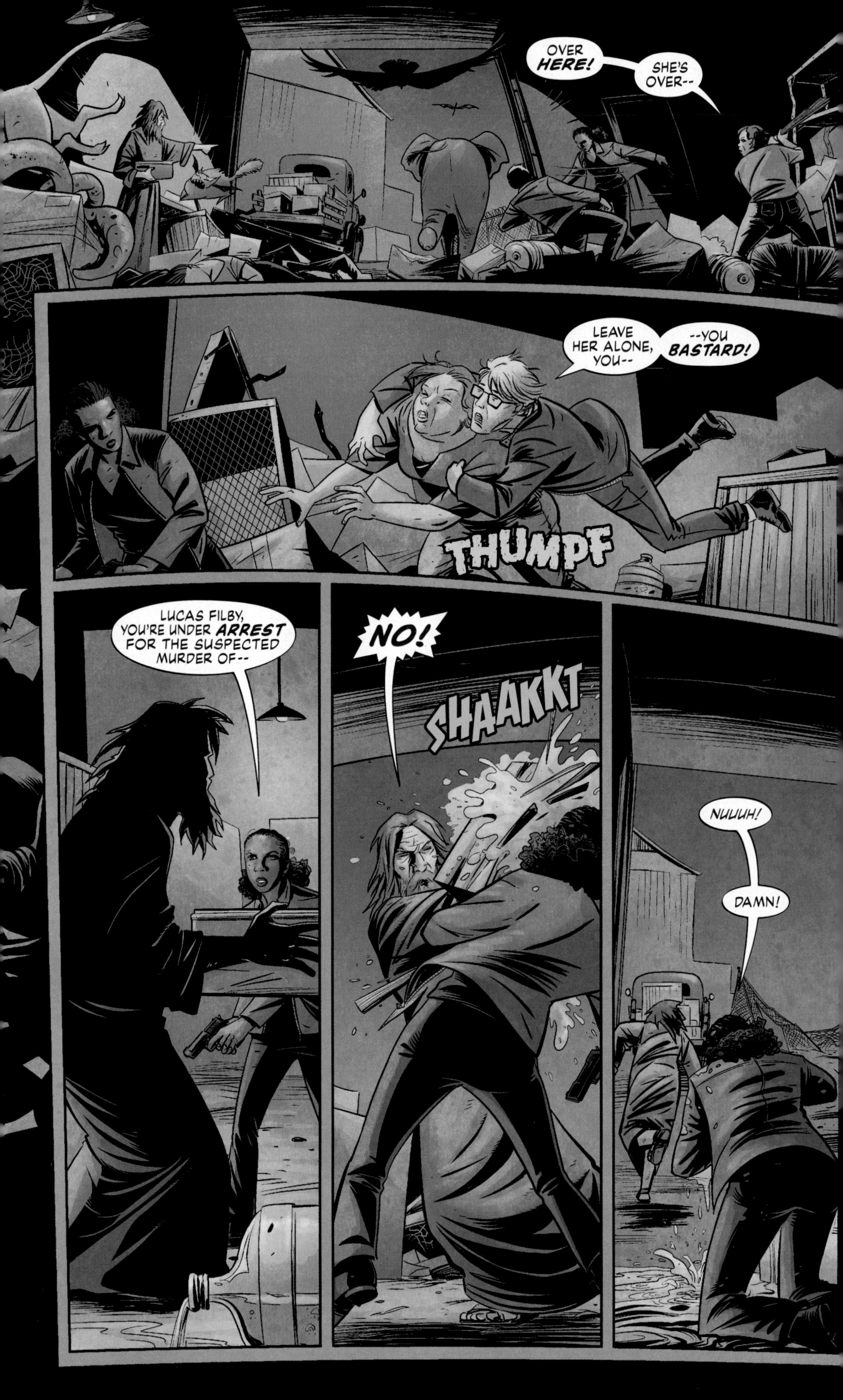
OVER HERE!
SHE'S OVER--
LEAVE HER ALONE, YOU--
--YOU BASTARD!
THUMPF
LUCAS FILBY, YOU'RE UNDER ARREST FOR THE SUSPECTED MURDER OF--
NO!
SHAAKKT
NUUUH!
DAMN!

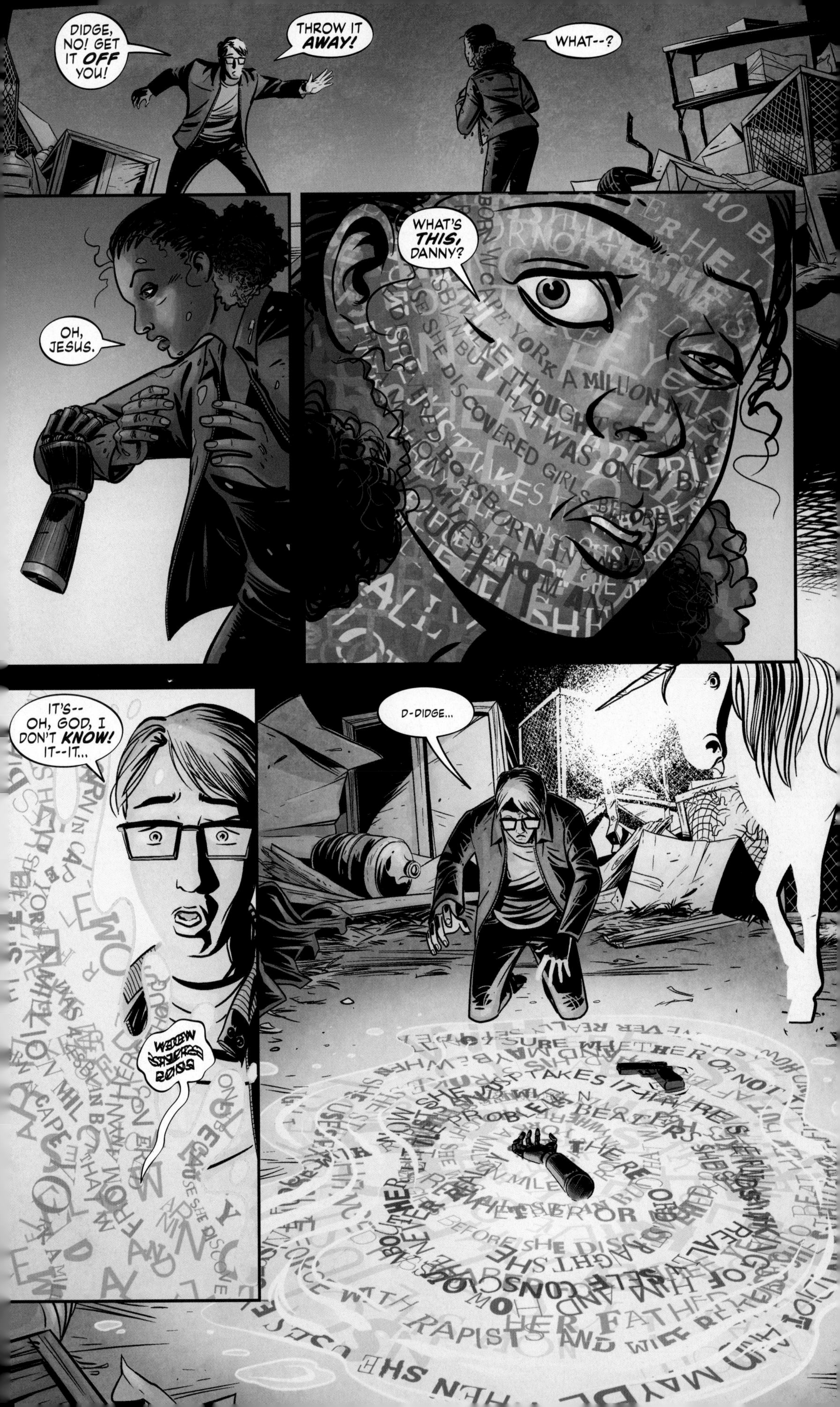
DIDGE, NO! GET IT OFF YOU!
THROW IT AWAY!
WHAT--?
OH, JESUS.
WHAT'S THIS, DANNY?
IT'S-- OH, GOD, I DON'T KNOW! IT--IT...
D-DIDGE...

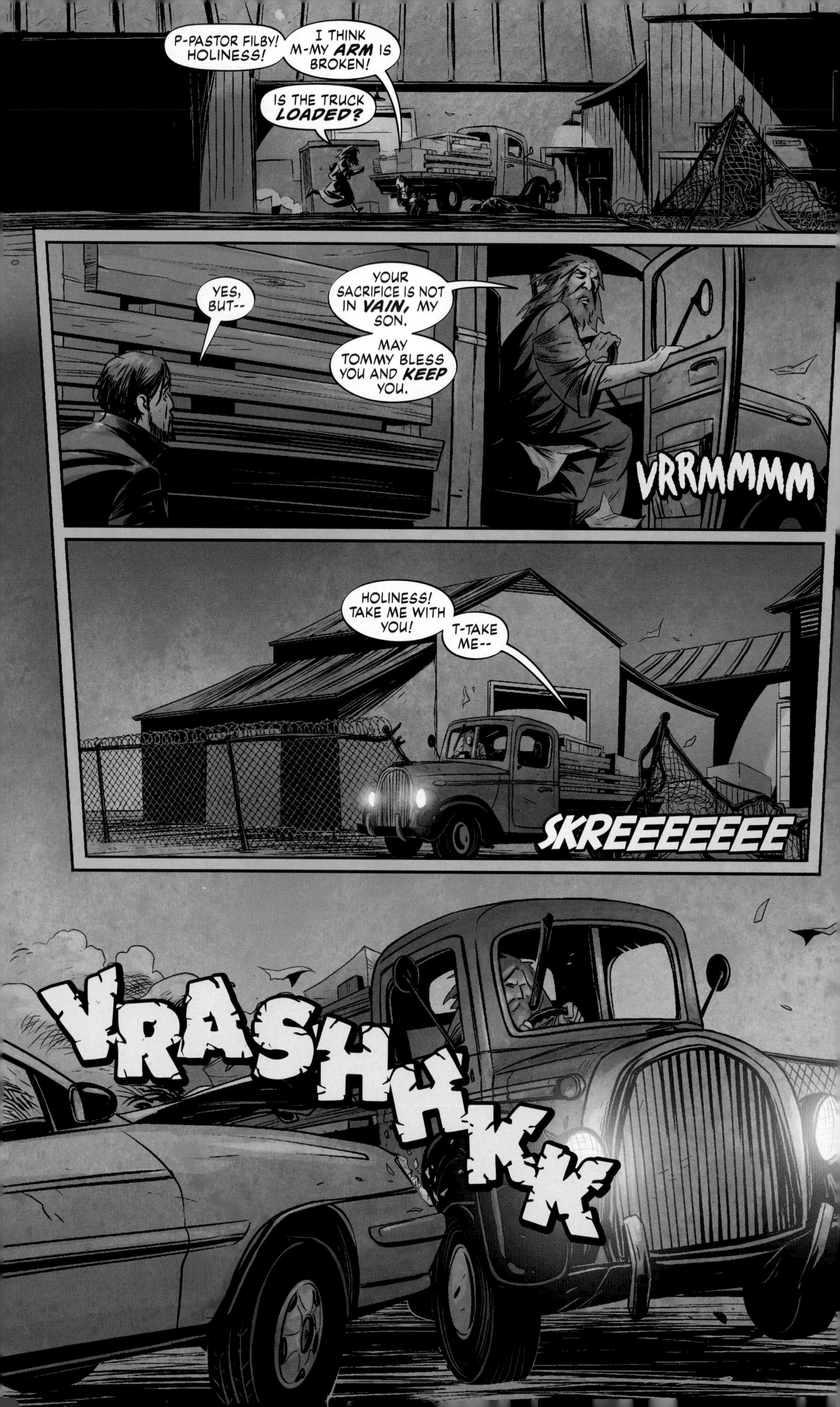
P-PASTOR FILBY! HOLINESS!
I THINK M-MY ARM IS BROKEN!
IS THE TRUCK LOADED?
YES, BUT--
YOUR SACRIFICE IS NOT IN VAIN, MY SON.
MAY TOMMY BLESS YOU AND KEEP YOU.
VRRMMMM
HOLINESS! TAKE ME WITH YOU!
T-TAKE ME--
SKREEEEEEEE
VRASHHKK

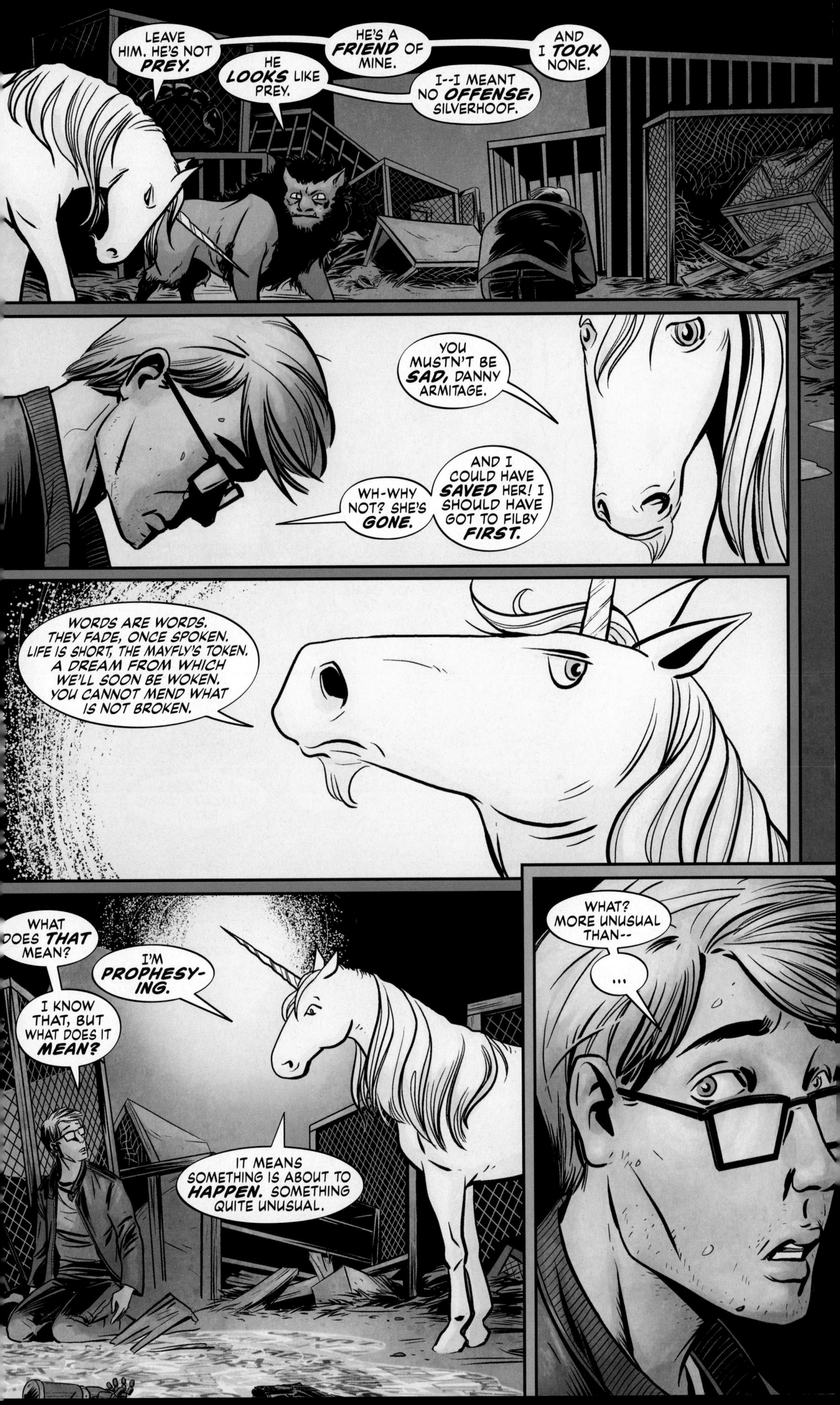
LEAVE HIM. HE'S NOT PREY.
HE LOOKS LIKE PREY.
HE'S A FRIEND OF MINE.
I--I MEANT NO OFFENSE, SILVERHOOF.
AND I TOOK NONE.
YOU MUSTN'T BE SAD, DANNY ARMITAGE.
WH-WHY NOT? SHE'S GONE.
AND I COULD HAVE SAVED HER! I SHOULD HAVE GOT TO FILBY FIRST.
WORDS ARE WORDS. THEY FADE, ONCE SPOKEN. LIFE IS SHORT, THE MAYFLY'S TOKEN. A DREAM FROM WHICH WE'LL SOON BE WOKEN. YOU CANNOT MEND WHAT IS NOT BROKEN.
WHAT DOES THAT MEAN?
I'M PROPHESY-ING.
I KNOW THAT, BUT WHAT DOES IT MEAN?
IT MEANS SOMETHING IS ABOUT TO HAPPEN. SOMETHING QUITE UNUSUAL.
WHAT? MORE UNUSUAL THAN--
...

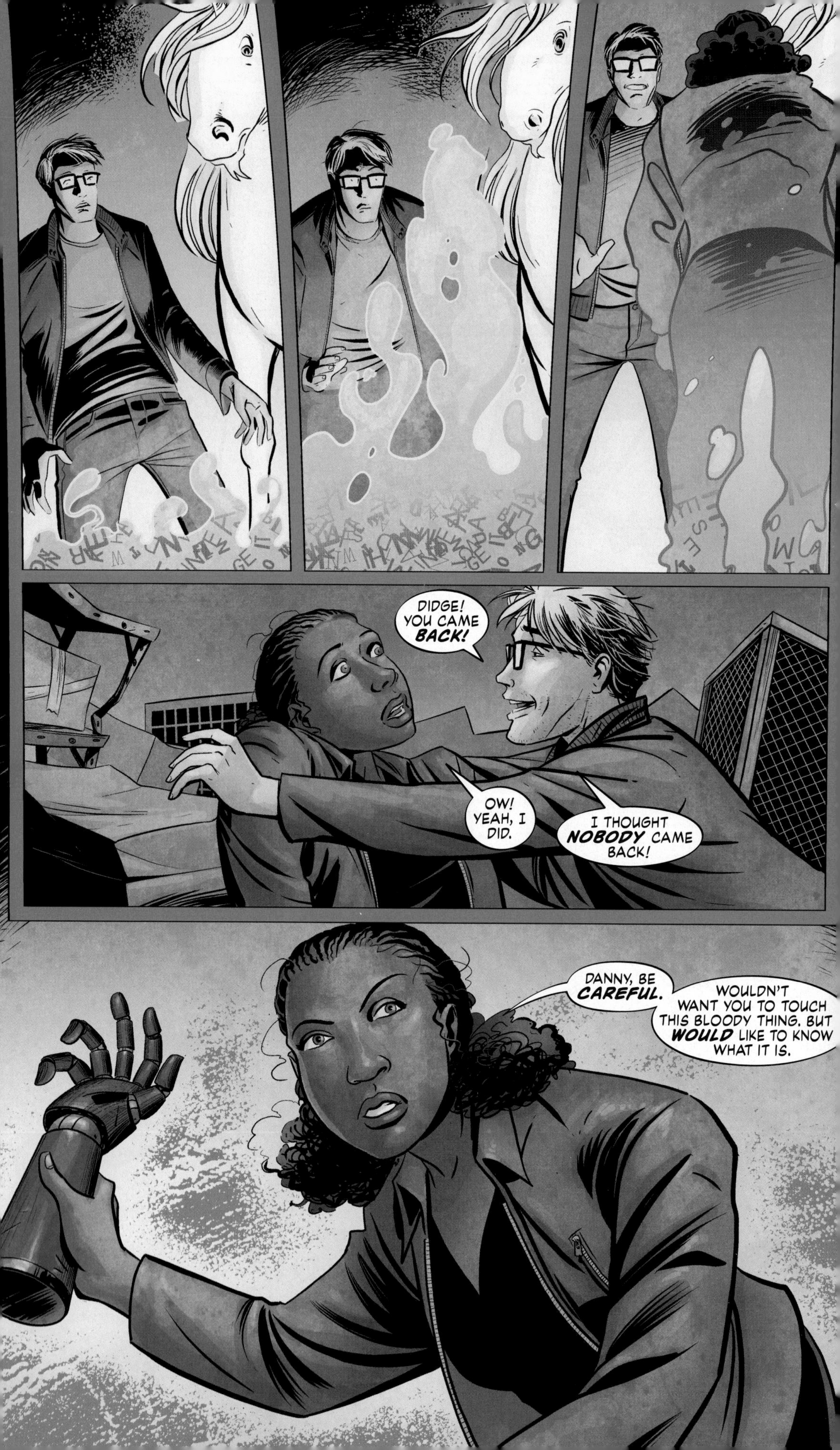
DIDGE! YOU CAME **BACK!**
OW! YEAH, I DID.
I THOUGHT **NOBODY** CAME BACK!
DANNY, BE **CAREFUL.**
WOULDN'T WANT YOU TO TOUCH THIS BLOODY THING. BUT **WOULD** LIKE TO KNOW WHAT IT IS.

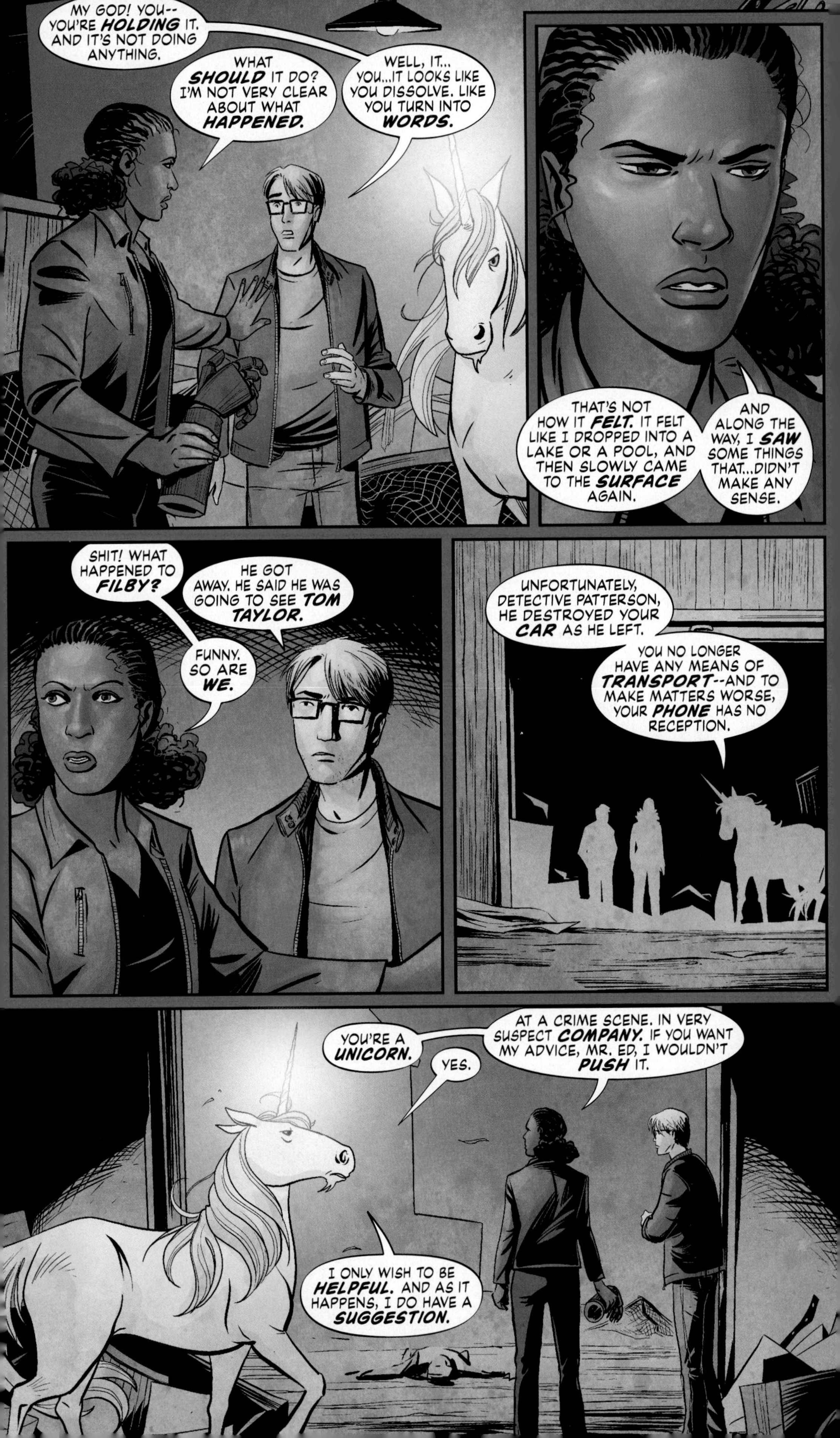
MY GOD! YOU-- YOU'RE HOLDING IT. AND IT'S NOT DOING ANYTHING.
WHAT SHOULD IT DO? I'M NOT VERY CLEAR ABOUT WHAT HAPPENED.
WELL, IT... YOU...IT LOOKS LIKE YOU DISSOLVE. LIKE YOU TURN INTO WORDS.
THAT'S NOT HOW IT FELT. IT FELT LIKE I DROPPED INTO A LAKE OR A POOL, AND THEN SLOWLY CAME TO THE SURFACE AGAIN.
AND ALONG THE WAY, I SAW SOME THINGS THAT...DIDN'T MAKE ANY SENSE.
SHIT! WHAT HAPPENED TO FILBY?
HE GOT AWAY. HE SAID HE WAS GOING TO SEE TOM TAYLOR.
FUNNY. SO ARE WE.
UNFORTUNATELY, DETECTIVE PATTERSON, HE DESTROYED YOUR CAR AS HE LEFT.
YOU NO LONGER HAVE ANY MEANS OF TRANSPORT--AND TO MAKE MATTERS WORSE, YOUR PHONE HAS NO RECEPTION.
YOU'RE A UNICORN.
YES.
AT A CRIME SCENE. IN VERY SUSPECT COMPANY. IF YOU WANT MY ADVICE, MR. ED, I WOULDN'T PUSH IT.
I ONLY WISH TO BE HELPFUL. AND AS IT HAPPENS, I DO HAVE A SUGGESTION.

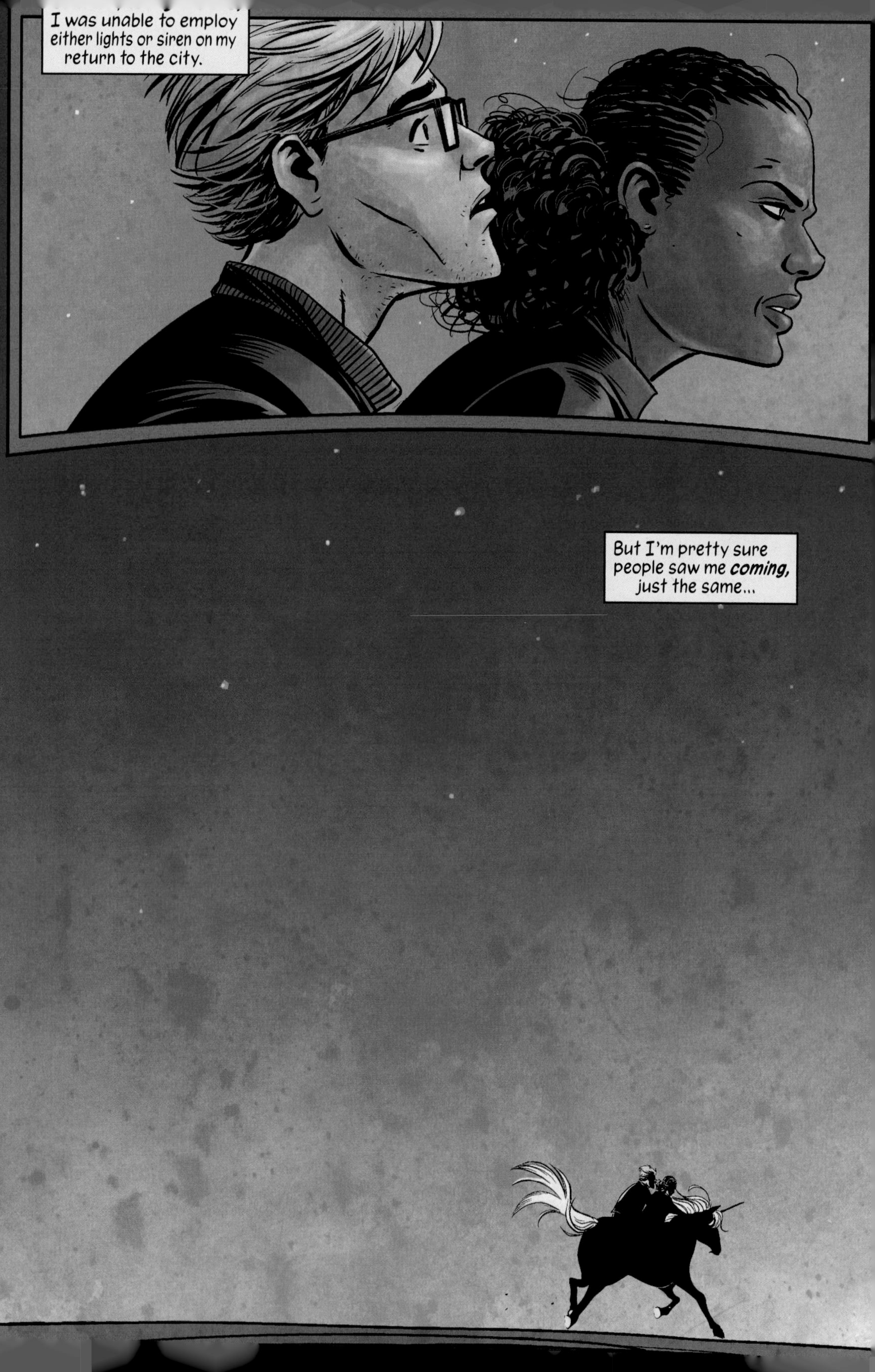
I was unable to employ either lights or siren on my return to the city.
But I'm pretty sure people saw me *coming,* just the same...

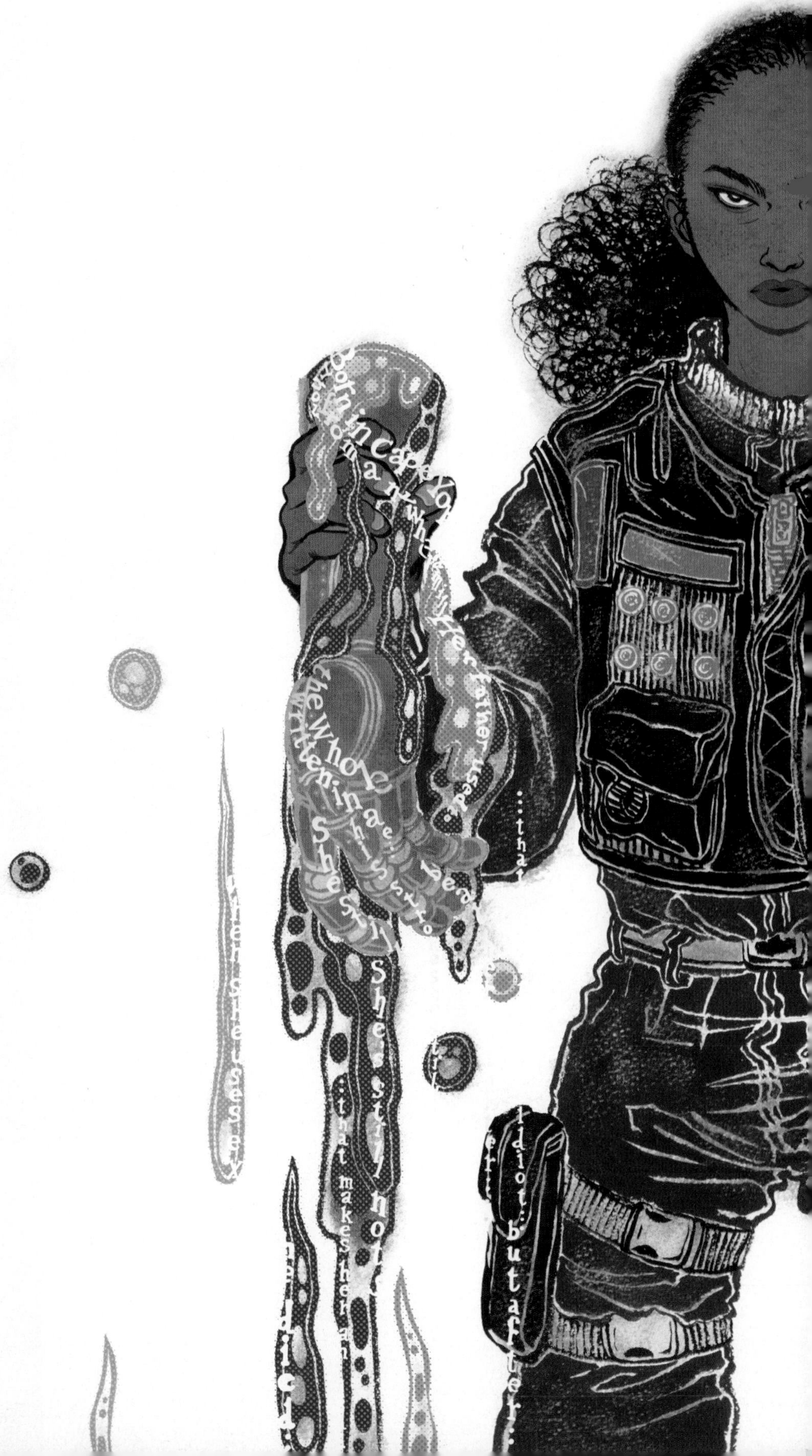

her father used
idiot... but after...

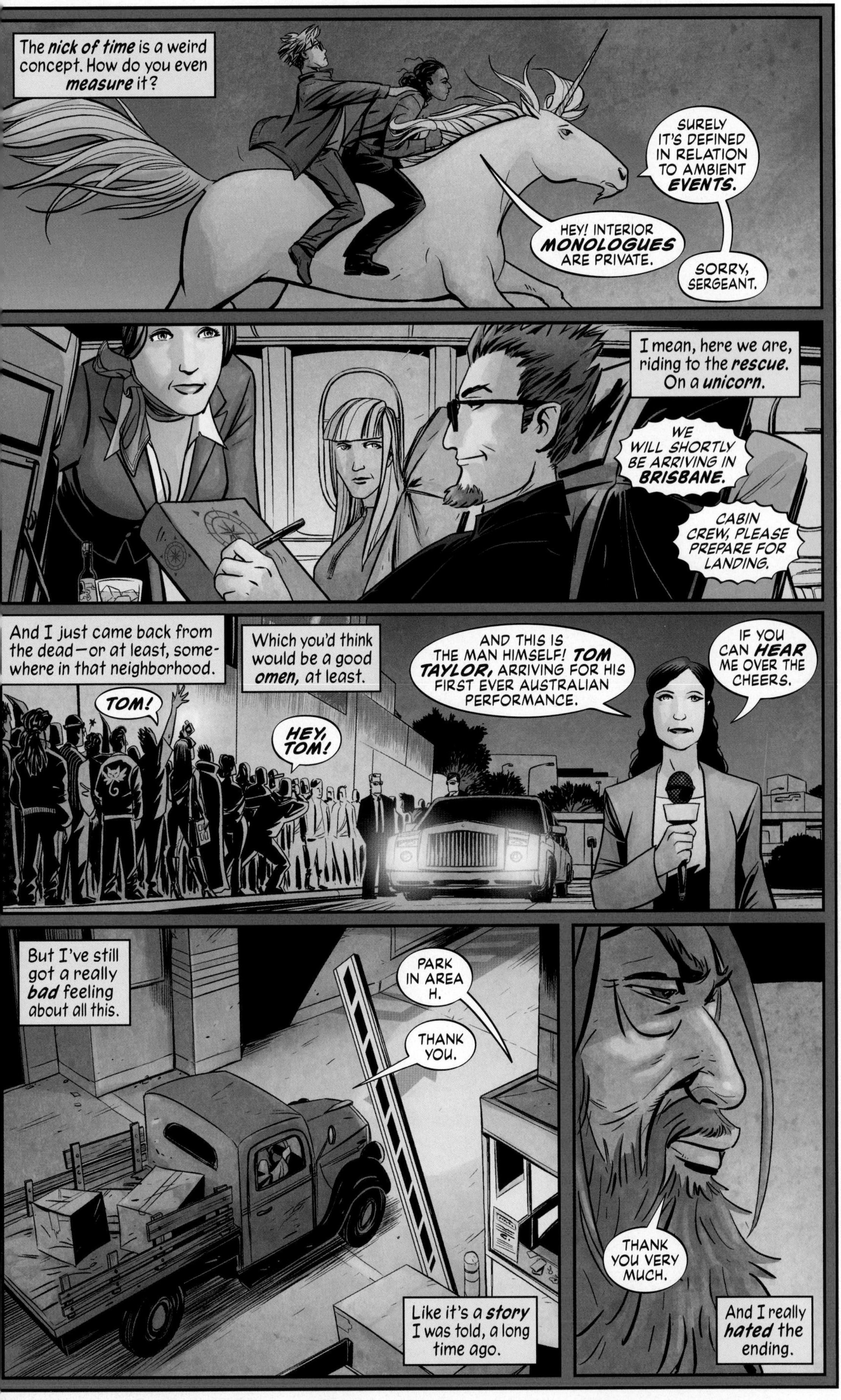

The nick of time is a weird concept. How do you even measure it?
SURELY IT'S DEFINED IN RELATION TO AMBIENT EVENTS.
HEY! INTERIOR MONOLOGUES ARE PRIVATE.
SORRY, SERGEANT.
I mean, here we are, riding to the rescue. On a unicorn.
WE WILL SHORTLY BE ARRIVING IN BRISBANE.
CABIN CREW, PLEASE PREPARE FOR LANDING.
And I just came back from the dead—or at least, somewhere in that neighborhood.
Which you'd think would be a good omen, at least.
AND THIS IS THE MAN HIMSELF! TOM TAYLOR, ARRIVING FOR HIS FIRST EVER AUSTRALIAN PERFORMANCE.
IF YOU CAN HEAR ME OVER THE CHEERS.
TOM!
HEY, TOM!
But I've still got a really bad feeling about all this.
PARK IN AREA H.
THANK YOU.
Like it's a story I was told, a long time ago.
THANK YOU VERY MUCH.
And I really hated the ending.

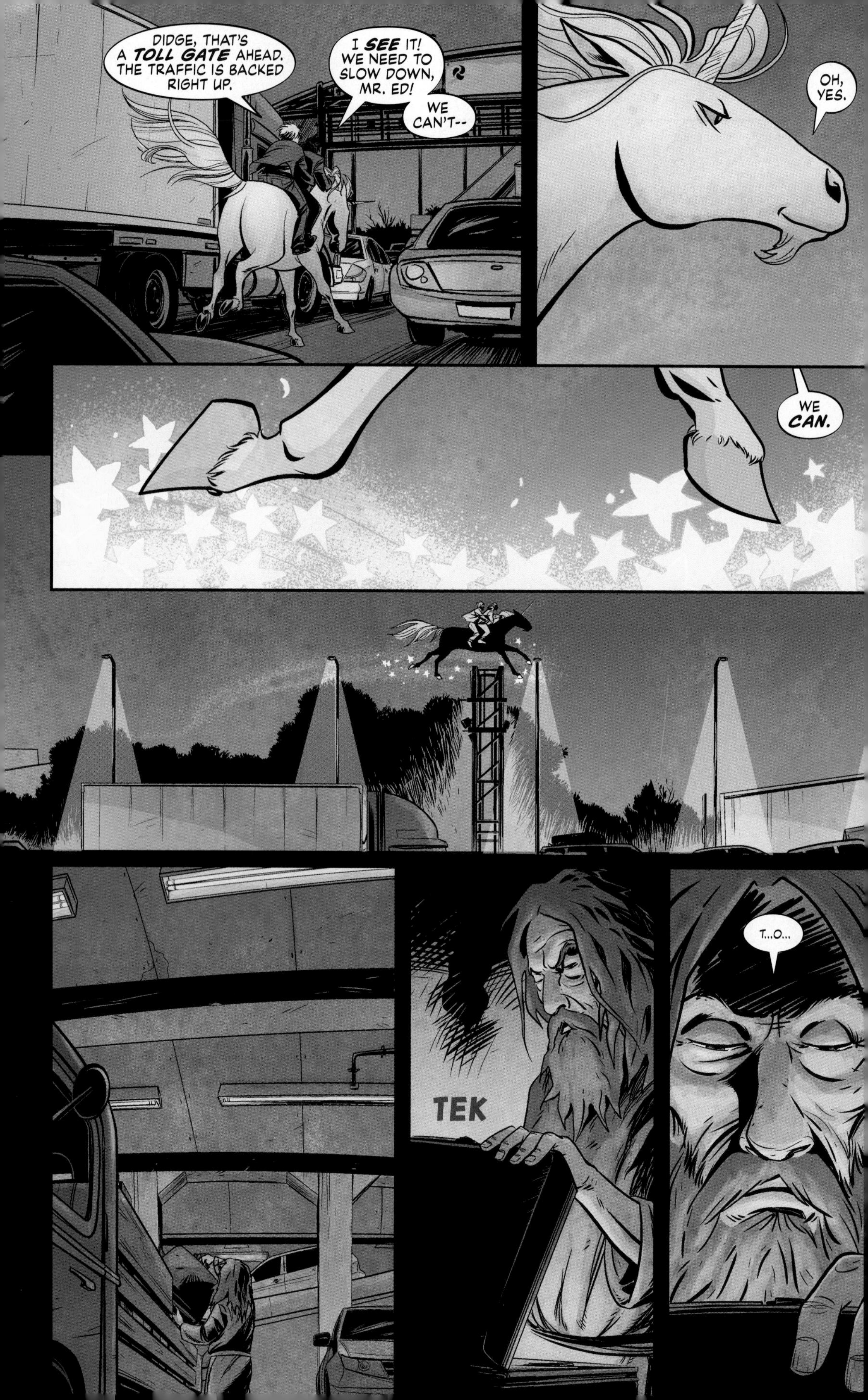
DIDGE, THAT'S A TOLL GATE AHEAD. THE TRAFFIC IS BACKED RIGHT UP.
I SEE IT! WE NEED TO SLOW DOWN, MR. ED!
WE CAN'T--
OH, YES.
WE CAN.
TEK
T...O...

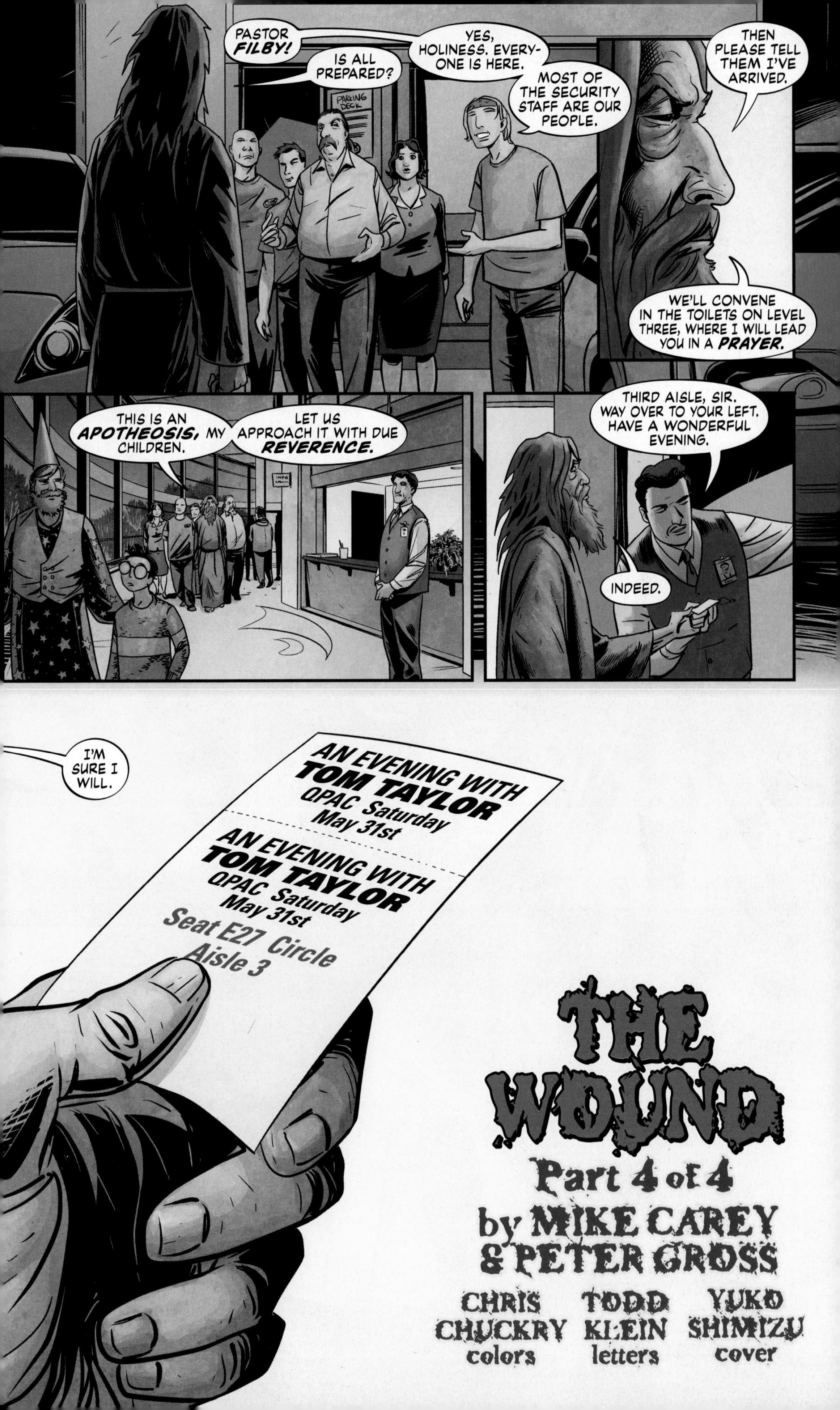

PASTOR FILBY!
IS ALL PREPARED?
YES, HOLINESS. EVERY-ONE IS HERE.
MOST OF THE SECURITY STAFF ARE OUR PEOPLE.
PARKING DECK
THEN PLEASE TELL THEM I'VE ARRIVED.
WE'LL CONVENE IN THE TOILETS ON LEVEL THREE, WHERE I WILL LEAD YOU IN A PRAYER.
THIS IS AN APOTHEOSIS, MY CHILDREN.
LET US APPROACH IT WITH DUE REVERENCE.
INFO
THIRD AISLE, SIR. WAY OVER TO YOUR LEFT. HAVE A WONDERFUL EVENING.
INDEED.
I'M SURE I WILL.
AN EVENING WITH TOM TAYLOR QPAC Saturday May 31st
AN EVENING WITH TOM TAYLOR QPAC Saturday May 31st
Seat E27 Circle Aisle 3
THE WOUND
Part 4 of 4
by MIKE CAREY & PETER GROSS
CHRIS CHUCKRY colors
TODD KLEIN letters
YUKO SHIMIZU cover

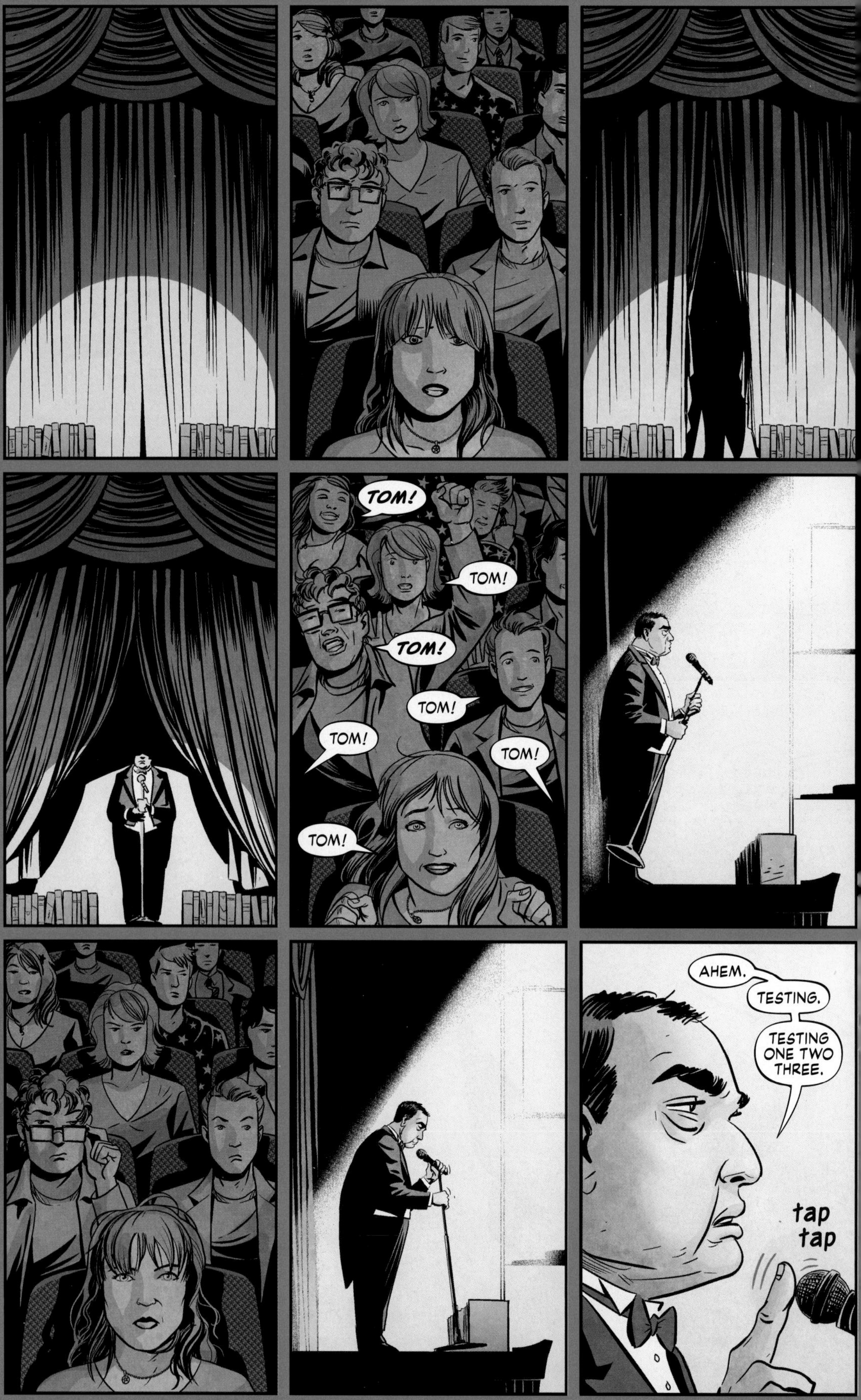
TOM!
TOM!
TOM!
TOM!
TOM!
TOM!
TOM!
AHEM.
TESTING.
TESTING ONE TWO THREE.
tap tap

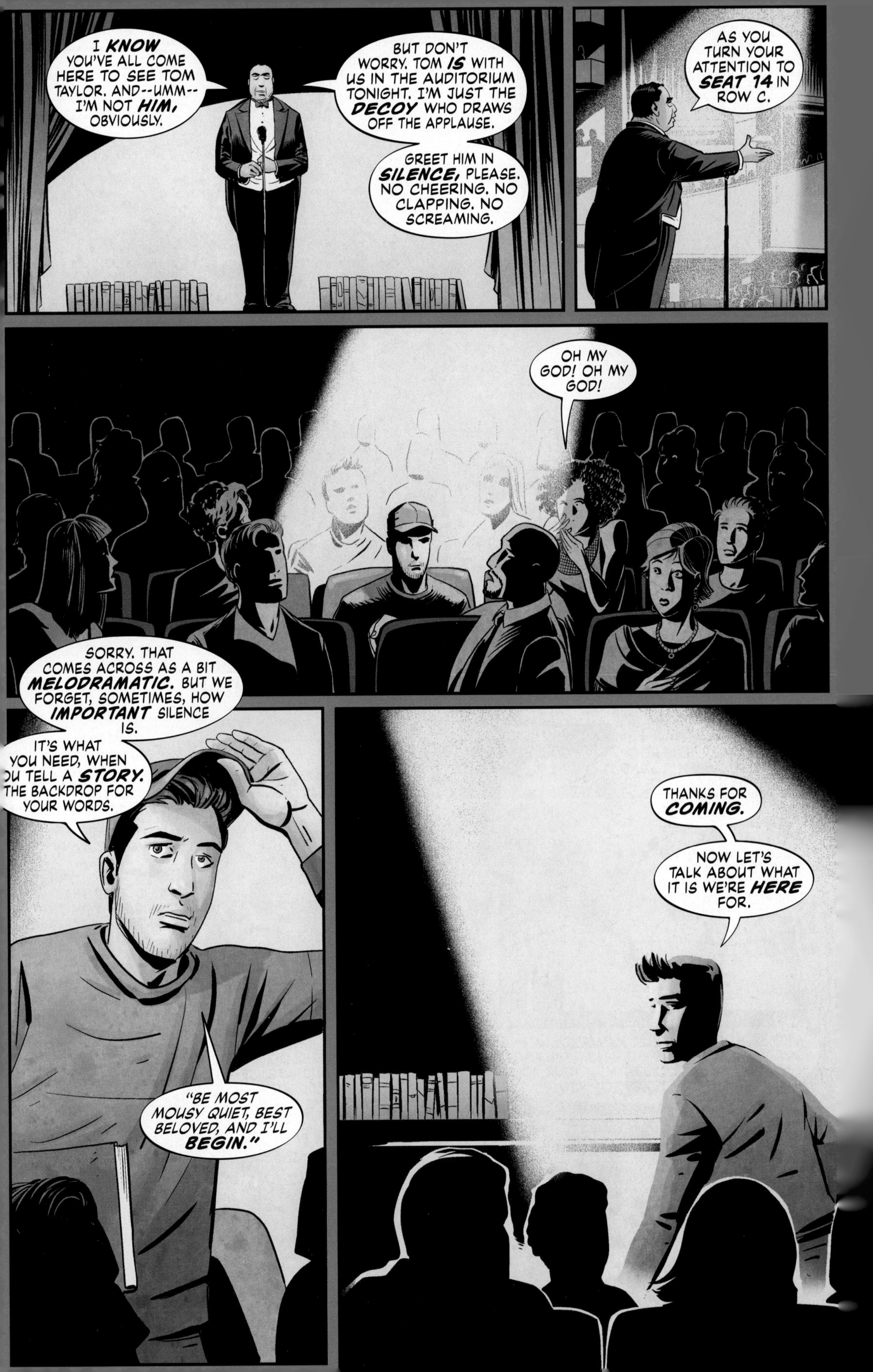
I KNOW YOU'VE ALL COME HERE TO SEE TOM TAYLOR. AND--UMM-- I'M NOT HIM, OBVIOUSLY.
BUT DON'T WORRY. TOM IS WITH US IN THE AUDITORIUM TONIGHT. I'M JUST THE DECOY WHO DRAWS OFF THE APPLAUSE.
GREET HIM IN SILENCE, PLEASE. NO CHEERING. NO CLAPPING. NO SCREAMING.
AS YOU TURN YOUR ATTENTION TO SEAT 14 IN ROW C.
OH MY GOD! OH MY GOD!
SORRY. THAT COMES ACROSS AS A BIT MELODRAMATIC. BUT WE FORGET, SOMETIMES, HOW IMPORTANT SILENCE IS.
IT'S WHAT YOU NEED, WHEN OU TELL A STORY. THE BACKDROP FOR YOUR WORDS.
"BE MOST MOUSY QUIET, BEST BELOVED, AND I'LL BEGIN."
THANKS FOR COMING.
NOW LET'S TALK ABOUT WHAT IT IS WE'RE HERE FOR.

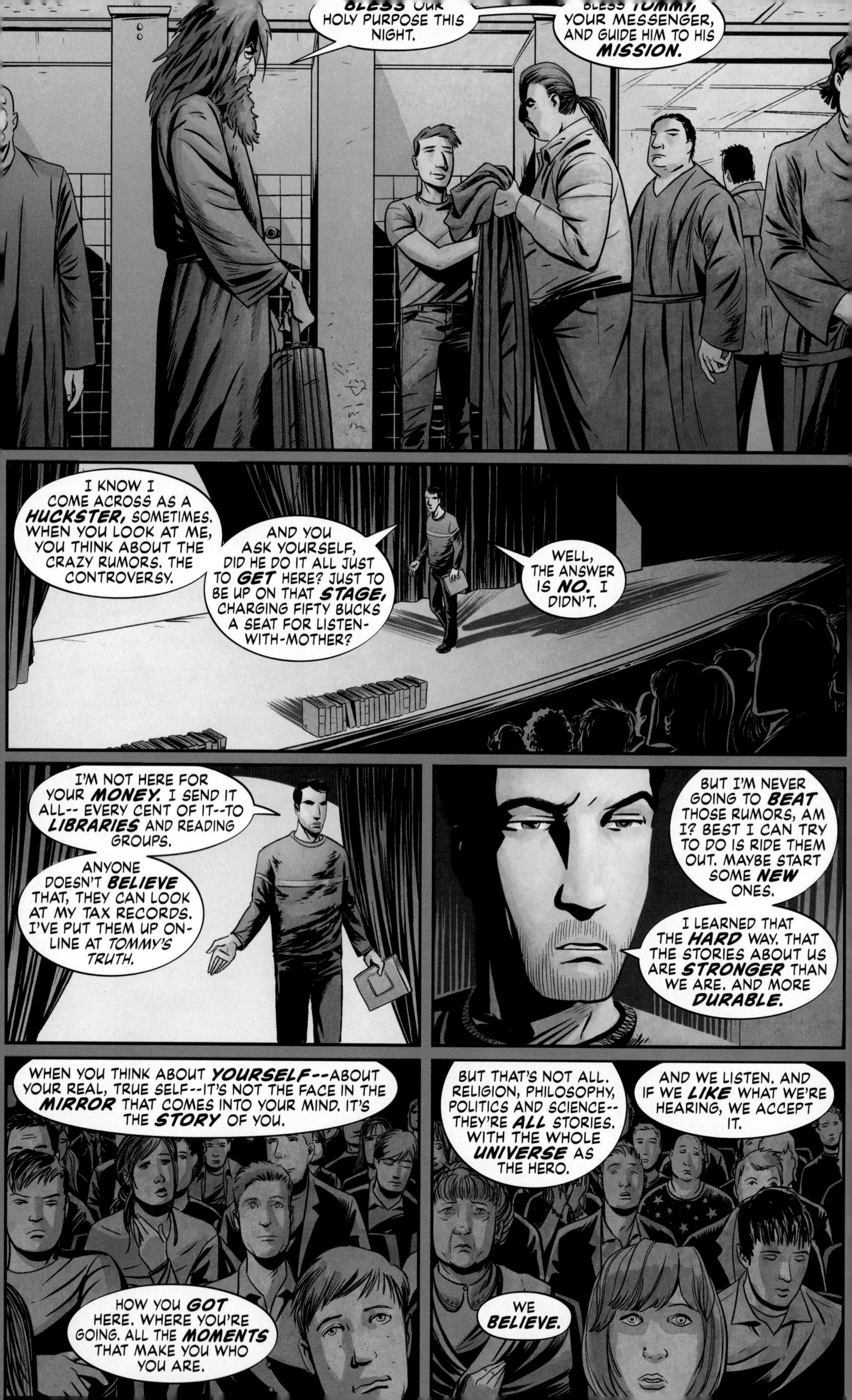
HOLY PURPOSE THIS NIGHT.
YOUR MESSENGER, AND GUIDE HIM TO HIS MISSION.
I KNOW I COME ACROSS AS A HUCKSTER, SOMETIMES. WHEN YOU LOOK AT ME, YOU THINK ABOUT THE CRAZY RUMORS. THE CONTROVERSY.
AND YOU ASK YOURSELF, DID HE DO IT ALL JUST TO GET HERE? JUST TO BE UP ON THAT STAGE, CHARGING FIFTY BUCKS A SEAT FOR LISTEN-WITH-MOTHER?
WELL, THE ANSWER IS NO. I DIDN'T.
I'M NOT HERE FOR YOUR MONEY. I SEND IT ALL-- EVERY CENT OF IT--TO LIBRARIES AND READING GROUPS.
ANYONE DOESN'T BELIEVE THAT, THEY CAN LOOK AT MY TAX RECORDS. I'VE PUT THEM UP ON-LINE AT TOMMY'S TRUTH.
BUT I'M NEVER GOING TO BEAT THOSE RUMORS, AM I? BEST I CAN TRY TO DO IS RIDE THEM OUT. MAYBE START SOME NEW ONES.
I LEARNED THAT THE HARD WAY. THAT THE STORIES ABOUT US ARE STRONGER THAN WE ARE. AND MORE DURABLE.
WHEN YOU THINK ABOUT YOURSELF--ABOUT YOUR REAL, TRUE SELF--IT'S NOT THE FACE IN THE MIRROR THAT COMES INTO YOUR MIND. IT'S THE STORY OF YOU.
HOW YOU GOT HERE. WHERE YOU'RE GOING. ALL THE MOMENTS THAT MAKE YOU WHO YOU ARE.
BUT THAT'S NOT ALL. RELIGION, PHILOSOPHY, POLITICS AND SCIENCE-- THEY'RE ALL STORIES. WITH THE WHOLE UNIVERSE AS THE HERO.
AND WE LISTEN. AND IF WE LIKE WHAT WE'RE HEARING, WE ACCEPT IT.
WE BELIEVE.

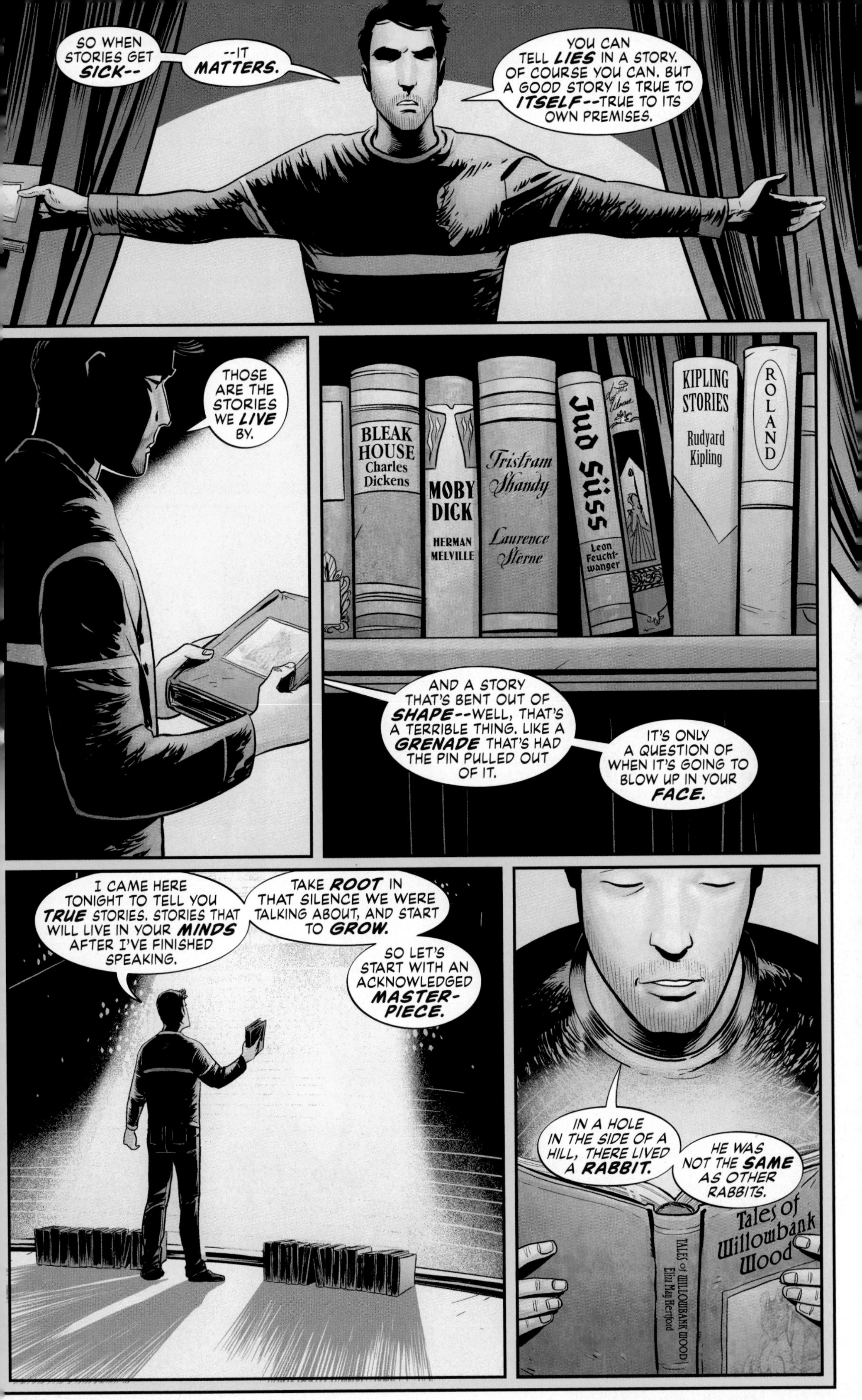

SO WHEN STORIES GET SICK--
--IT MATTERS.
YOU CAN TELL LIES IN A STORY. OF COURSE YOU CAN. BUT A GOOD STORY IS TRUE TO ITSELF--TRUE TO ITS OWN PREMISES.
THOSE ARE THE STORIES WE LIVE BY.
BLEAK HOUSE Charles Dickens
MOBY DICK HERMAN MELVILLE
Tristram Shandy Laurence Sterne
Jud Süss Leon Feucht-wanger
KIPLING STORIES Rudyard Kipling
ROLAND
AND A STORY THAT'S BENT OUT OF SHAPE--WELL, THAT'S A TERRIBLE THING. LIKE A GRENADE THAT'S HAD THE PIN PULLED OUT OF IT.
IT'S ONLY A QUESTION OF WHEN IT'S GOING TO BLOW UP IN YOUR FACE.
I CAME HERE TONIGHT TO TELL YOU TRUE STORIES. STORIES THAT WILL LIVE IN YOUR MINDS AFTER I'VE FINISHED SPEAKING.
TAKE ROOT IN THAT SILENCE WE WERE TALKING ABOUT, AND START TO GROW.
SO LET'S START WITH AN ACKNOWLEDGED MASTER-PIECE.
IN A HOLE IN THE SIDE OF A HILL, THERE LIVED A RABBIT.
HE WAS NOT THE SAME AS OTHER RABBITS.
Tales of Willowbank Wood
TALES of WILLOWBANK WOOD Eliza May Hertford

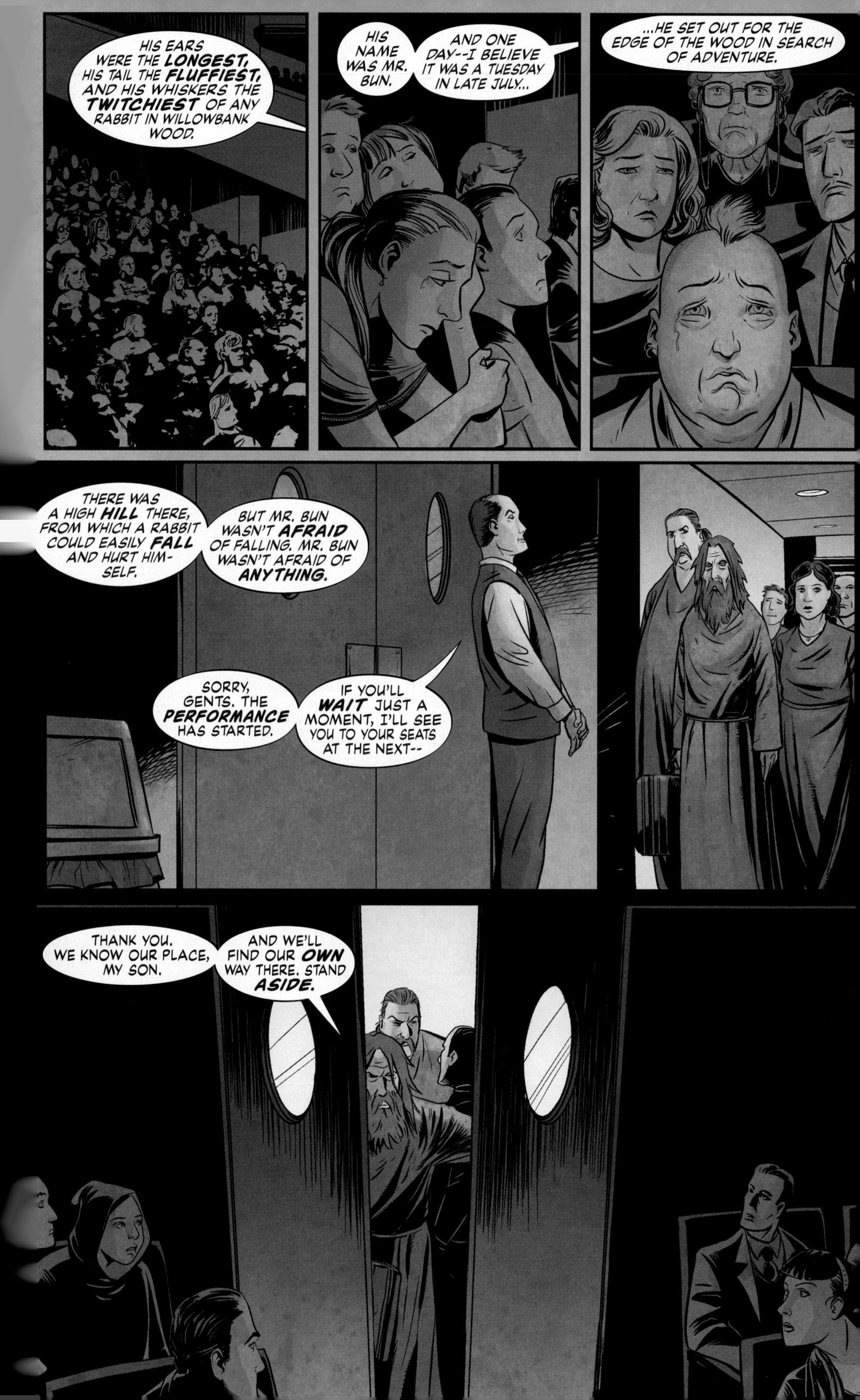
HIS EARS WERE THE LONGEST, HIS TAIL THE FLUFFIEST, AND HIS WHISKERS THE TWITCHIEST OF ANY RABBIT IN WILLOWBANK WOOD.
HIS NAME WAS MR. BUN.
AND ONE DAY--I BELIEVE IT WAS A TUESDAY IN LATE JULY...
...HE SET OUT FOR THE EDGE OF THE WOOD IN SEARCH OF ADVENTURE.
THERE WAS A HIGH HILL THERE, FROM WHICH A RABBIT COULD EASILY FALL AND HURT HIM-SELF.
BUT MR. BUN WASN'T AFRAID OF FALLING. MR. BUN WASN'T AFRAID OF ANYTHING.
SORRY, GENTS. THE PERFORMANCE HAS STARTED.
IF YOU'LL WAIT JUST A MOMENT, I'LL SEE YOU TO YOUR SEATS AT THE NEXT--
THANK YOU. WE KNOW OUR PLACE, MY SON.
AND WE'LL FIND OUR OWN WAY THERE. STAND ASIDE.

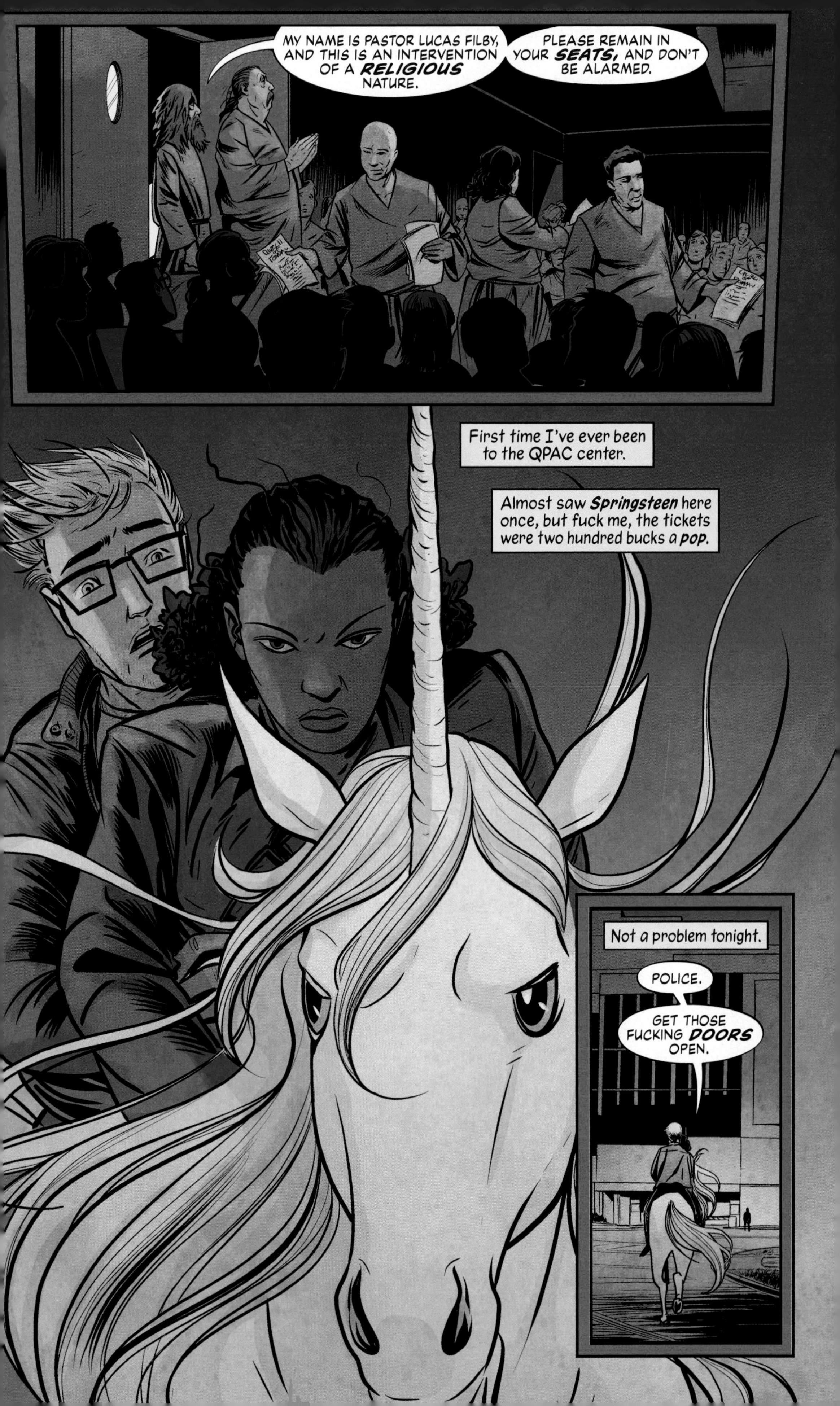
MY NAME IS PASTOR LUCAS FILBY, AND THIS IS AN INTERVENTION OF A **RELIGIOUS** NATURE.
PLEASE REMAIN IN YOUR **SEATS,** AND DON'T BE ALARMED.
First time I've ever been to the QPAC center.
Almost saw **Springsteen** here once, but fuck me, the tickets were two hundred bucks a **pop**.
Not a problem tonight.
POLICE.
GET THOSE FUCKING **DOORS** OPEN.

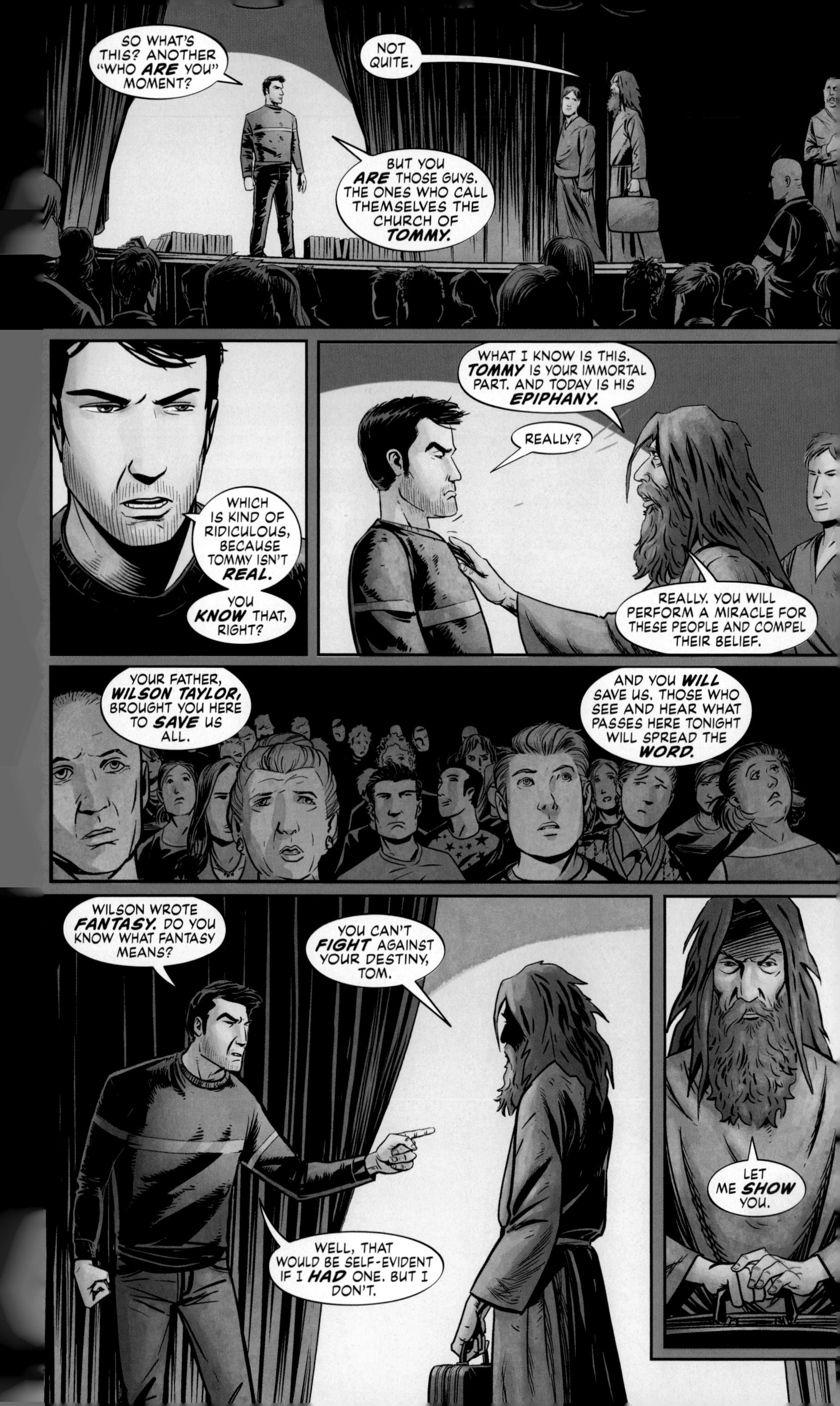

SO WHAT'S THIS? ANOTHER "WHO ARE YOU" MOMENT?
NOT QUITE.
BUT YOU ARE THOSE GUYS. THE ONES WHO CALL THEMSELVES THE CHURCH OF TOMMY.
WHICH IS KIND OF RIDICULOUS, BECAUSE TOMMY ISN'T REAL.
YOU KNOW THAT, RIGHT?
WHAT I KNOW IS THIS. TOMMY IS YOUR IMMORTAL PART. AND TODAY IS HIS EPIPHANY.
REALLY?
REALLY. YOU WILL PERFORM A MIRACLE FOR THESE PEOPLE AND COMPEL THEIR BELIEF.
YOUR FATHER, WILSON TAYLOR, BROUGHT YOU HERE TO SAVE US ALL.
AND YOU WILL SAVE US. THOSE WHO SEE AND HEAR WHAT PASSES HERE TONIGHT WILL SPREAD THE WORD.
WILSON WROTE FANTASY. DO YOU KNOW WHAT FANTASY MEANS?
YOU CAN'T FIGHT AGAINST YOUR DESTINY, TOM.
WELL, THAT WOULD BE SELF-EVIDENT IF I HAD ONE. BUT I DON'T.
LET ME SHOW YOU.

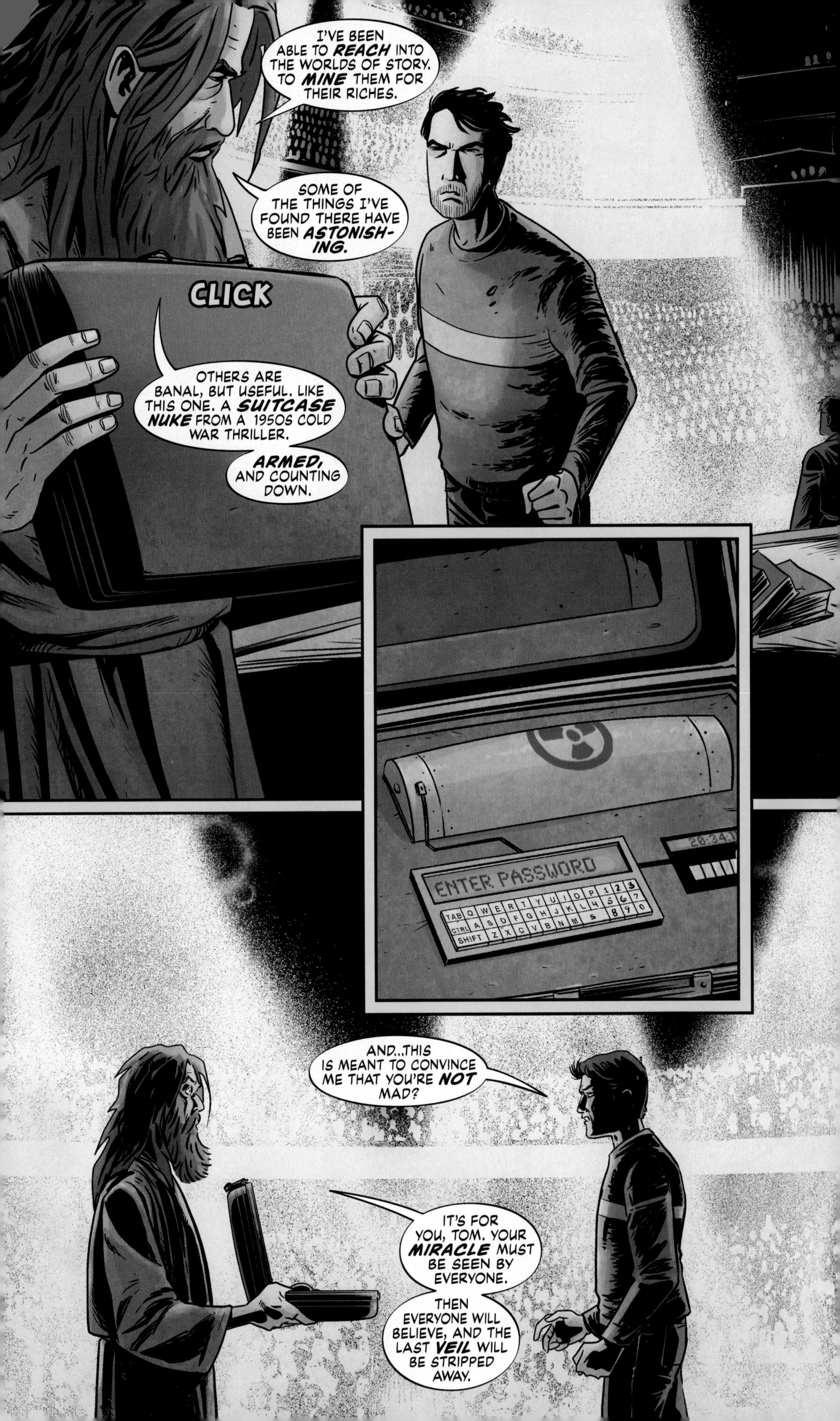
I'VE BEEN ABLE TO REACH INTO THE WORLDS OF STORY. TO MINE THEM FOR THEIR RICHES.
SOME OF THE THINGS I'VE FOUND THERE HAVE BEEN ASTONISHING.
CLICK
OTHERS ARE BANAL, BUT USEFUL. LIKE THIS ONE. A SUITCASE NUKE FROM A 1950S COLD WAR THRILLER.
ARMED, AND COUNTING DOWN.
ENTER PASSWORD
AND...THIS IS MEANT TO CONVINCE ME THAT YOU'RE NOT MAD?
IT'S FOR YOU, TOM. YOUR MIRACLE MUST BE SEEN BY EVERYONE.
THEN EVERYONE WILL BELIEVE, AND THE LAST VEIL WILL BE STRIPPED AWAY.

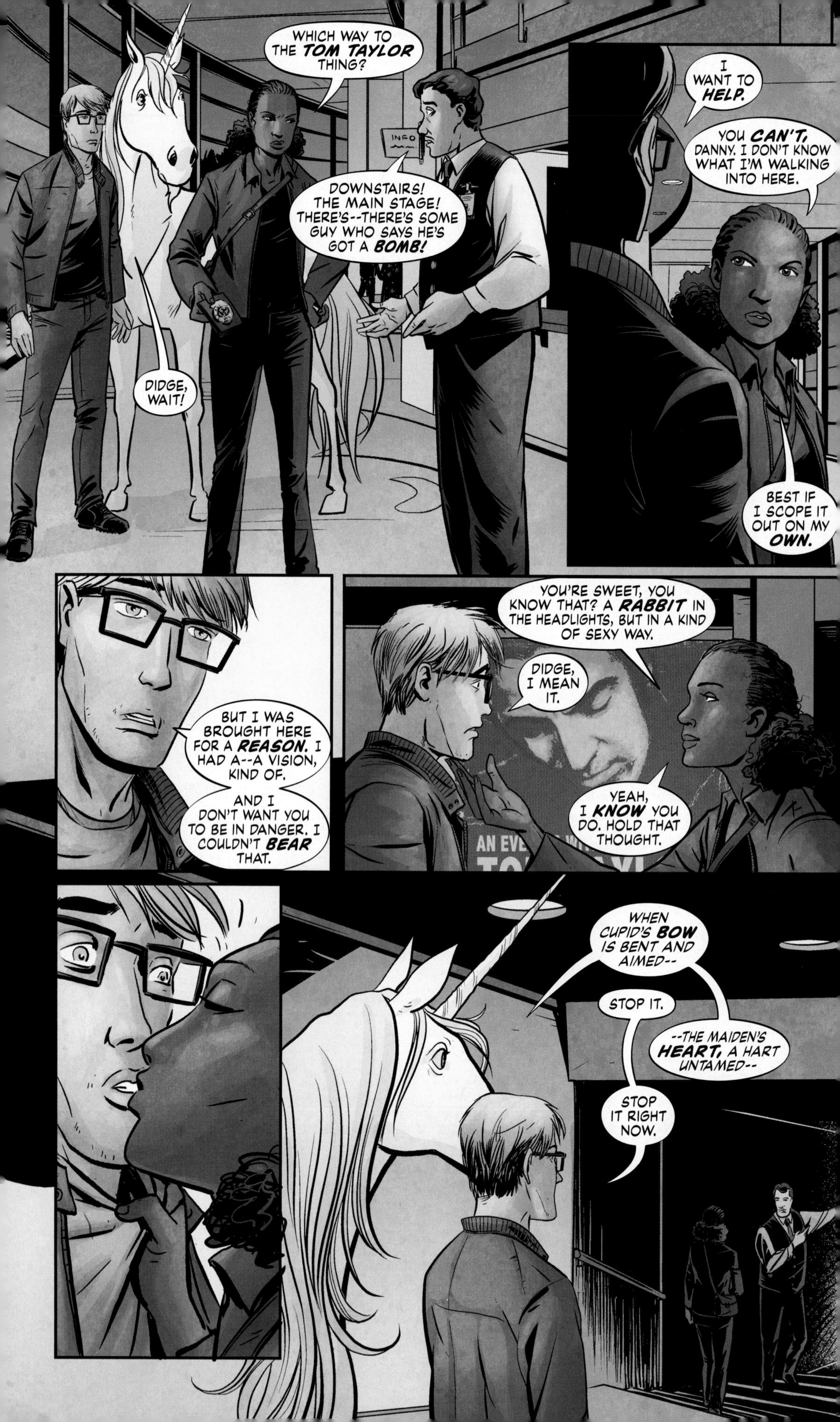
WHICH WAY TO THE TOM TAYLOR THING?
DOWNSTAIRS! THE MAIN STAGE! THERE'S--THERE'S SOME GUY WHO SAYS HE'S GOT A BOMB!
INFO
DIDGE, WAIT!
I WANT TO HELP.
YOU CAN'T, DANNY. I DON'T KNOW WHAT I'M WALKING INTO HERE.
BEST IF I SCOPE IT OUT ON MY OWN.
BUT I WAS BROUGHT HERE FOR A REASON. I HAD A--A VISION, KIND OF.
AND I DON'T WANT YOU TO BE IN DANGER. I COULDN'T BEAR THAT.
YOU'RE SWEET, YOU KNOW THAT? A RABBIT IN THE HEADLIGHTS, BUT IN A KIND OF SEXY WAY.
DIDGE, I MEAN IT.
YEAH, I KNOW YOU DO. HOLD THAT THOUGHT.
WHEN CUPID'S BOW IS BENT AND AIMED--
STOP IT.
--THE MAIDEN'S HEART, A HART UNTAMED--
STOP IT RIGHT NOW.

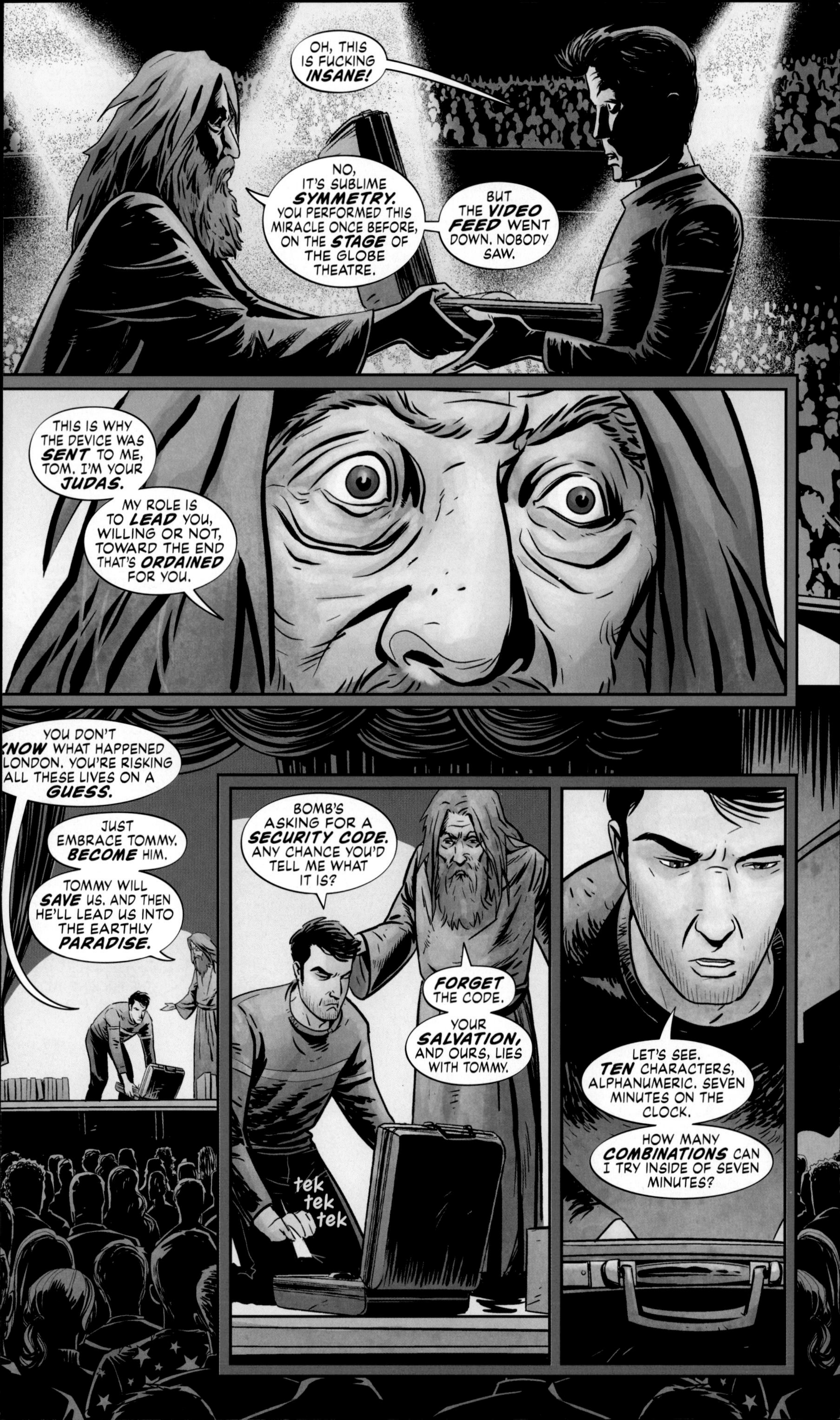
OH, THIS IS FUCKING INSANE!
NO, IT'S SUBLIME SYMMETRY. YOU PERFORMED THIS MIRACLE ONCE BEFORE, ON THE STAGE OF THE GLOBE THEATRE.
BUT THE VIDEO FEED WENT DOWN. NOBODY SAW.
THIS IS WHY THE DEVICE WAS SENT TO ME, TOM. I'M YOUR JUDAS.
MY ROLE IS TO LEAD YOU, WILLING OR NOT, TOWARD THE END THAT'S ORDAINED FOR YOU.
YOU DON'T KNOW WHAT HAPPENED LONDON. YOU'RE RISKING ALL THESE LIVES ON A GUESS.
JUST EMBRACE TOMMY. BECOME HIM.
TOMMY WILL SAVE US. AND THEN HE'LL LEAD US INTO THE EARTHLY PARADISE.
BOMB'S ASKING FOR A SECURITY CODE. ANY CHANCE YOU'D TELL ME WHAT IT IS?
FORGET THE CODE.
YOUR SALVATION, AND OURS, LIES WITH TOMMY.
tek tek tek
LET'S SEE. TEN CHARACTERS, ALPHANUMERIC. SEVEN MINUTES ON THE CLOCK.
HOW MANY COMBINATIONS CAN I TRY INSIDE OF SEVEN MINUTES?

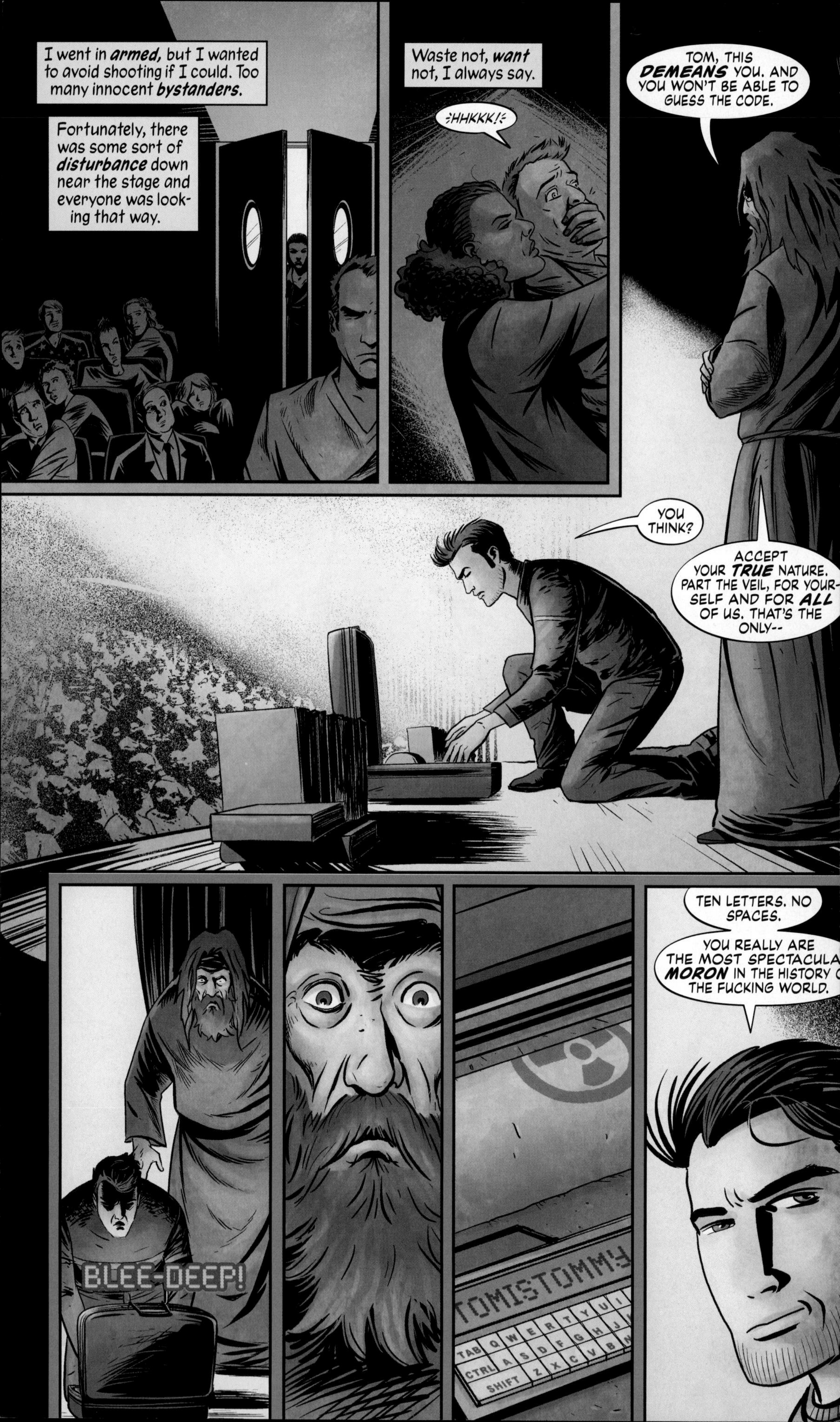
I went in *armed,* but I wanted to avoid shooting if I could. Too many innocent *bystanders.*
Fortunately, there was some sort of *disturbance* down near the stage and everyone was looking that way.
Waste not, *want* not, I always say.
HHKKK!
TOM, THIS **DEMEANS** YOU. AND YOU WON'T BE ABLE TO GUESS THE CODE.
YOU THINK?
ACCEPT YOUR **TRUE** NATURE. PART THE VEIL, FOR YOURSELF AND FOR **ALL** OF US. THAT'S THE ONLY--
BLEE-DEEP!
TOMISTOMMY
TAB Q W E R T Y U I
CTRL A S D F G H J
SHIFT Z X C V B N
TEN LETTERS. NO SPACES.
YOU REALLY ARE THE MOST SPECTACULA **MORON** IN THE HISTORY O THE FUCKING WORLD.

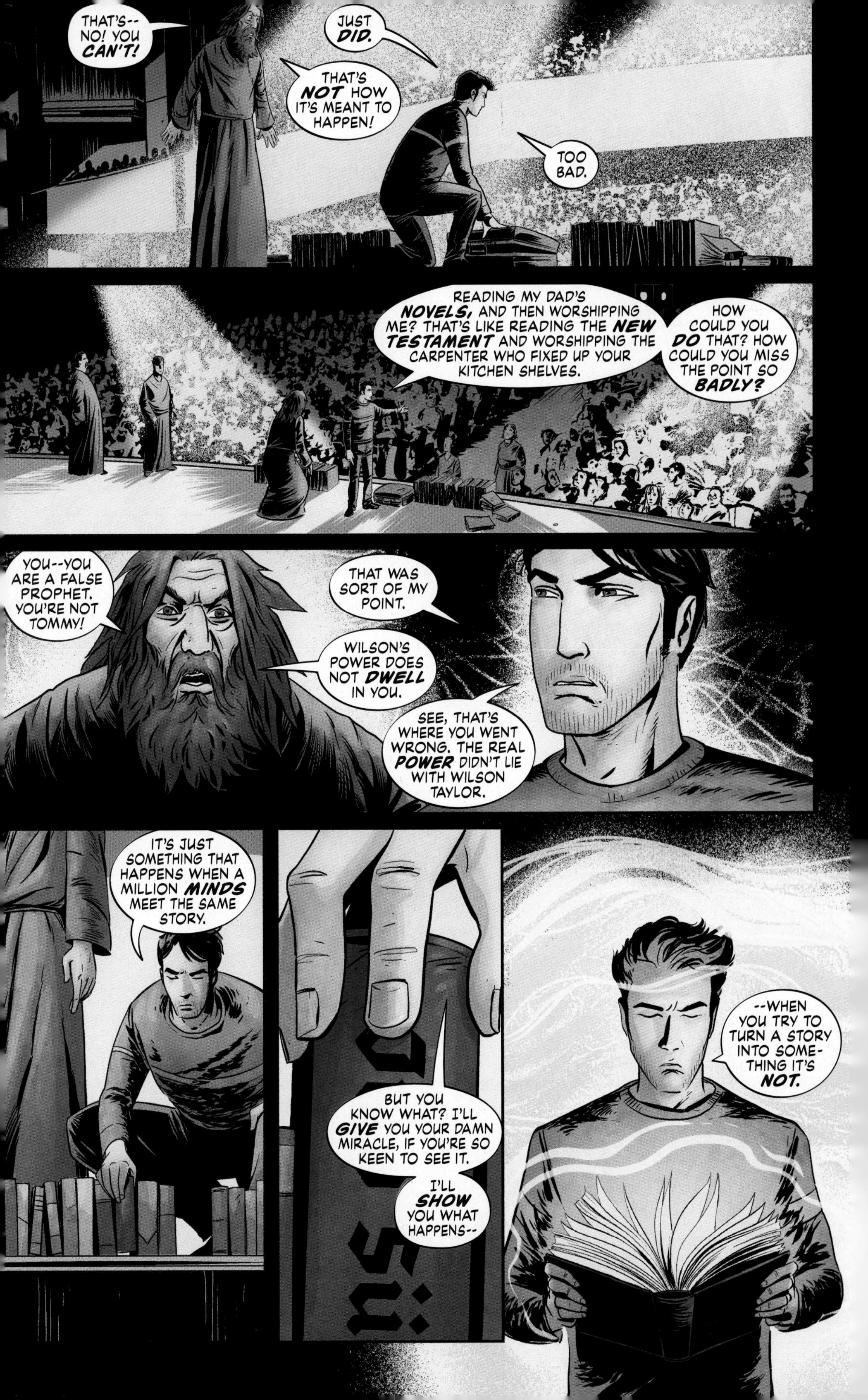
THAT'S--
NO! YOU CAN'T!
JUST DID.
THAT'S NOT HOW IT'S MEANT TO HAPPEN!
TOO BAD.
READING MY DAD'S NOVELS, AND THEN WORSHIPPING ME? THAT'S LIKE READING THE NEW TESTAMENT AND WORSHIPPING THE CARPENTER WHO FIXED UP YOUR KITCHEN SHELVES.
HOW COULD YOU DO THAT? HOW COULD YOU MISS THE POINT SO BADLY?
YOU--YOU ARE A FALSE PROPHET. YOU'RE NOT TOMMY!
THAT WAS SORT OF MY POINT.
WILSON'S POWER DOES NOT DWELL IN YOU.
SEE, THAT'S WHERE YOU WENT WRONG. THE REAL POWER DIDN'T LIE WITH WILSON TAYLOR.
IT'S JUST SOMETHING THAT HAPPENS WHEN A MILLION MINDS MEET THE SAME STORY.
BUT YOU KNOW WHAT? I'LL GIVE YOU YOUR DAMN MIRACLE, IF YOU'RE SO KEEN TO SEE IT.
I'LL SHOW YOU WHAT HAPPENS--
--WHEN YOU TRY TO TURN A STORY INTO SOME-THING IT'S NOT.

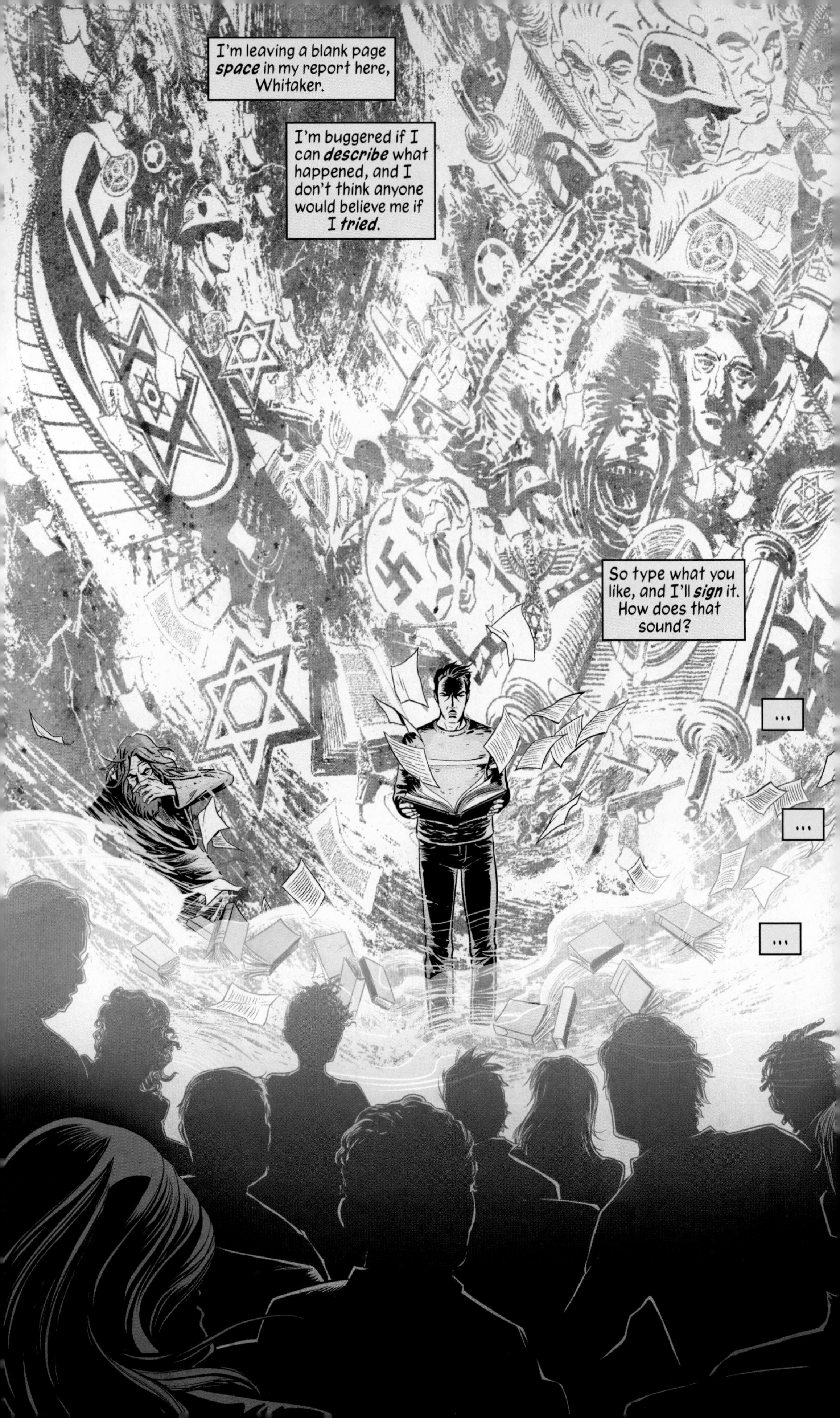
I'm leaving a blank page *space* in my report here, Whitaker.
I'm buggered if I can *describe* what happened, and I don't think anyone would believe me if I *tried*.
So type what you like, and I'll *sign* it. How does that sound?
...
...
...

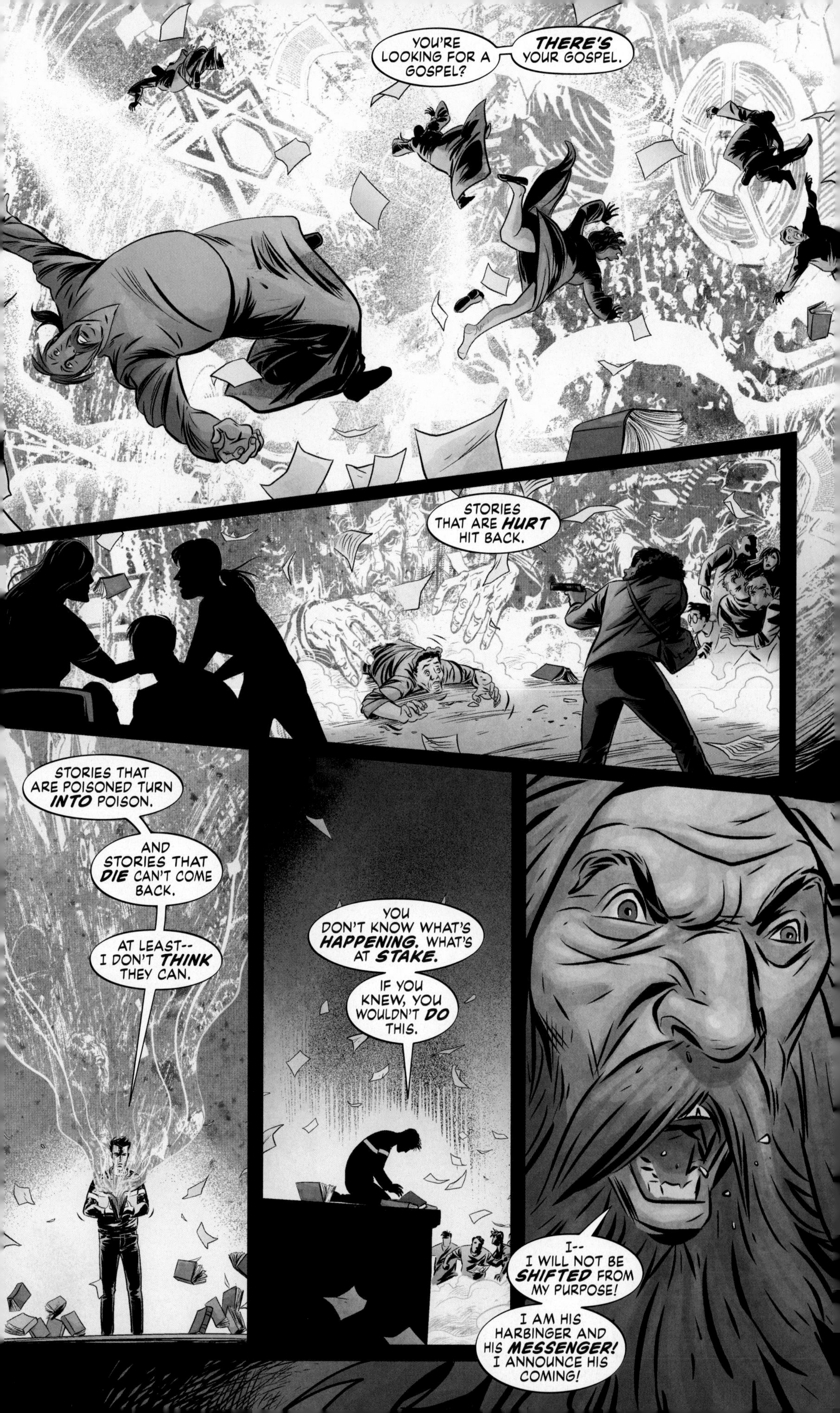
YOU'RE LOOKING FOR A GOSPEL?
THERE'S YOUR GOSPEL.
STORIES THAT ARE HURT HIT BACK.
STORIES THAT ARE POISONED TURN INTO POISON.
AND STORIES THAT DIE CAN'T COME BACK.
AT LEAST-- I DON'T THINK THEY CAN.
YOU DON'T KNOW WHAT'S HAPPENING. WHAT'S AT STAKE.
IF YOU KNEW, YOU WOULDN'T DO THIS.
I-- I WILL NOT BE SHIFTED FROM MY PURPOSE!
I AM HIS HARBINGER AND HIS MESSENGER! I ANNOUNCE HIS COMING!

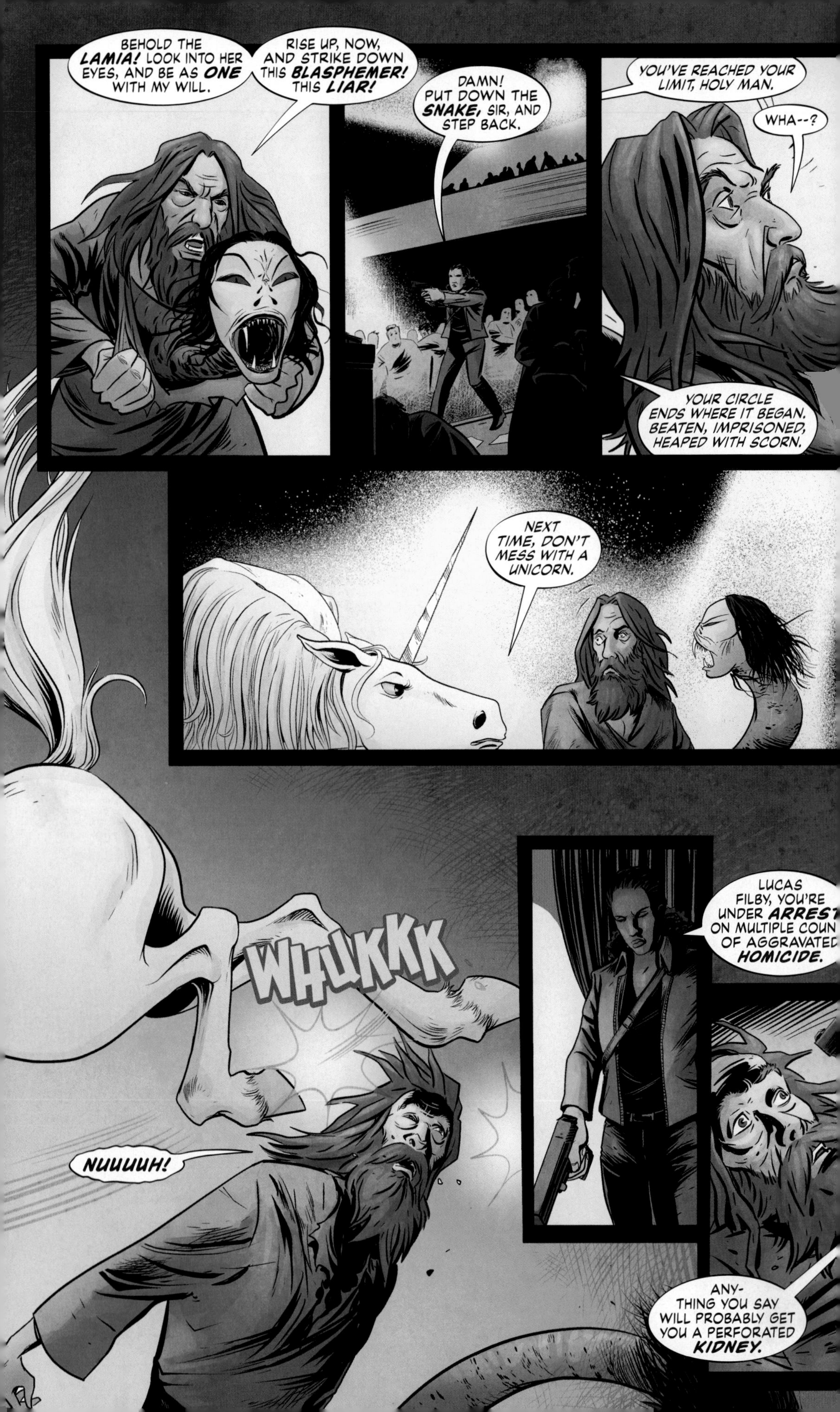
BEHOLD THE LAMIA! LOOK INTO HER EYES, AND BE AS ONE WITH MY WILL.
RISE UP, NOW, AND STRIKE DOWN THIS BLASPHEMER! THIS LIAR!
DAMN! PUT DOWN THE SNAKE, SIR, AND STEP BACK.
YOU'VE REACHED YOUR LIMIT, HOLY MAN.
WHA--?
YOUR CIRCLE ENDS WHERE IT BEGAN. BEATEN, IMPRISONED, HEAPED WITH SCORN.
NEXT TIME, DON'T MESS WITH A UNICORN.
WHUKKK
NUUUUH!
LUCAS FILBY, YOU'RE UNDER ARREST ON MULTIPLE COUN OF AGGRAVATED HOMICIDE.
ANY-THING YOU SAY WILL PROBABLY GET YOU A PERFORATED KIDNEY.

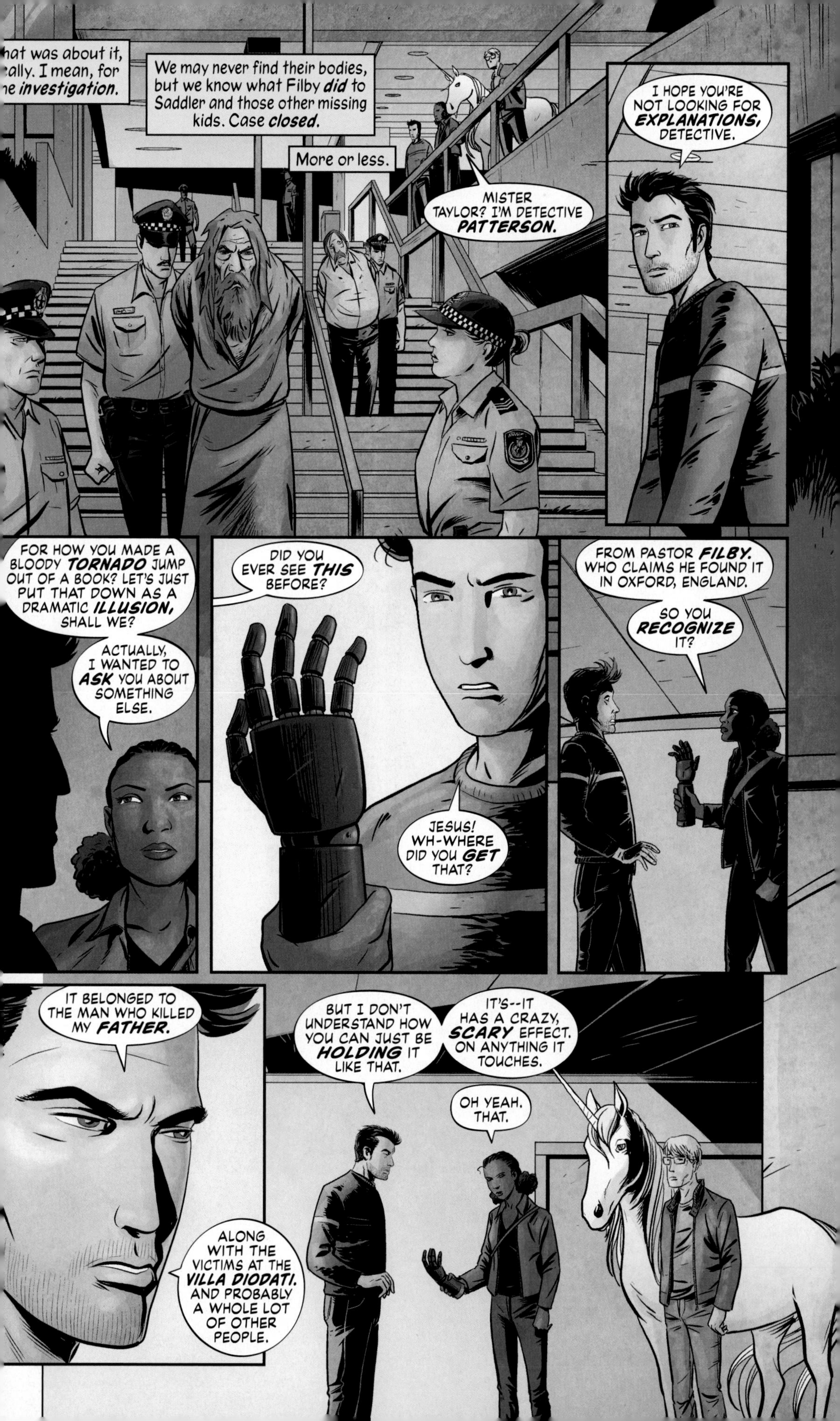

hat was about it, ally. I mean, for e *investigation*.
We may never find their bodies, but we know what Filby *did* to Saddler and those other missing kids. Case *closed*.
More or less.
MISTER TAYLOR? I'M DETECTIVE ***PATTERSON.***
I HOPE YOU'RE NOT LOOKING FOR ***EXPLANATIONS,*** DETECTIVE.
FOR HOW YOU MADE A BLOODY ***TORNADO*** JUMP OUT OF A BOOK? LET'S JUST PUT THAT DOWN AS A DRAMATIC ***ILLUSION,*** SHALL WE?
ACTUALLY, I WANTED TO ***ASK*** YOU ABOUT SOMETHING ELSE.
DID YOU EVER SEE ***THIS*** BEFORE?
JESUS! WH-WHERE DID YOU ***GET*** THAT?
FROM PASTOR ***FILBY.*** WHO CLAIMS HE FOUND IT IN OXFORD, ENGLAND.
SO YOU ***RECOGNIZE*** IT?
IT BELONGED TO THE MAN WHO KILLED MY ***FATHER.***
ALONG WITH THE VICTIMS AT THE ***VILLA DIODATI.*** AND PROBABLY A WHOLE LOT OF OTHER PEOPLE.
BUT I DON'T UNDERSTAND HOW YOU CAN JUST BE ***HOLDING*** IT LIKE THAT.
IT'S--IT HAS A CRAZY, ***SCARY*** EFFECT. ON ANYTHING IT TOUCHES.
OH YEAH. THAT.

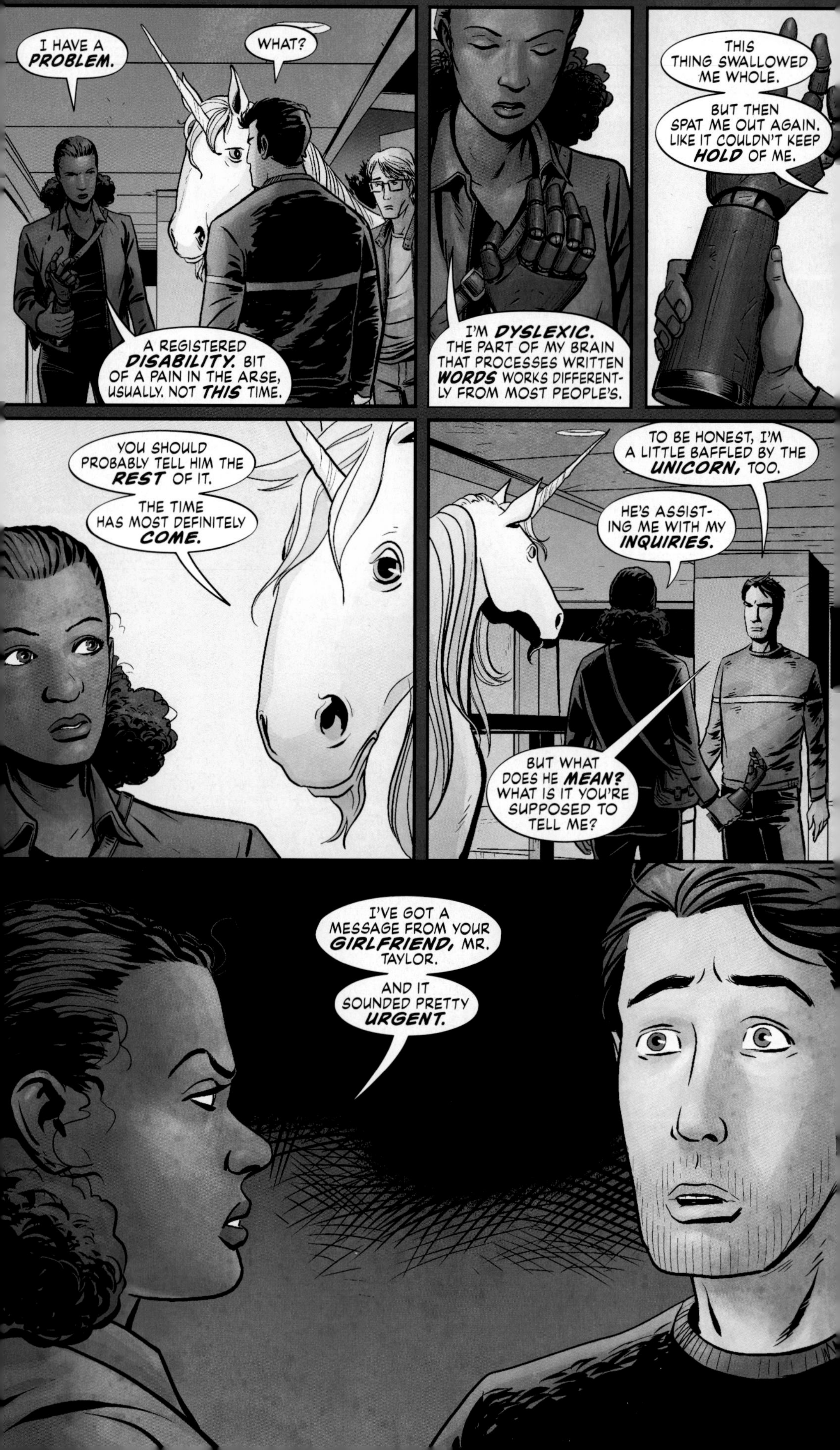
I HAVE A PROBLEM.
WHAT?
A REGISTERED DISABILITY. BIT OF A PAIN IN THE ARSE, USUALLY. NOT THIS TIME.
I'M DYSLEXIC. THE PART OF MY BRAIN THAT PROCESSES WRITTEN WORDS WORKS DIFFERENTLY FROM MOST PEOPLE'S.
THIS THING SWALLOWED ME WHOLE.
BUT THEN SPAT ME OUT AGAIN. LIKE IT COULDN'T KEEP HOLD OF ME.
YOU SHOULD PROBABLY TELL HIM THE REST OF IT.
THE TIME HAS MOST DEFINITELY COME.
TO BE HONEST, I'M A LITTLE BAFFLED BY THE UNICORN, TOO.
HE'S ASSISTING ME WITH MY INQUIRIES.
BUT WHAT DOES HE MEAN? WHAT IS IT YOU'RE SUPPOSED TO TELL ME?
I'VE GOT A MESSAGE FROM YOUR GIRLFRIEND, MR. TAYLOR.
AND IT SOUNDED PRETTY URGENT.

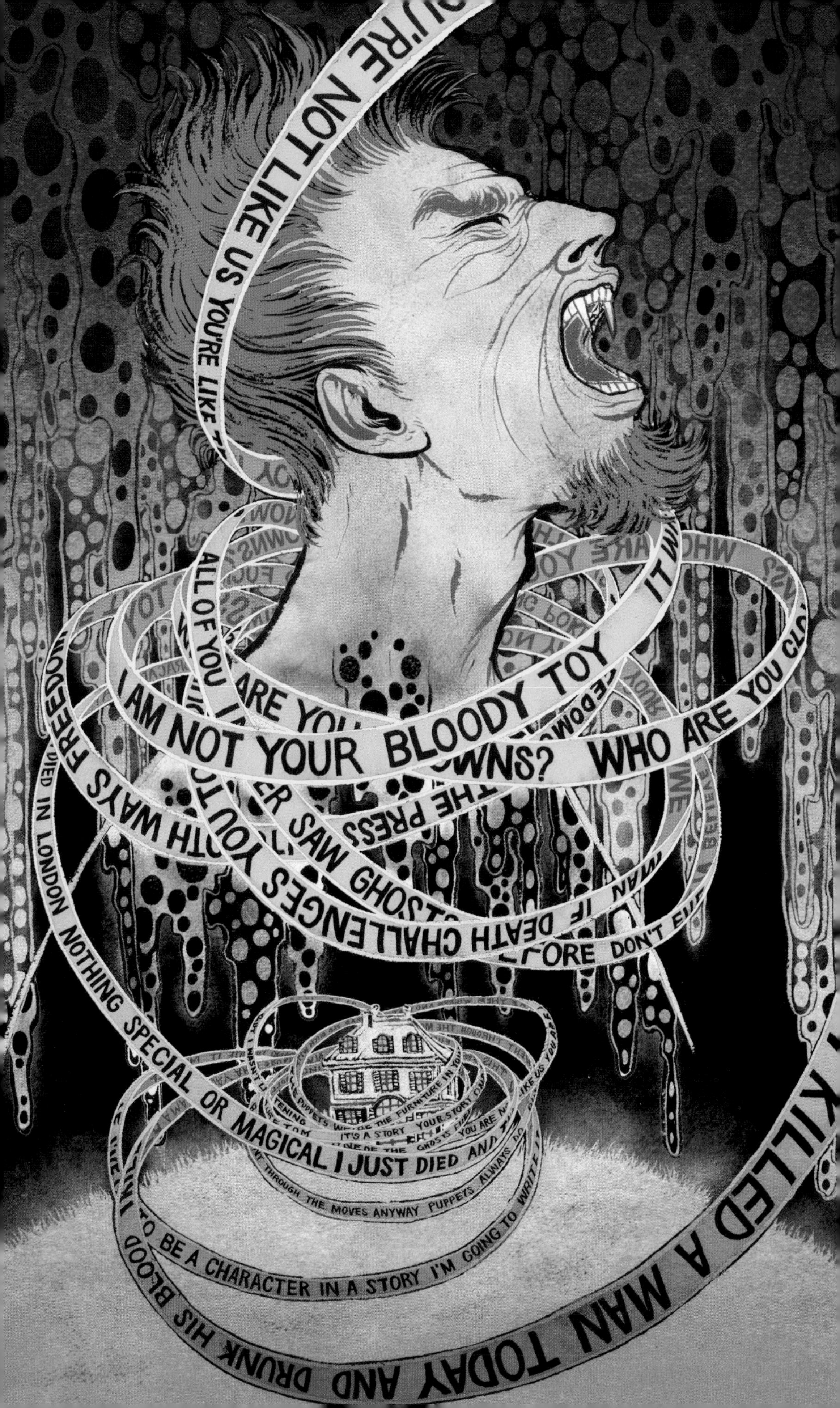

NOT LIKE US YOU'RE LIKE
I AM NOT YOUR BLOODY TOY
OWNS?
WHO ARE YOU
ALL OF YOU
ARE YOU
SAW GHOSTS
THE PRESS
YOUTH WAYS
CHALLENGES IF DEATH
DON'T
DIED IN LONDON NOTHING SPECIAL OR MAGICAL I JUST DIED AND
THROUGH THE MOVES ANYWAY PUPPETS ALWAYS
IT'S A STORY YOUR STORY
TO BE A CHARACTER IN A STORY I'M GOING TO
KILLED A MAN TODAY AND DRUNK HIS BLOOD

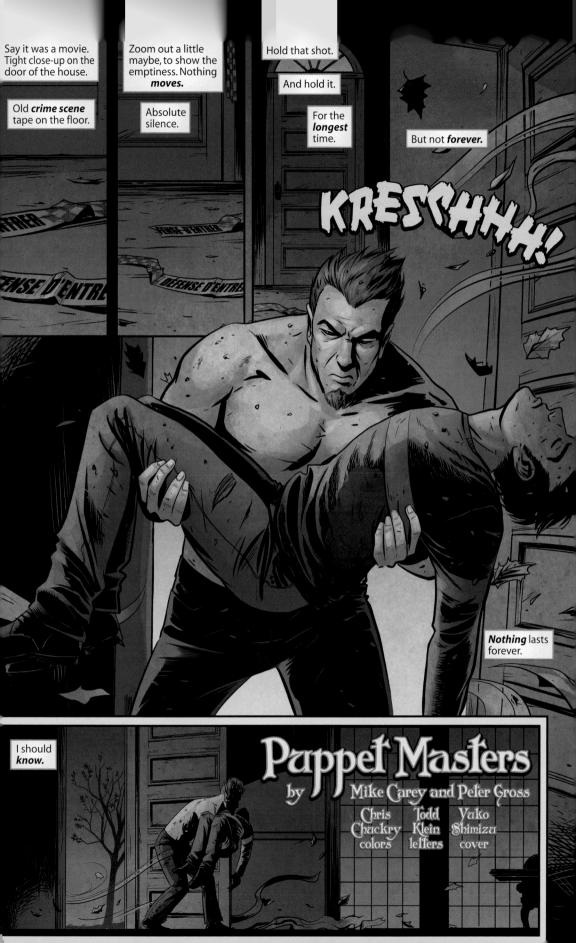

Say it was a movie. Tight close-up on the door of the house.

Old **crime scene** tape on the floor.

Zoom out a little maybe, to show the emptiness. Nothing **moves.**

Absolute silence.

Hold that shot.

And hold it.

For the **longest** time.

But not **forever.**

KRESCHHH!

Nothing lasts forever.

I should **know.**

Puppet Masters

by Mike Carey and Peter Gross

Chris Chuckry colors

Todd Klein letters

Yuko Shimizu cover

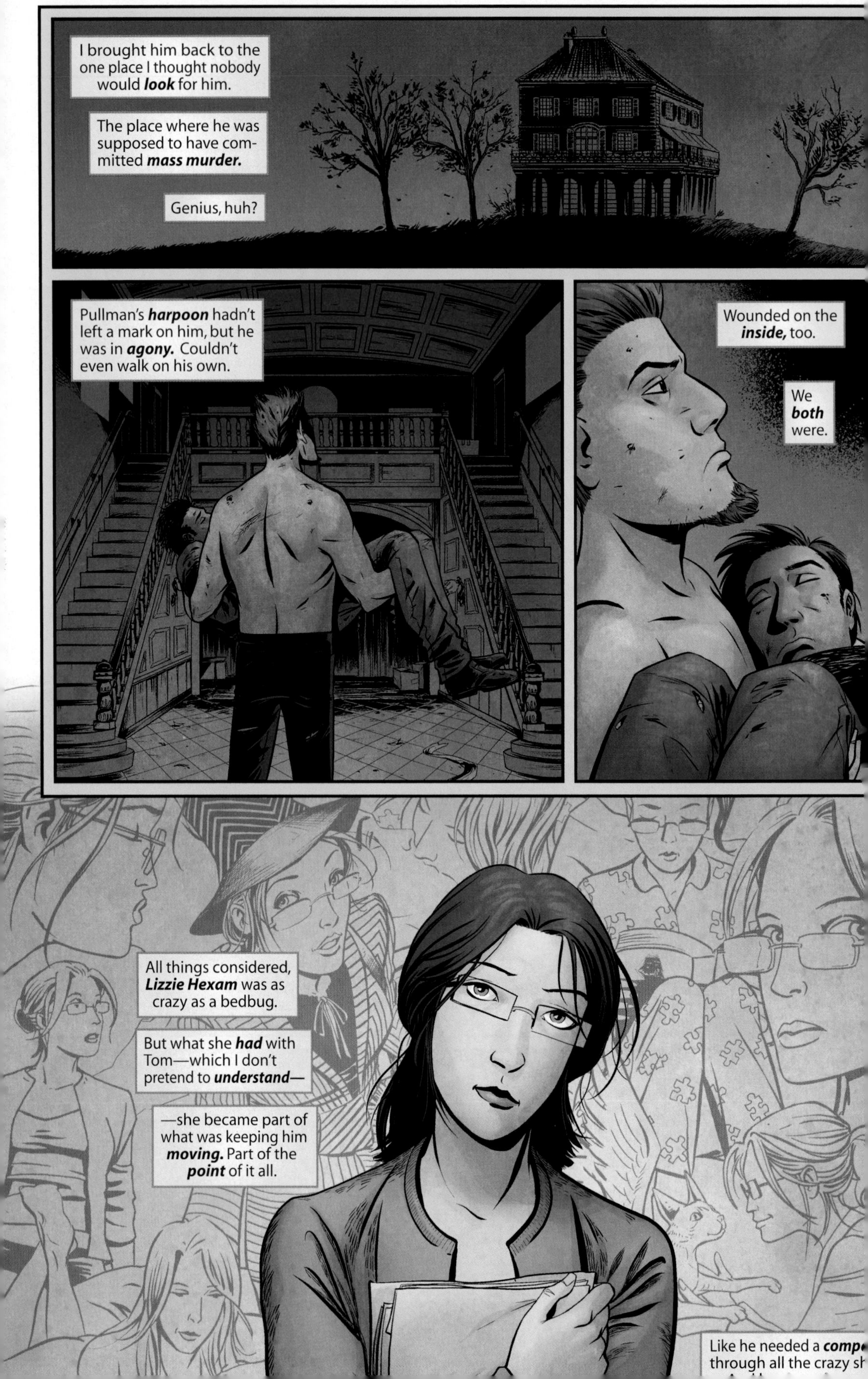
I brought him back to the one place I thought nobody would *look* for him.
The place where he was supposed to have committed *mass murder.*
Genius, huh?
Pullman's *harpoon* hadn't left a mark on him, but he was in *agony.* Couldn't even walk on his own.
Wounded on the *inside,* too.
We *both* were.
All things considered, *Lizzie Hexam* was as crazy as a bedbug.
But what she *had* with Tom—which I don't pretend to *understand*—
—she became part of what was keeping him *moving.* Part of the *point* of it all.
Like he needed a
through all the crazy

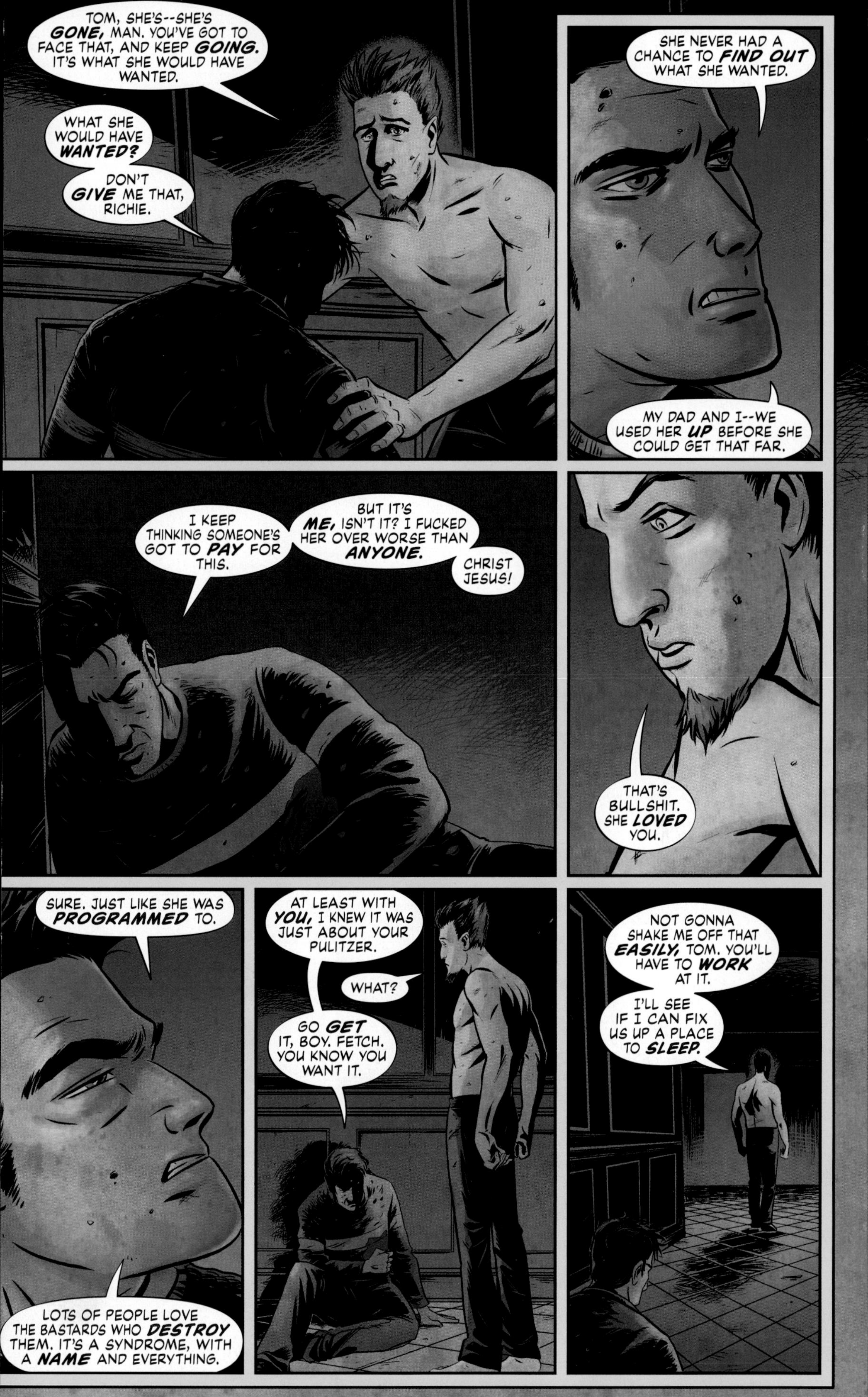
TOM, SHE'S--SHE'S GONE, MAN. YOU'VE GOT TO FACE THAT, AND KEEP GOING. IT'S WHAT SHE WOULD HAVE WANTED.
WHAT SHE WOULD HAVE WANTED?
DON'T GIVE ME THAT, RICHIE.
SHE NEVER HAD A CHANCE TO FIND OUT WHAT SHE WANTED.
MY DAD AND I--WE USED HER UP BEFORE SHE COULD GET THAT FAR.
I KEEP THINKING SOMEONE'S GOT TO PAY FOR THIS.
BUT IT'S ME, ISN'T IT? I FUCKED HER OVER WORSE THAN ANYONE.
CHRIST JESUS!
THAT'S BULLSHIT. SHE LOVED YOU.
SURE. JUST LIKE SHE WAS PROGRAMMED TO.
LOTS OF PEOPLE LOVE THE BASTARDS WHO DESTROY THEM. IT'S A SYNDROME, WITH A NAME AND EVERYTHING.
AT LEAST WITH YOU, I KNEW IT WAS JUST ABOUT YOUR PULITZER.
WHAT?
GO GET IT, BOY. FETCH. YOU KNOW YOU WANT IT.
NOT GONNA SHAKE ME OFF THAT EASILY, TOM. YOU'LL HAVE TO WORK AT IT.
I'LL SEE IF I CAN FIX US UP A PLACE TO SLEEP.

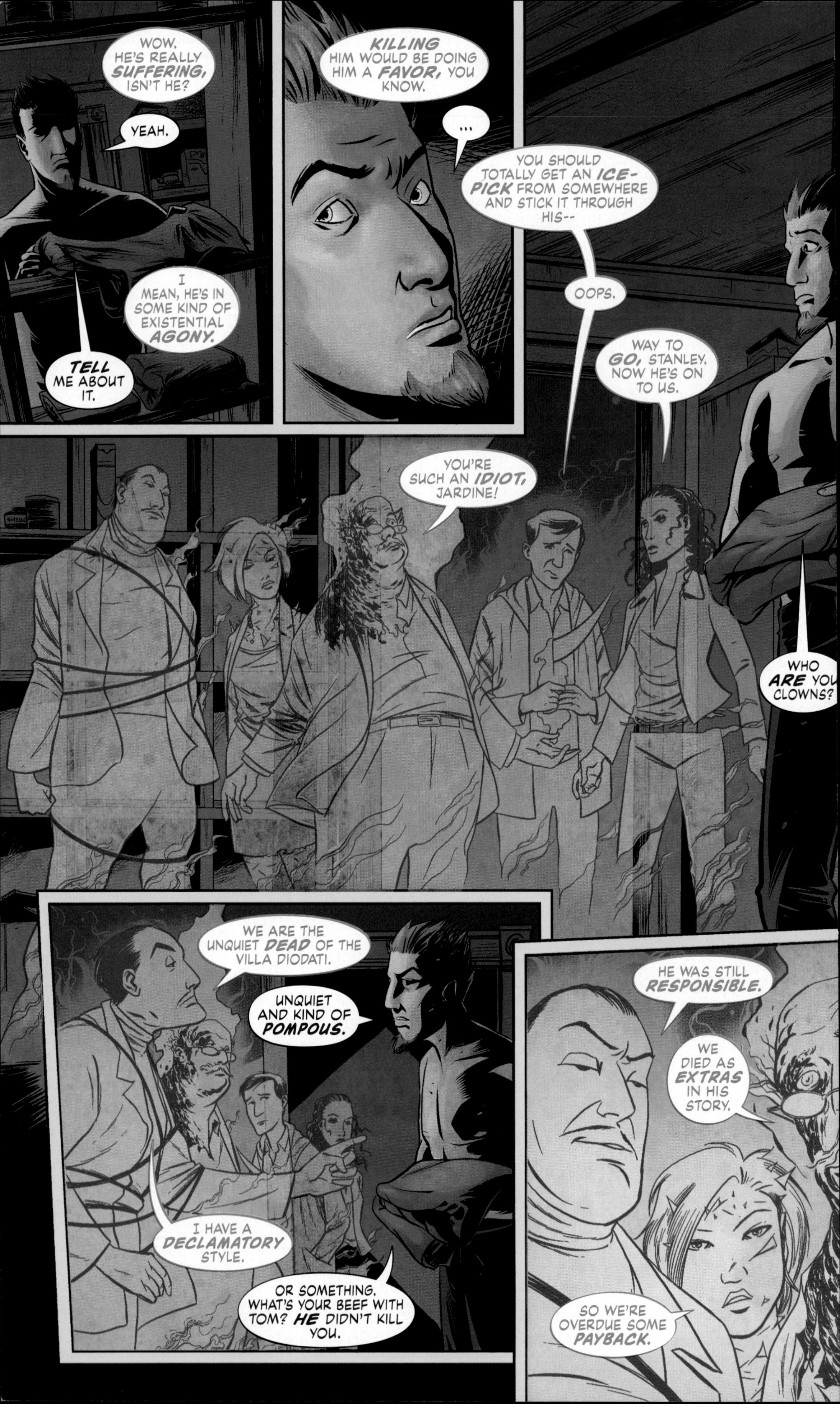

WOW. HE'S REALLY SUFFERING, ISN'T HE?
YEAH.
I MEAN, HE'S IN SOME KIND OF EXISTENTIAL AGONY.
TELL ME ABOUT IT.
KILLING HIM WOULD BE DOING HIM A FAVOR, YOU KNOW.
...
YOU SHOULD TOTALLY GET AN ICE-PICK FROM SOMEWHERE AND STICK IT THROUGH HIS--
OOPS.
WAY TO GO, STANLEY. NOW HE'S ON TO US.
YOU'RE SUCH AN IDIOT, JARDINE!
WHO ARE YOU CLOWNS?
WE ARE THE UNQUIET DEAD OF THE VILLA DIODATI.
UNQUIET AND KIND OF POMPOUS.
I HAVE A DECLAMATORY STYLE.
OR SOMETHING. WHAT'S YOUR BEEF WITH TOM? HE DIDN'T KILL YOU.
HE WAS STILL RESPONSIBLE.
WE DIED AS EXTRAS IN HIS STORY.
SO WE'RE OVERDUE SOME PAYBACK.

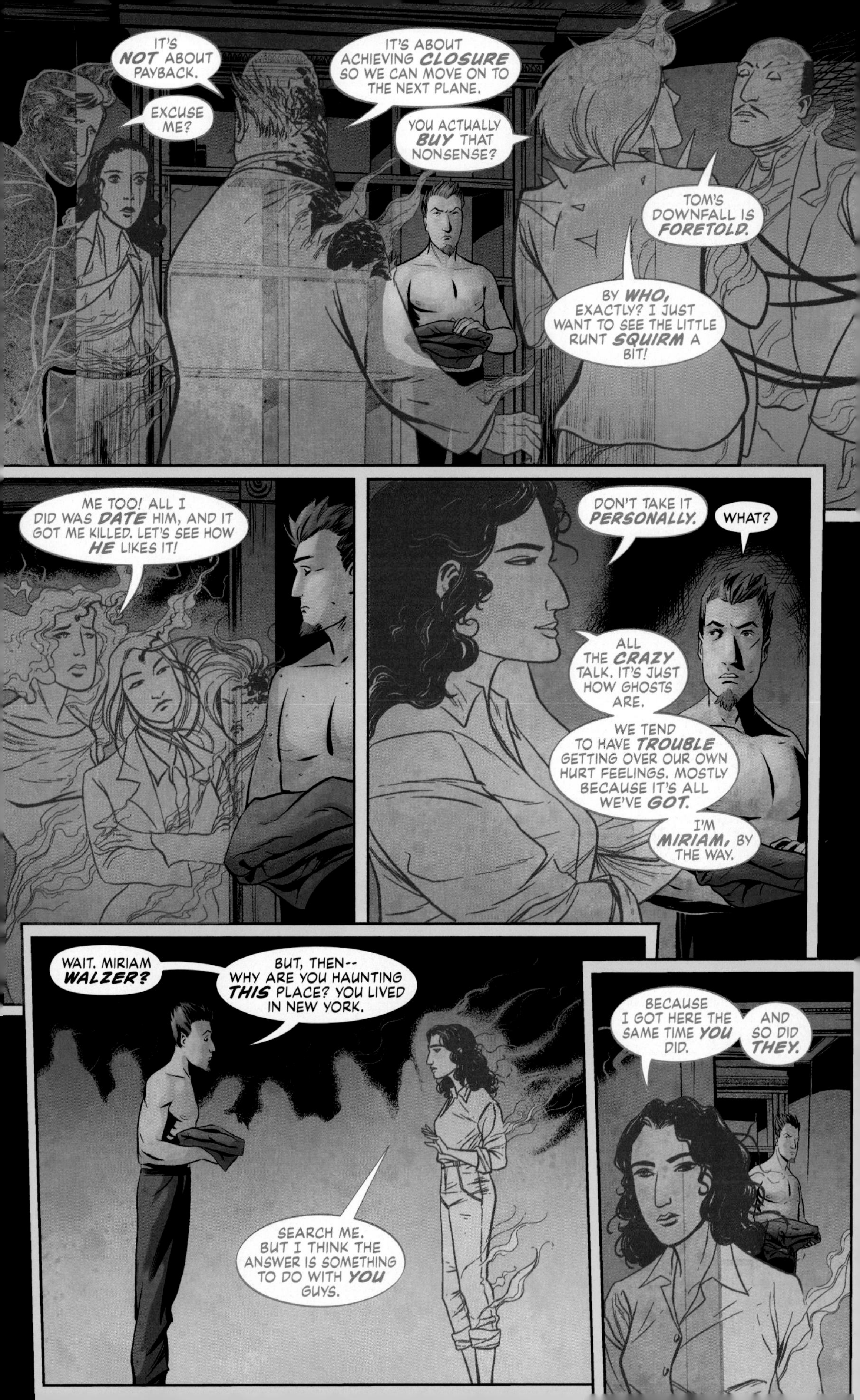
IT'S NOT ABOUT PAYBACK.
EXCUSE ME?
IT'S ABOUT ACHIEVING CLOSURE SO WE CAN MOVE ON TO THE NEXT PLANE.
YOU ACTUALLY BUY THAT NONSENSE?
TOM'S DOWNFALL IS FORETOLD.
BY WHO, EXACTLY? I JUST WANT TO SEE THE LITTLE RUNT SQUIRM A BIT!
ME TOO! ALL I DID WAS DATE HIM, AND IT GOT ME KILLED. LET'S SEE HOW HE LIKES IT!
DON'T TAKE IT PERSONALLY.
WHAT?
ALL THE CRAZY TALK. IT'S JUST HOW GHOSTS ARE.
WE TEND TO HAVE TROUBLE GETTING OVER OUR OWN HURT FEELINGS. MOSTLY BECAUSE IT'S ALL WE'VE GOT.
I'M MIRIAM, BY THE WAY.
WAIT. MIRIAM WALZER?
BUT, THEN-- WHY ARE YOU HAUNTING THIS PLACE? YOU LIVED IN NEW YORK.
SEARCH ME. BUT I THINK THE ANSWER IS SOMETHING TO DO WITH YOU GUYS.
BECAUSE I GOT HERE THE SAME TIME YOU DID.
AND SO DID THEY.

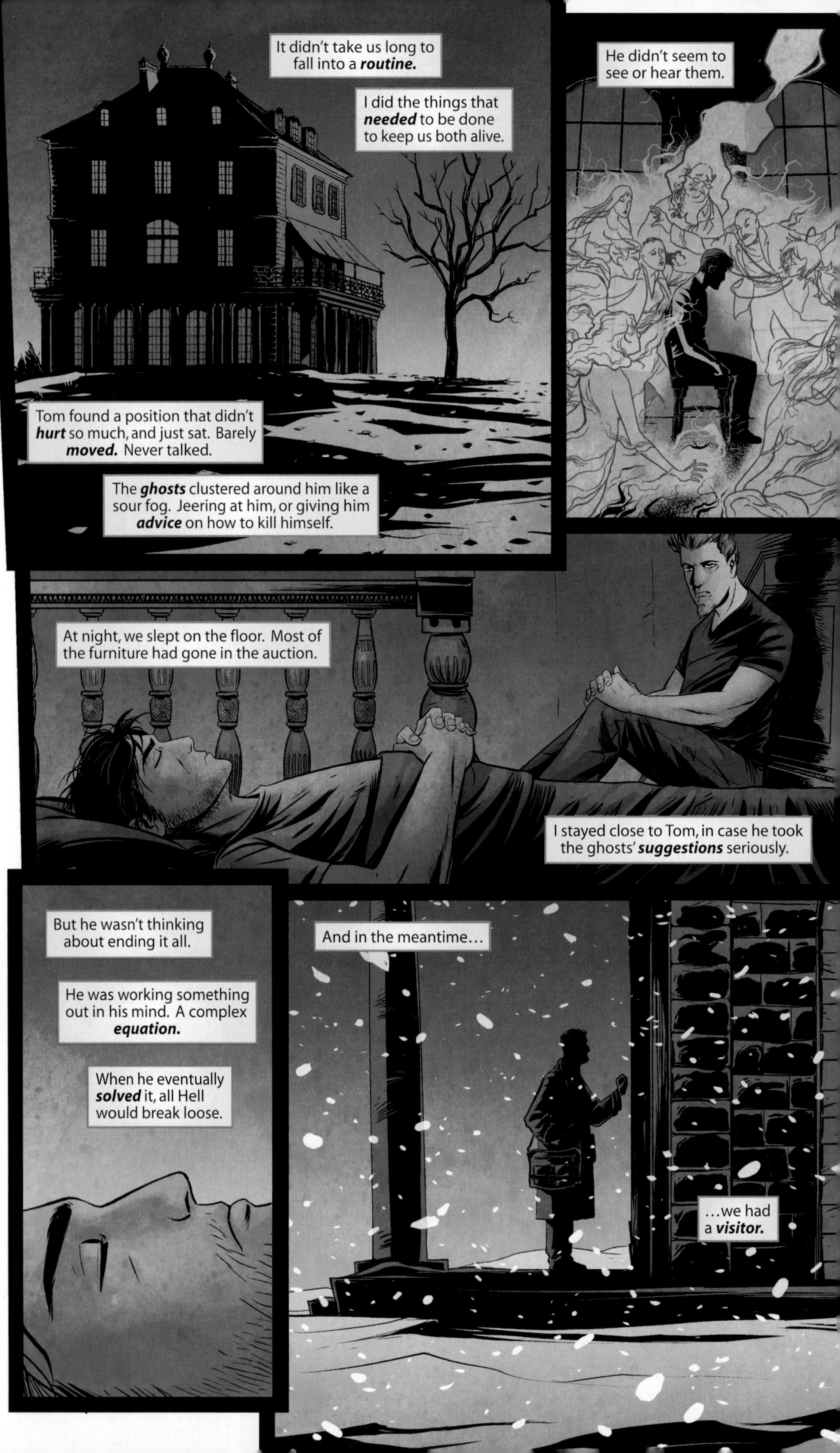
It didn't take us long to fall into a ***routine.***
I did the things that ***needed*** to be done to keep us both alive.
Tom found a position that didn't ***hurt*** so much, and just sat. Barely ***moved.*** Never talked.
The ***ghosts*** clustered around him like a sour fog. Jeering at him, or giving him ***advice*** on how to kill himself.
He didn't seem to see or hear them.
At night, we slept on the floor. Most of the furniture had gone in the auction.
I stayed close to Tom, in case he took the ghosts' ***suggestions*** seriously.
But he wasn't thinking about ending it all.
He was working something out in his mind. A complex ***equation.***
When he eventually ***solved*** it, all Hell would break loose.
And in the meantime…
…we had a ***visitor.***

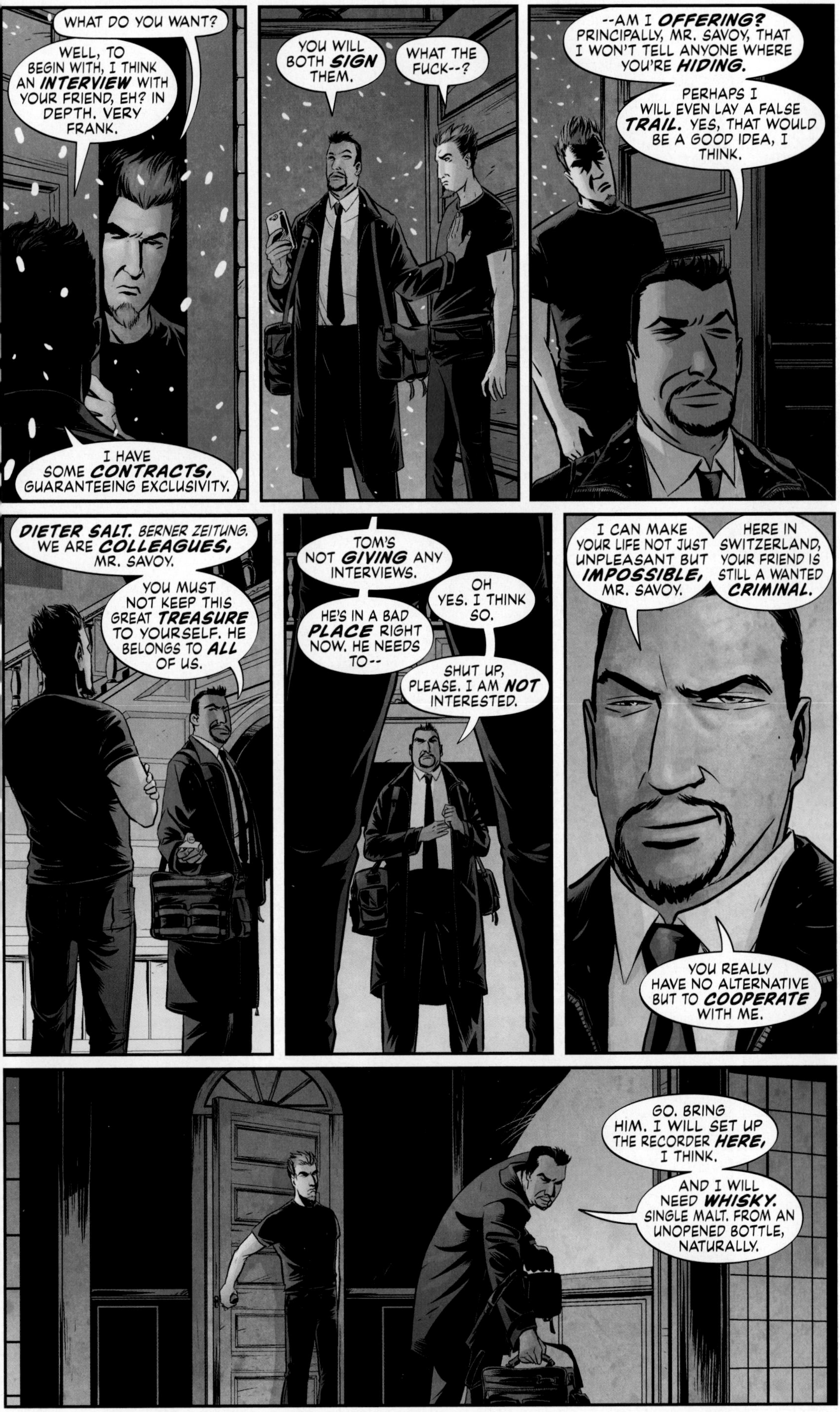
WHAT DO YOU WANT?
WELL, TO BEGIN WITH, I THINK AN INTERVIEW WITH YOUR FRIEND, EH? IN DEPTH. VERY FRANK.
I HAVE SOME CONTRACTS, GUARANTEEING EXCLUSIVITY.
YOU WILL BOTH SIGN THEM.
WHAT THE FUCK--?
--AM I OFFERING? PRINCIPALLY, MR. SAVOY, THAT I WON'T TELL ANYONE WHERE YOU'RE HIDING.
PERHAPS I WILL EVEN LAY A FALSE TRAIL. YES, THAT WOULD BE A GOOD IDEA, I THINK.
DIETER SALT. BERNER ZEITUNG. WE ARE COLLEAGUES, MR. SAVOY.
YOU MUST NOT KEEP THIS GREAT TREASURE TO YOURSELF. HE BELONGS TO ALL OF US.
TOM'S NOT GIVING ANY INTERVIEWS.
HE'S IN A BAD PLACE RIGHT NOW. HE NEEDS TO--
OH YES. I THINK SO.
SHUT UP, PLEASE. I AM NOT INTERESTED.
I CAN MAKE YOUR LIFE NOT JUST UNPLEASANT BUT IMPOSSIBLE, MR. SAVOY.
HERE IN SWITZERLAND, YOUR FRIEND IS STILL A WANTED CRIMINAL.
YOU REALLY HAVE NO ALTERNATIVE BUT TO COOPERATE WITH ME.
GO. BRING HIM. I WILL SET UP THE RECORDER HERE, I THINK.
AND I WILL NEED WHISKY. SINGLE MALT. FROM AN UNOPENED BOTTLE, NATURALLY.

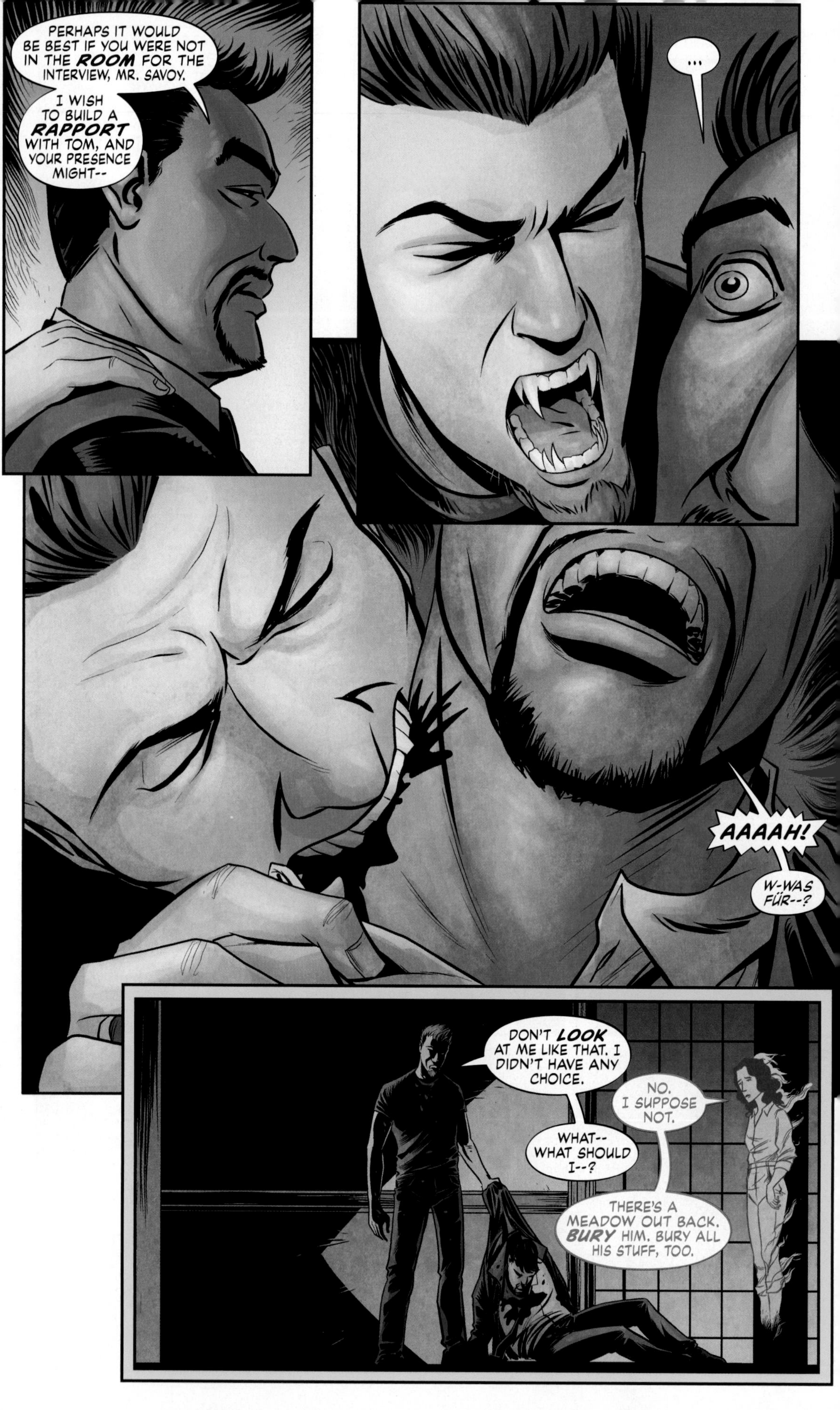
PERHAPS IT WOULD BE BEST IF YOU WERE NOT IN THE ROOM FOR THE INTERVIEW, MR. SAVOY.
I WISH TO BUILD A RAPPORT WITH TOM, AND YOUR PRESENCE MIGHT--
...
AAAAH!
W-WAS FÜR--?
DON'T LOOK AT ME LIKE THAT. I DIDN'T HAVE ANY CHOICE.
NO. I SUPPOSE NOT.
WHAT-- WHAT SHOULD I--?
THERE'S A MEADOW OUT BACK. BURY HIM. BURY ALL HIS STUFF, TOO.

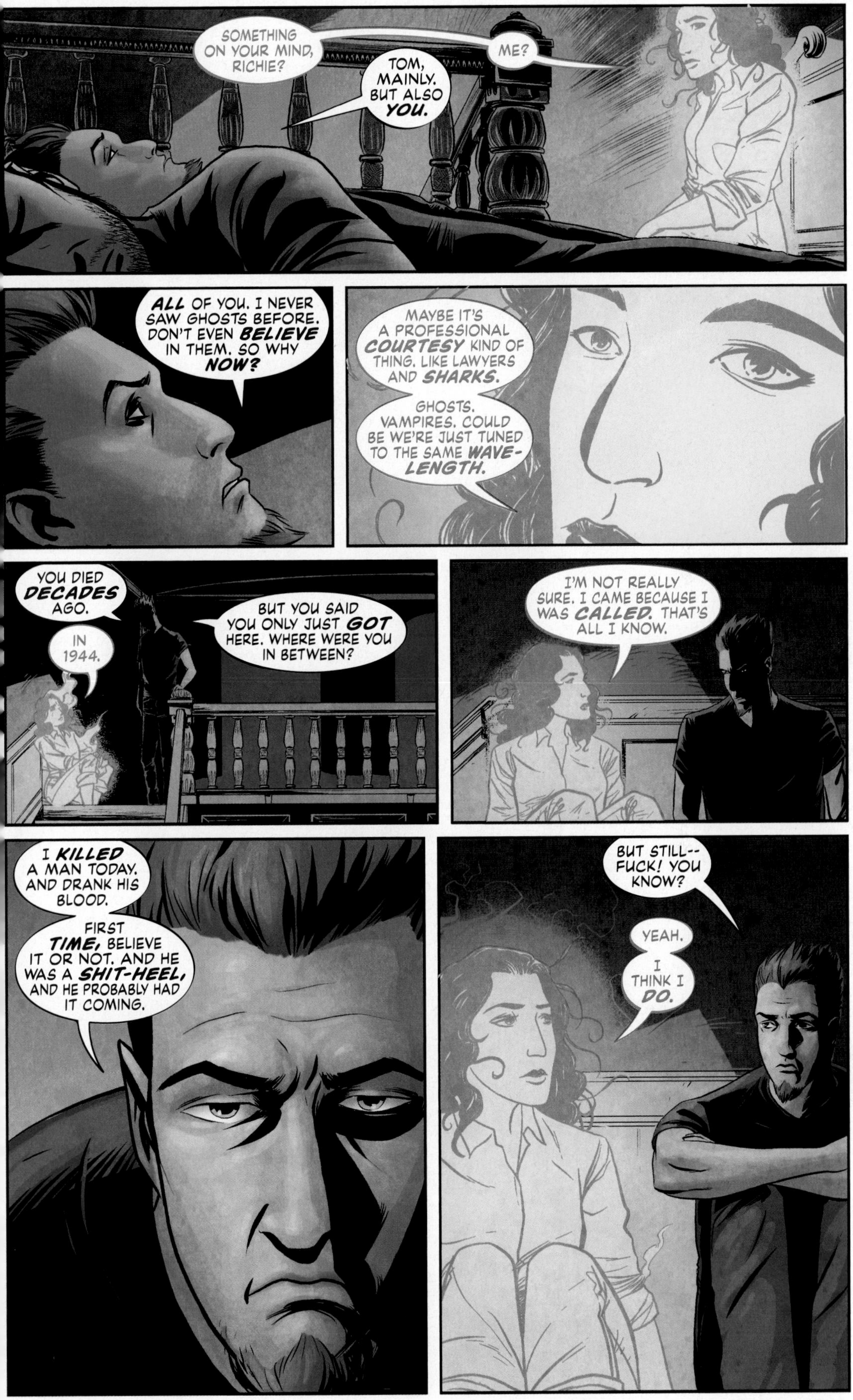
SOMETHING ON YOUR MIND, RICHIE?
ME?
TOM, MAINLY. BUT ALSO *YOU.*
ALL OF YOU. I NEVER SAW GHOSTS BEFORE. DON'T EVEN *BELIEVE* IN THEM. SO WHY *NOW?*
MAYBE IT'S A PROFESSIONAL *COURTESY* KIND OF THING. LIKE LAWYERS AND *SHARKS.*
GHOSTS. VAMPIRES. COULD BE WE'RE JUST TUNED TO THE SAME *WAVE-LENGTH.*
YOU DIED *DECADES* AGO.
IN 1944.
BUT YOU SAID YOU ONLY JUST *GOT* HERE. WHERE WERE YOU IN BETWEEN?
I'M NOT REALLY SURE. I CAME BECAUSE I WAS *CALLED.* THAT'S ALL I KNOW.
I *KILLED* A MAN TODAY. AND DRANK HIS BLOOD.
FIRST *TIME,* BELIEVE IT OR NOT. AND HE WAS A *SHIT-HEEL,* AND HE PROBABLY HAD IT COMING.
BUT STILL-- FUCK! YOU KNOW?
YEAH.
I THINK I *DO.*

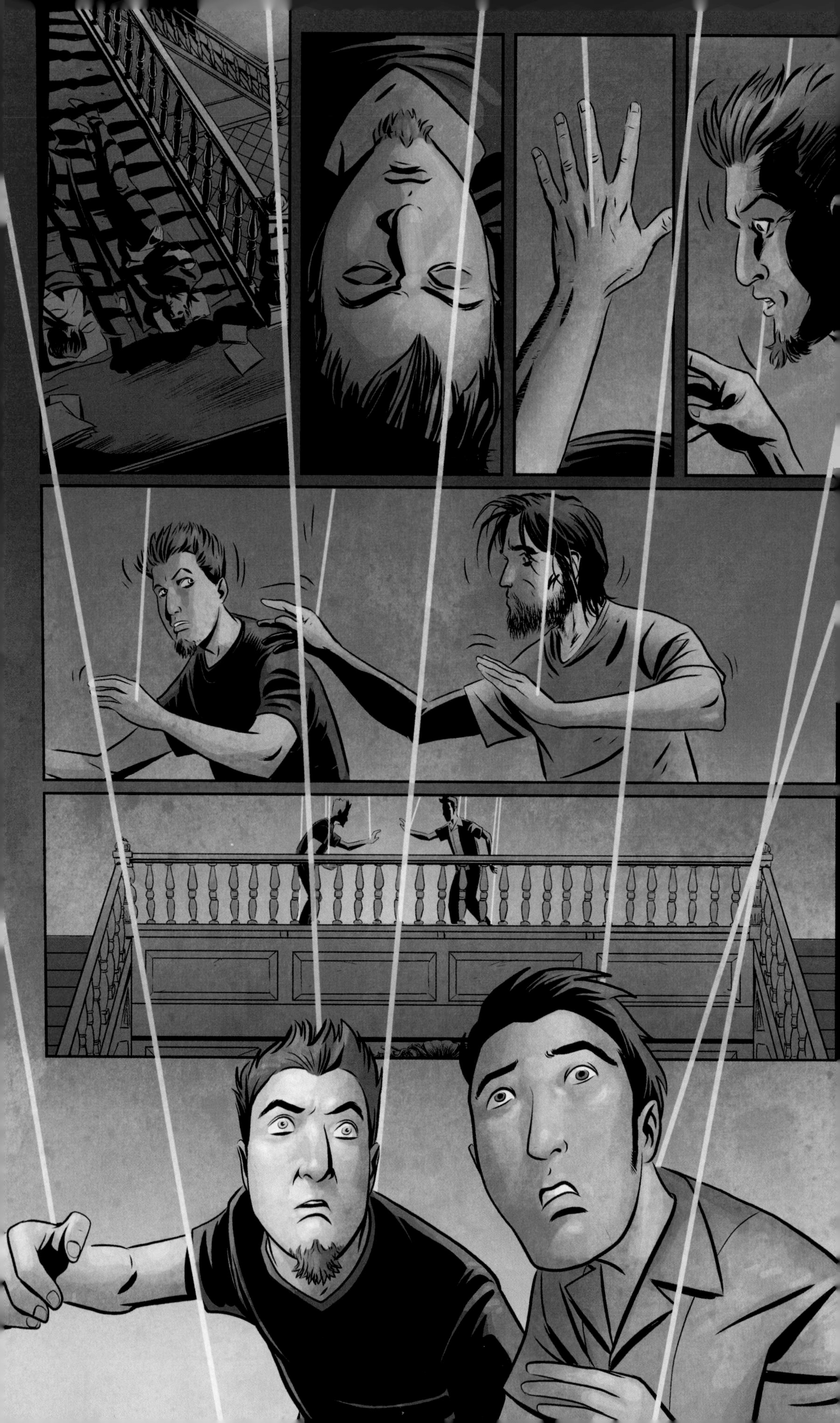

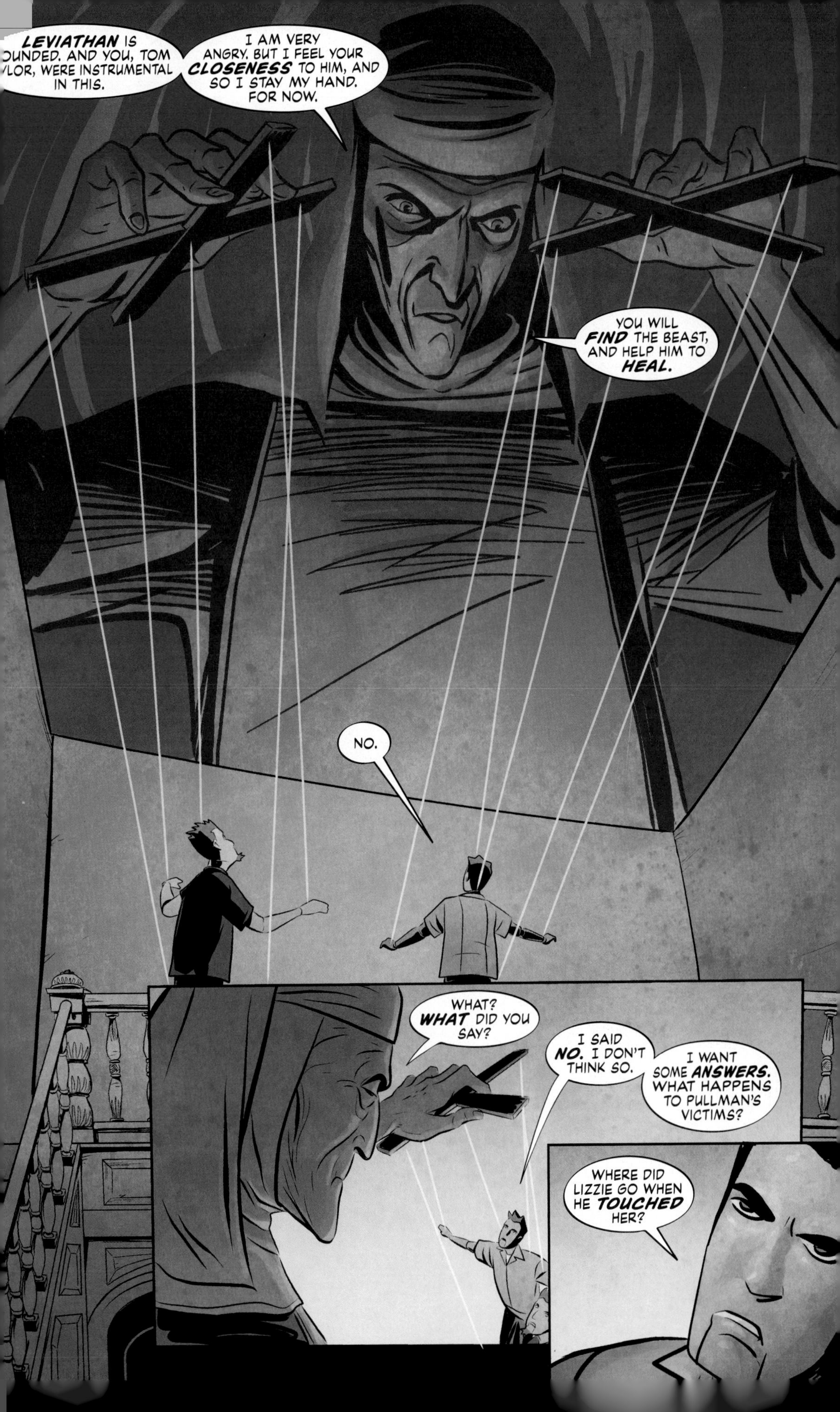

LEVIATHAN IS OUNDED. AND YOU, TOM YLOR, WERE INSTRUMENTAL IN THIS.
I AM VERY ANGRY. BUT I FEEL YOUR CLOSENESS TO HIM, AND SO I STAY MY HAND. FOR NOW.
YOU WILL FIND THE BEAST, AND HELP HIM TO HEAL.
NO.
WHAT? WHAT DID YOU SAY?
I SAID NO. I DON'T THINK SO.
I WANT SOME ANSWERS. WHAT HAPPENS TO PULLMAN'S VICTIMS?
WHERE DID LIZZIE GO WHEN HE TOUCHED HER?

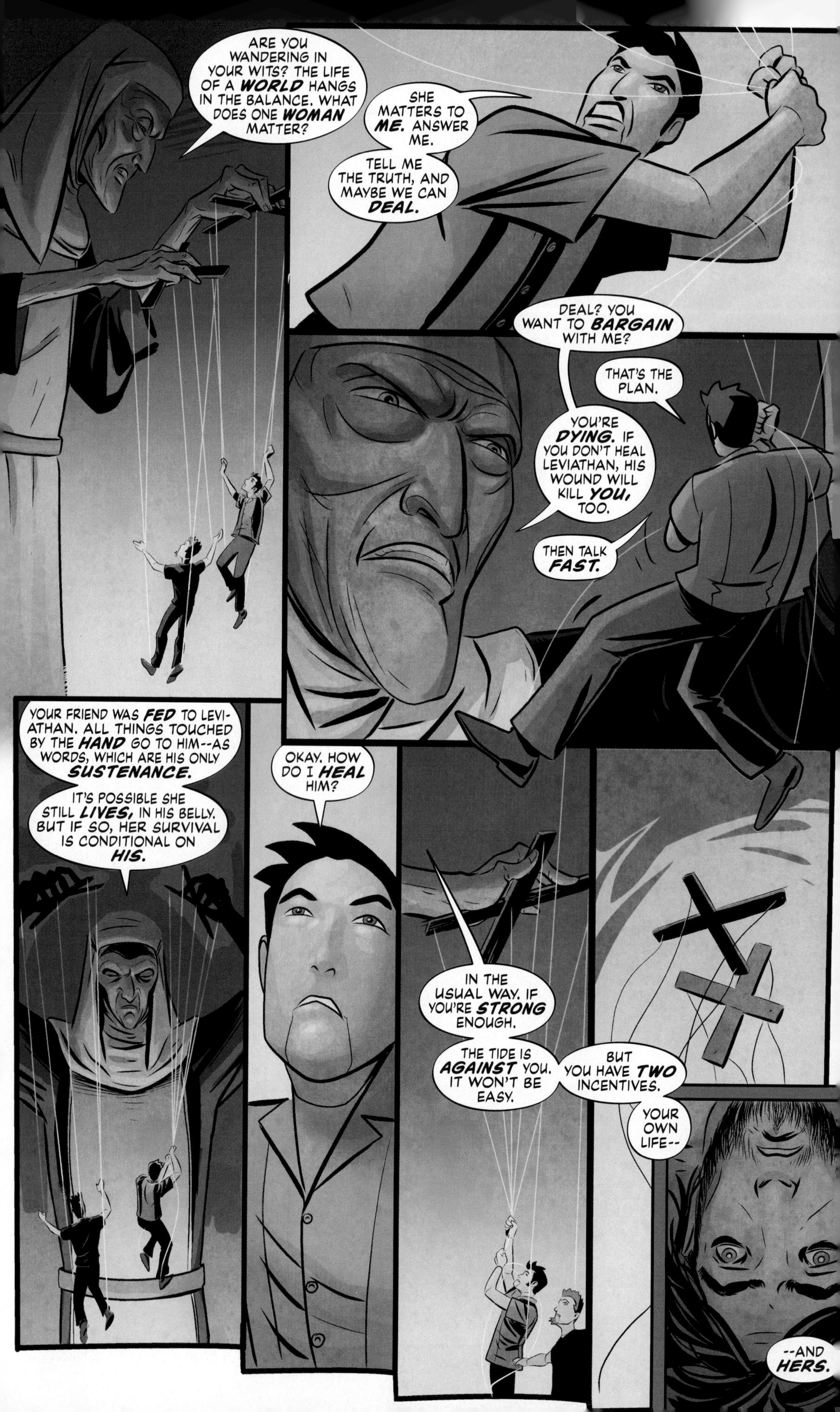

ARE YOU WANDERING IN YOUR WITS? THE LIFE OF A WORLD HANGS IN THE BALANCE. WHAT DOES ONE WOMAN MATTER?
SHE MATTERS TO ME. ANSWER ME.
TELL ME THE TRUTH, AND MAYBE WE CAN DEAL.
DEAL? YOU WANT TO BARGAIN WITH ME?
THAT'S THE PLAN.
YOU'RE DYING. IF YOU DON'T HEAL LEVIATHAN, HIS WOUND WILL KILL YOU, TOO.
THEN TALK FAST.
YOUR FRIEND WAS FED TO LEVIATHAN. ALL THINGS TOUCHED BY THE HAND GO TO HIM--AS WORDS, WHICH ARE HIS ONLY SUSTENANCE.
IT'S POSSIBLE SHE STILL LIVES, IN HIS BELLY. BUT IF SO, HER SURVIVAL IS CONDITIONAL ON HIS.
OKAY. HOW DO I HEAL HIM?
IN THE USUAL WAY. IF YOU'RE STRONG ENOUGH.
THE TIDE IS AGAINST YOU. IT WON'T BE EASY.
BUT YOU HAVE TWO INCENTIVES.
YOUR OWN LIFE--
--AND HERS.

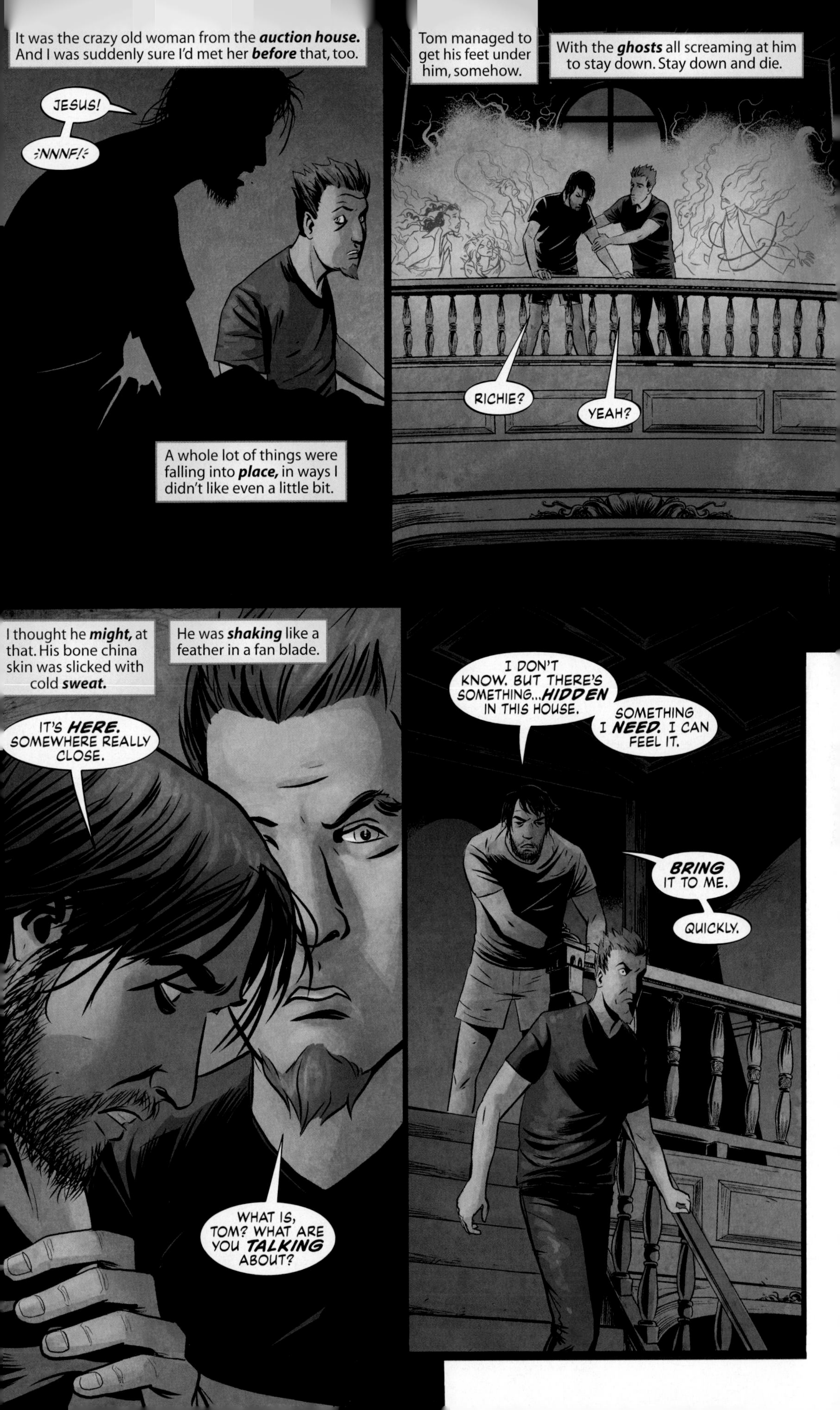
It was the crazy old woman from the auction house. And I was suddenly sure I'd met her before that, too.
JESUS!
NNNF!
A whole lot of things were falling into place, in ways I didn't like even a little bit.
Tom managed to get his feet under him, somehow.
With the ghosts all screaming at him to stay down. Stay down and die.
RICHIE?
YEAH?
I thought he might, at that. His bone china skin was slicked with cold sweat.
He was shaking like a feather in a fan blade.
IT'S HERE. SOMEWHERE REALLY CLOSE.
WHAT IS, TOM? WHAT ARE YOU TALKING ABOUT?
I DON'T KNOW. BUT THERE'S SOMETHING...HIDDEN IN THIS HOUSE.
SOMETHING I NEED. I CAN FEEL IT.
BRING IT TO ME.
QUICKLY.

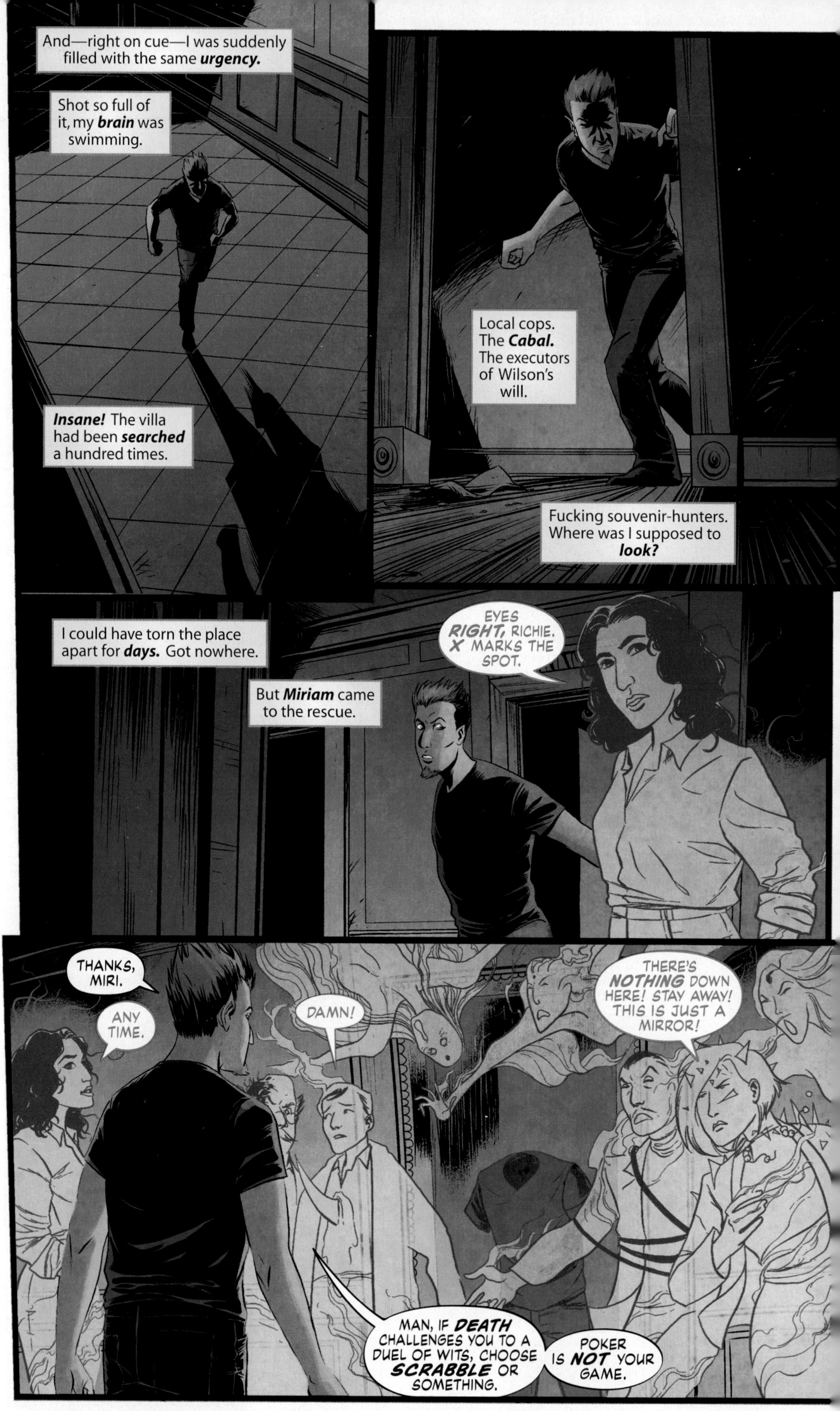

And—right on cue—I was suddenly filled with the same ***urgency.***
Shot so full of it, my ***brain*** was swimming.
Insane! The villa had been ***searched*** a hundred times.
Local cops. The ***Cabal.*** The executors of Wilson's will.
Fucking souvenir-hunters. Where was I supposed to ***look?***
I could have torn the place apart for ***days.*** Got nowhere.
But ***Miriam*** came to the rescue.
EYES ***RIGHT,*** RICHIE. ***X*** MARKS THE SPOT.
THANKS, MIRI.
ANY TIME.
DAMN!
THERE'S ***NOTHING*** DOWN HERE! STAY AWAY! THIS IS JUST A MIRROR!
MAN, IF ***DEATH*** CHALLENGES YOU TO A DUEL OF WITS, CHOOSE ***SCRABBLE*** OR SOMETHING.
POKER IS ***NOT*** YOUR GAME.

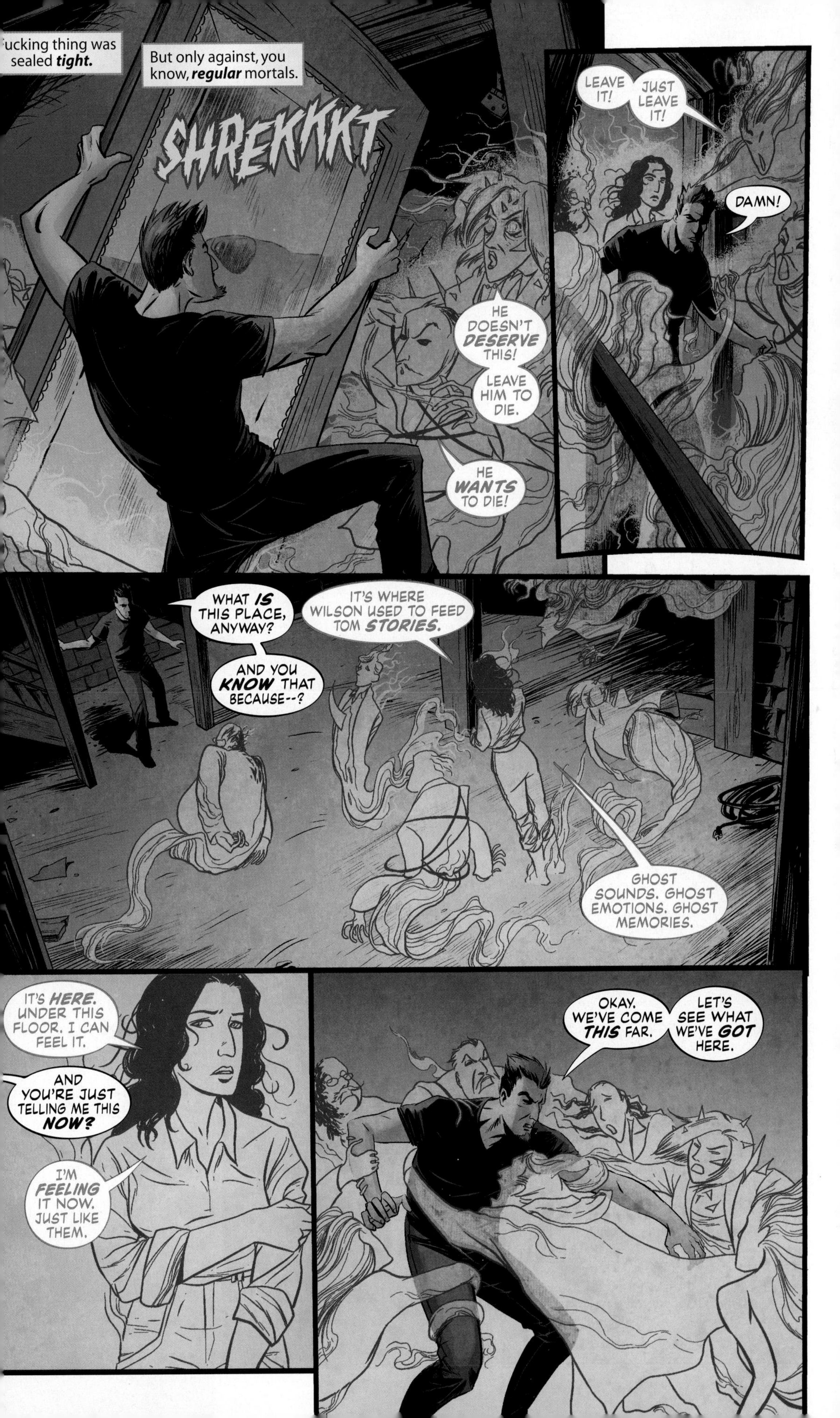
Fucking thing was sealed **tight.**
But only against, you know, ***regular*** mortals.
SHREKKKT
HE DOESN'T *DESERVE* THIS!
LEAVE HIM TO DIE.
HE *WANTS* TO DIE!
LEAVE IT!
JUST LEAVE IT!
DAMN!
WHAT *IS* THIS PLACE, ANYWAY?
IT'S WHERE WILSON USED TO FEED TOM *STORIES.*
AND YOU *KNOW* THAT BECAUSE--?
GHOST SOUNDS. GHOST EMOTIONS. GHOST MEMORIES.
IT'S *HERE.* UNDER THIS FLOOR. I CAN FEEL IT.
AND YOU'RE JUST TELLING ME THIS *NOW?*
I'M *FEELING* IT NOW. JUST LIKE THEM.
OKAY. WE'VE COME *THIS* FAR.
LET'S SEE WHAT WE'VE *GOT* HERE.

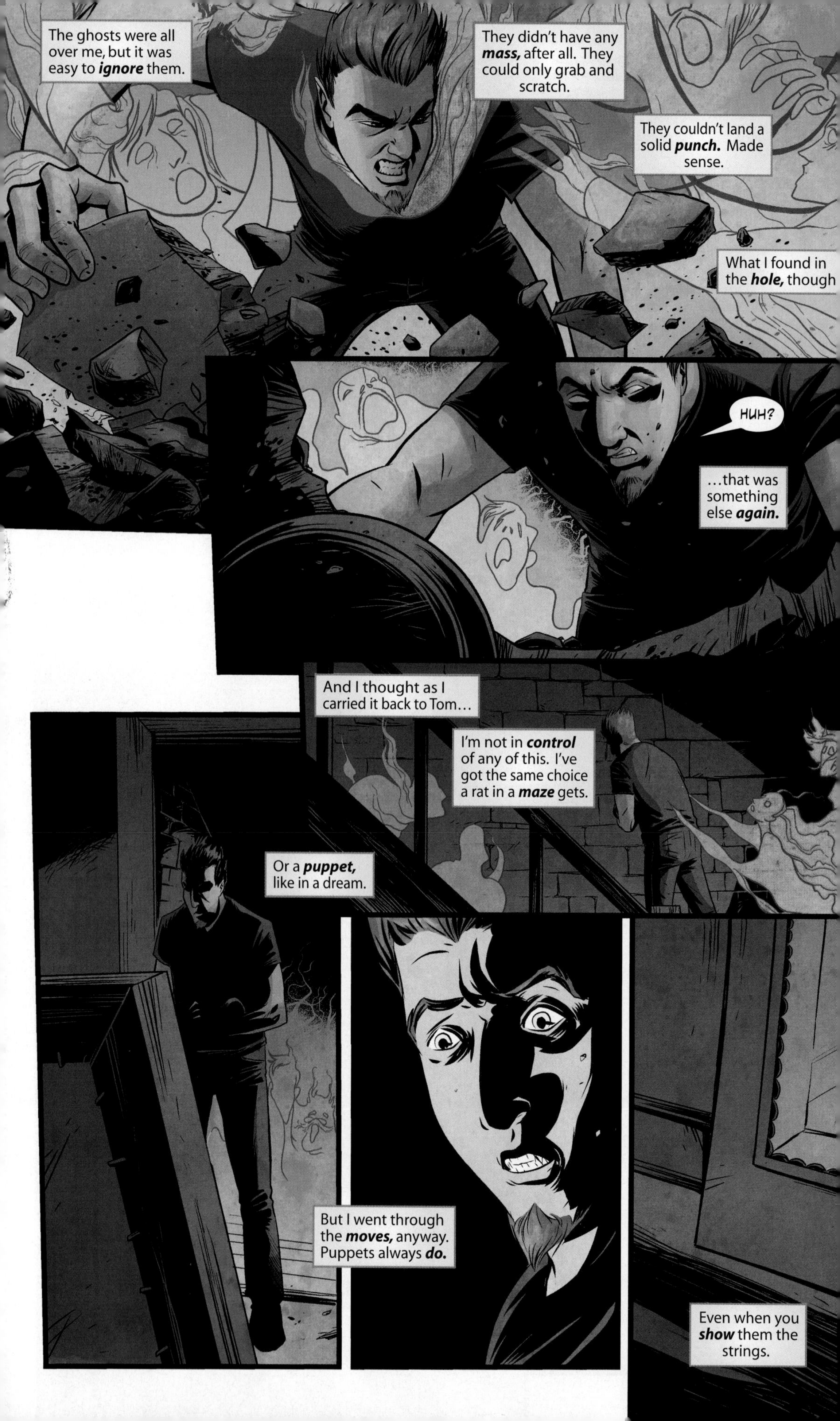
The ghosts were all over me, but it was easy to *ignore* them.
They didn't have any *mass,* after all. They could only grab and scratch.
They couldn't land a solid *punch.* Made sense.
What I found in the *hole,* though
HUH?
...that was something else *again.*
And I thought as I carried it back to Tom...
I'm not in *control* of any of this. I've got the same choice a rat in a *maze* gets.
Or a *puppet,* like in a dream.
But I went through the *moves,* anyway. Puppets always *do.*
Even when you *show* them the strings.

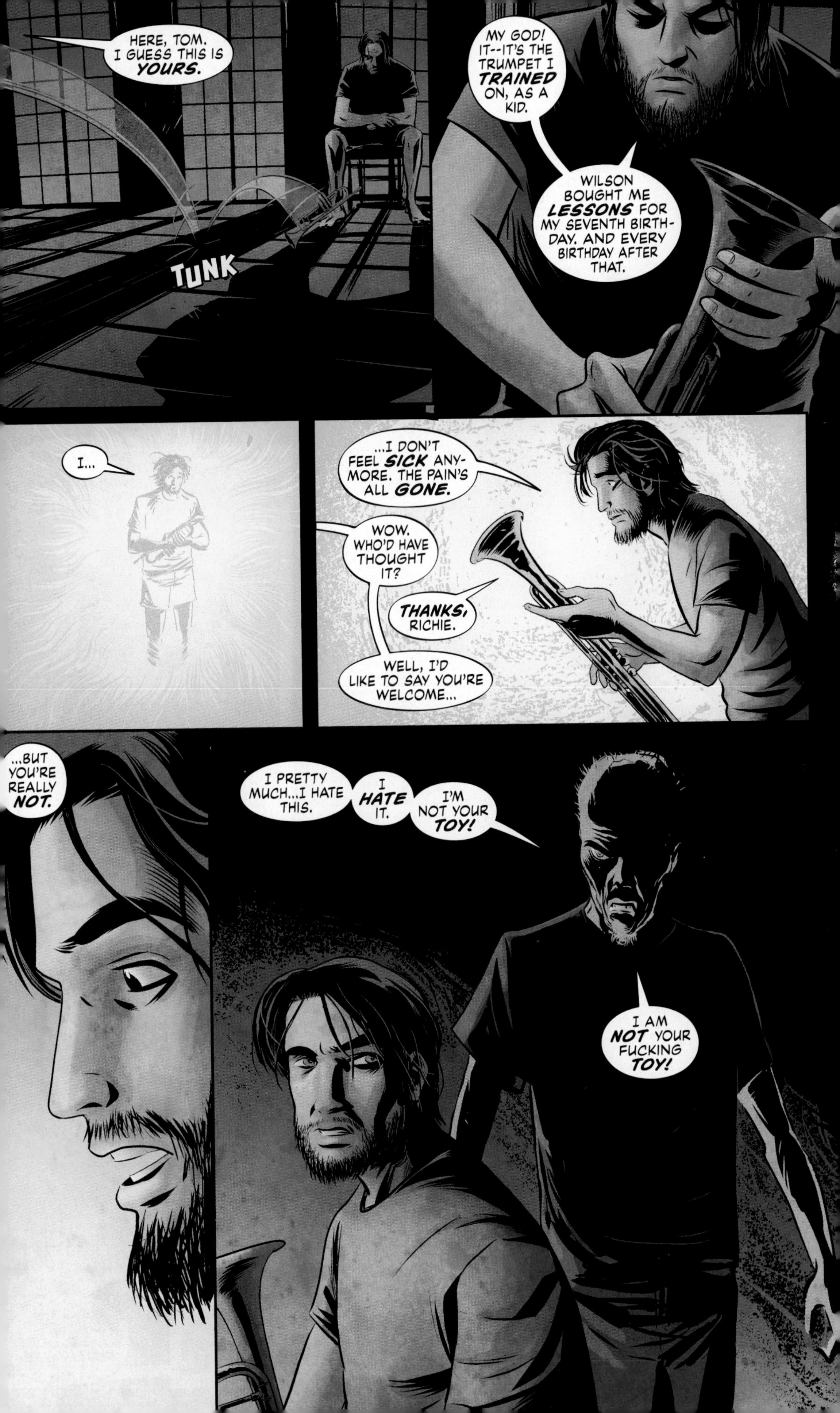
HERE, TOM. I GUESS THIS IS YOURS.
TUNK
MY GOD! IT--IT'S THE TRUMPET I TRAINED ON, AS A KID.
WILSON BOUGHT ME LESSONS FOR MY SEVENTH BIRTHDAY. AND EVERY BIRTHDAY AFTER THAT.
I...
...I DON'T FEEL SICK ANYMORE. THE PAIN'S ALL GONE.
WOW. WHO'D HAVE THOUGHT IT?
THANKS, RICHIE.
WELL, I'D LIKE TO SAY YOU'RE WELCOME...
...BUT YOU'RE REALLY NOT.
I PRETTY MUCH...I HATE THIS.
I HATE IT.
I'M NOT YOUR TOY!
I AM NOT YOUR FUCKING TOY!

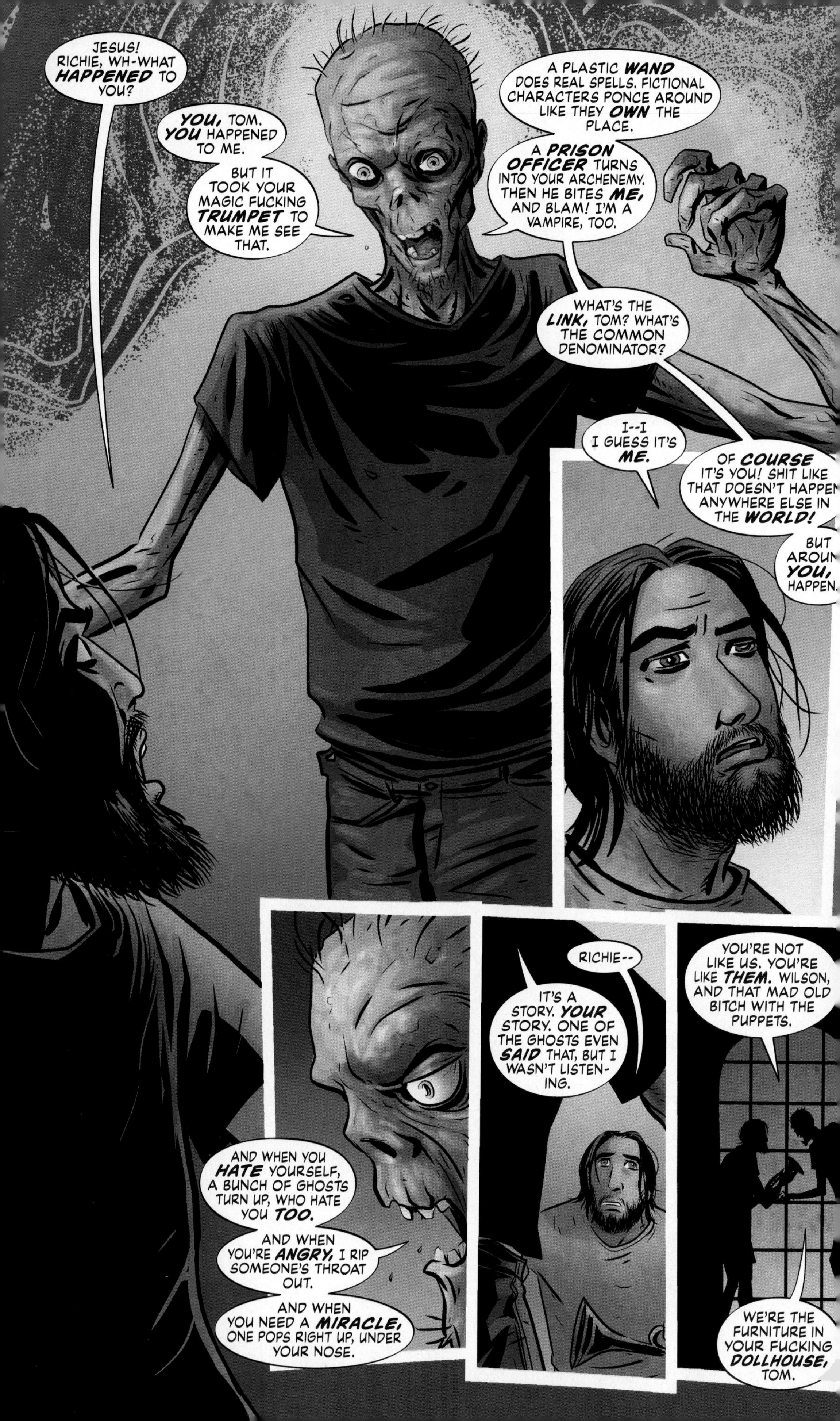
JESUS! RICHIE, WH-WHAT HAPPENED TO YOU?
YOU, TOM. YOU HAPPENED TO ME.
BUT IT TOOK YOUR MAGIC FUCKING TRUMPET TO MAKE ME SEE THAT.
A PLASTIC WAND DOES REAL SPELLS. FICTIONAL CHARACTERS PONCE AROUND LIKE THEY OWN THE PLACE.
A PRISON OFFICER TURNS INTO YOUR ARCHENEMY. THEN HE BITES ME, AND BLAM! I'M A VAMPIRE, TOO.
WHAT'S THE LINK, TOM? WHAT'S THE COMMON DENOMINATOR?
I--I I GUESS IT'S ME.
OF COURSE IT'S YOU! SHIT LIKE THAT DOESN'T HAPPEN ANYWHERE ELSE IN THE WORLD!
BUT AROUN YOU, HAPPEN.
AND WHEN YOU HATE YOURSELF, A BUNCH OF GHOSTS TURN UP, WHO HATE YOU TOO.
AND WHEN YOU'RE ANGRY, I RIP SOMEONE'S THROAT OUT.
AND WHEN YOU NEED A MIRACLE, ONE POPS RIGHT UP, UNDER YOUR NOSE.
RICHIE--
IT'S A STORY. YOUR STORY. ONE OF THE GHOSTS EVEN SAID THAT, BUT I WASN'T LISTEN-ING.
YOU'RE NOT LIKE US. YOU'RE LIKE THEM. WILSON, AND THAT MAD OLD BITCH WITH THE PUPPETS.
WE'RE THE FURNITURE IN YOUR FUCKING DOLLHOUSE, TOM.

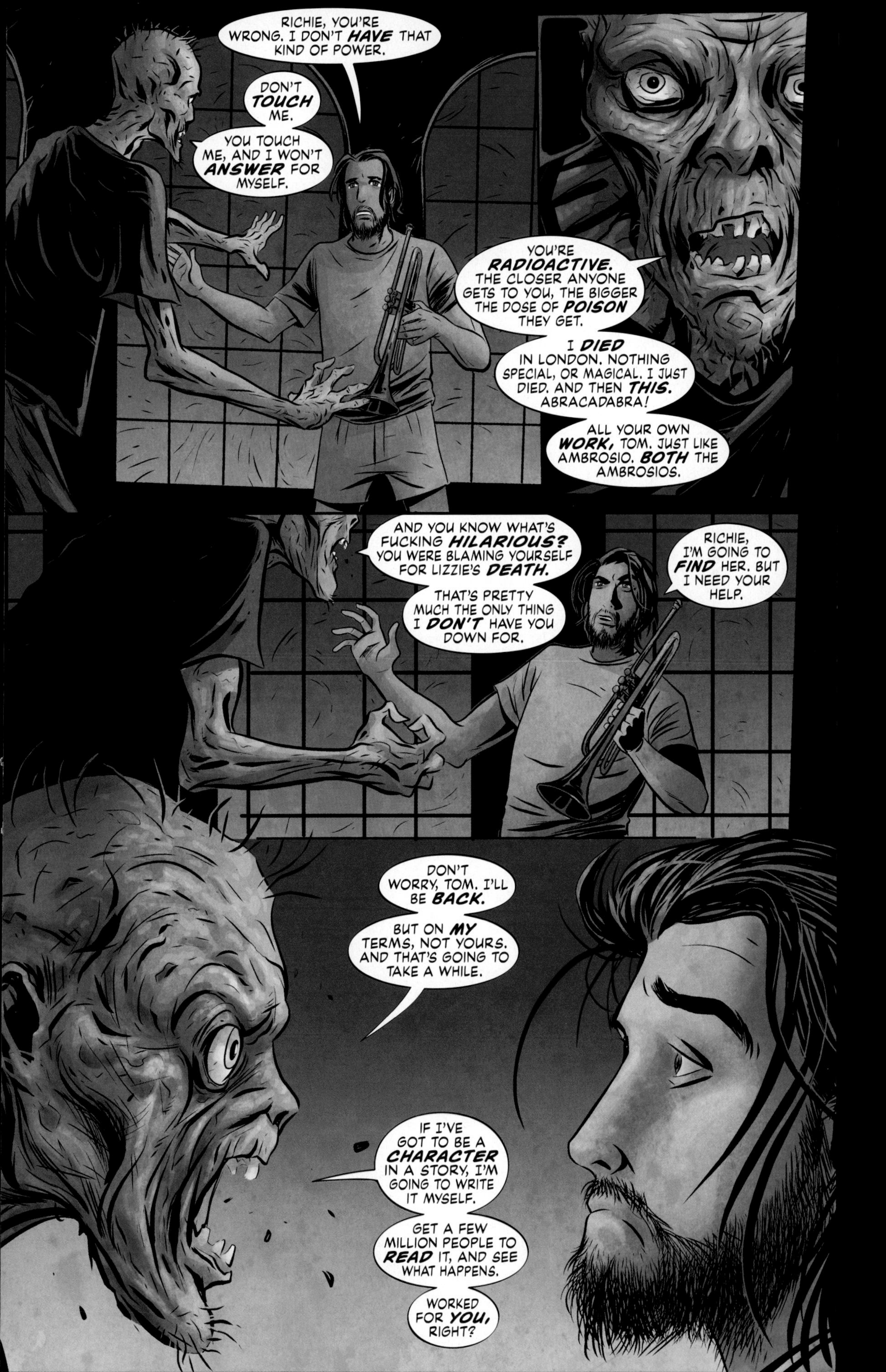
RICHIE, YOU'RE WRONG. I DON'T HAVE THAT KIND OF POWER.
DON'T TOUCH ME.
YOU TOUCH ME, AND I WON'T ANSWER FOR MYSELF.
YOU'RE RADIOACTIVE. THE CLOSER ANYONE GETS TO YOU, THE BIGGER THE DOSE OF POISON THEY GET.
I DIED IN LONDON. NOTHING SPECIAL, OR MAGICAL. I JUST DIED. AND THEN THIS. ABRACADABRA!
ALL YOUR OWN WORK, TOM. JUST LIKE AMBROSIO. BOTH THE AMBROSIOS.
AND YOU KNOW WHAT'S FUCKING HILARIOUS? YOU WERE BLAMING YOURSELF FOR LIZZIE'S DEATH.
THAT'S PRETTY MUCH THE ONLY THING I DON'T HAVE YOU DOWN FOR.
RICHIE, I'M GOING TO FIND HER. BUT I NEED YOUR HELP.
DON'T WORRY, TOM. I'LL BE BACK.
BUT ON MY TERMS, NOT YOURS. AND THAT'S GOING TO TAKE A WHILE.
IF I'VE GOT TO BE A CHARACTER IN A STORY, I'M GOING TO WRITE IT MYSELF.
GET A FEW MILLION PEOPLE TO READ IT, AND SEE WHAT HAPPENS.
WORKED FOR YOU, RIGHT?

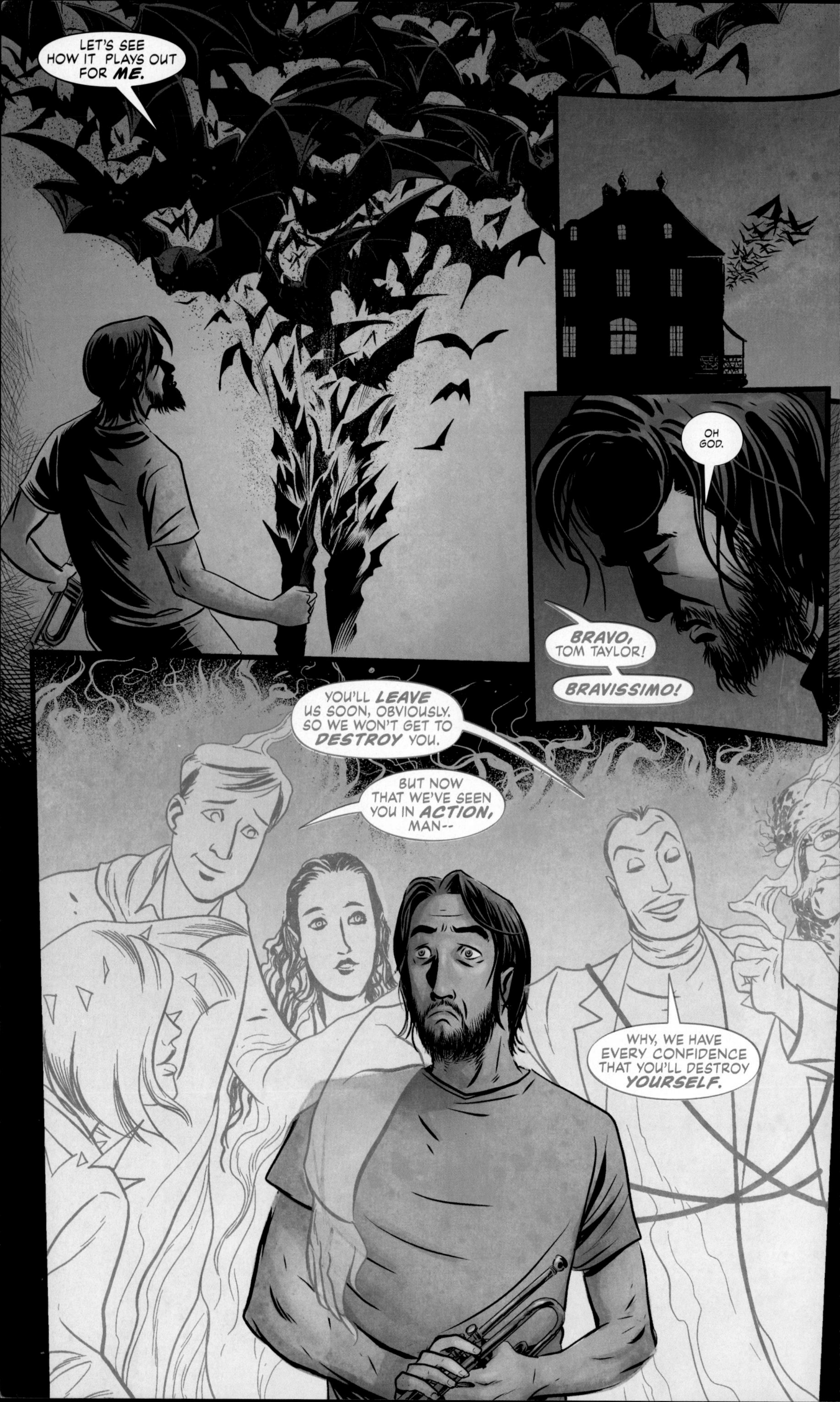

LET'S SEE HOW IT PLAYS OUT FOR **ME.**
OH GOD.
BRAVO, TOM TAYLOR!
BRAVISSIMO!
YOU'LL **LEAVE** US SOON, OBVIOUSLY. SO WE WON'T GET TO **DESTROY** YOU.
BUT NOW THAT WE'VE SEEN YOU IN **ACTION,** MAN--
WHY, WE HAVE EVERY CONFIDENCE THAT YOU'LL DESTROY **YOURSELF.**

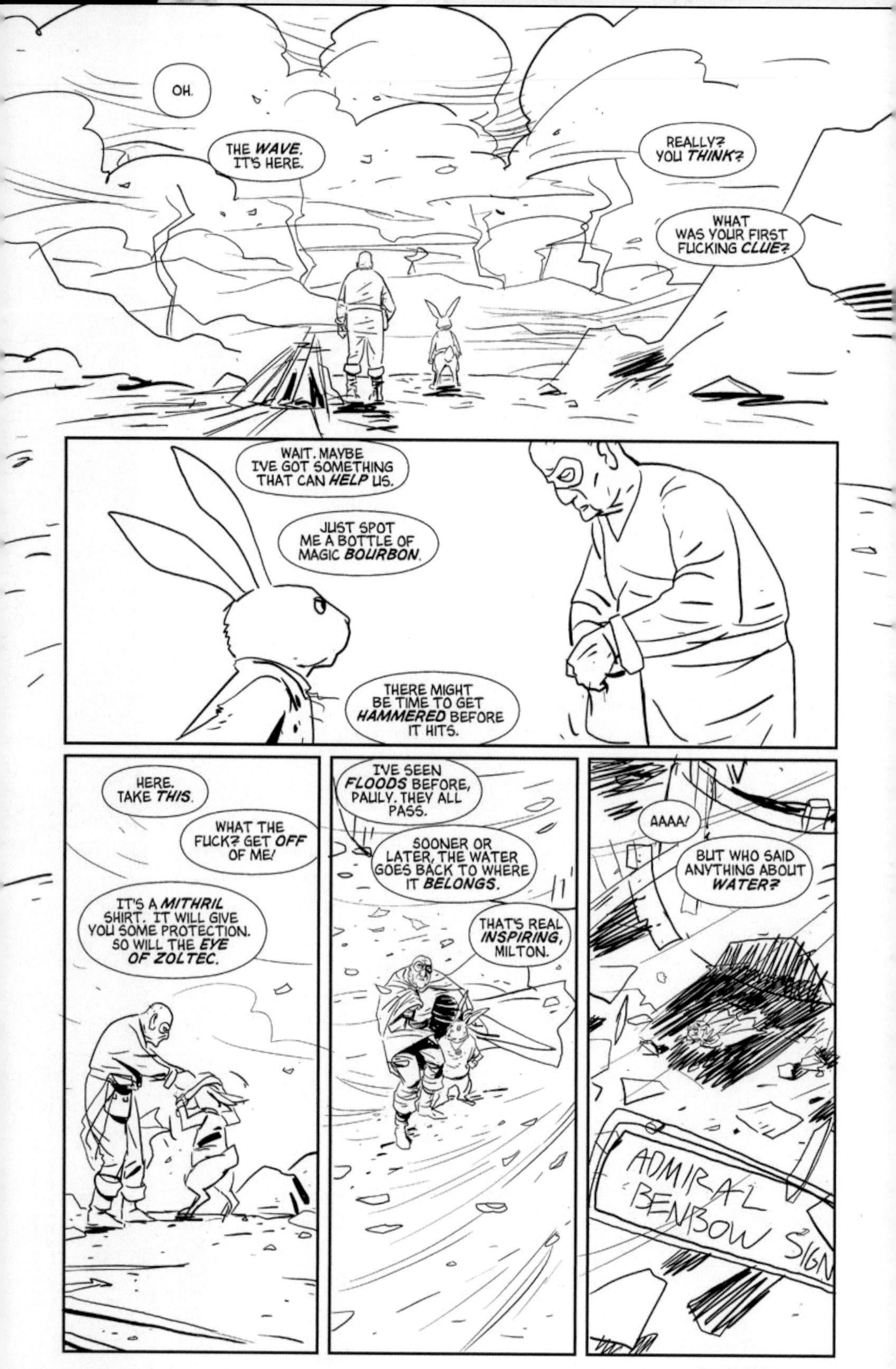
OH.
THE WAVE. IT'S HERE.
REALLY? YOU THINK?
WHAT WAS YOUR FIRST FUCKING CLUE?
WAIT. MAYBE I'VE GOT SOMETHING THAT CAN HELP US.
JUST SPOT ME A BOTTLE OF MAGIC BOURBON.
THERE MIGHT BE TIME TO GET HAMMERED BEFORE IT HITS.
HERE. TAKE THIS.
WHAT THE FUCK? GET OFF OF ME!
IT'S A MITHRIL SHIRT. IT WILL GIVE YOU SOME PROTECTION. SO WILL THE EYE OF ZOLTEC.
I'VE SEEN FLOODS BEFORE, PAULY. THEY ALL PASS.
SOONER OR LATER, THE WATER GOES BACK TO WHERE IT BELONGS.
THAT'S REAL INSPIRING, MILTON.
AAAA!
BUT WHO SAID ANYTHING ABOUT WATER?
ADMIRAL BENBOW SIGN

Layouts by Peter Gross

Issue #36

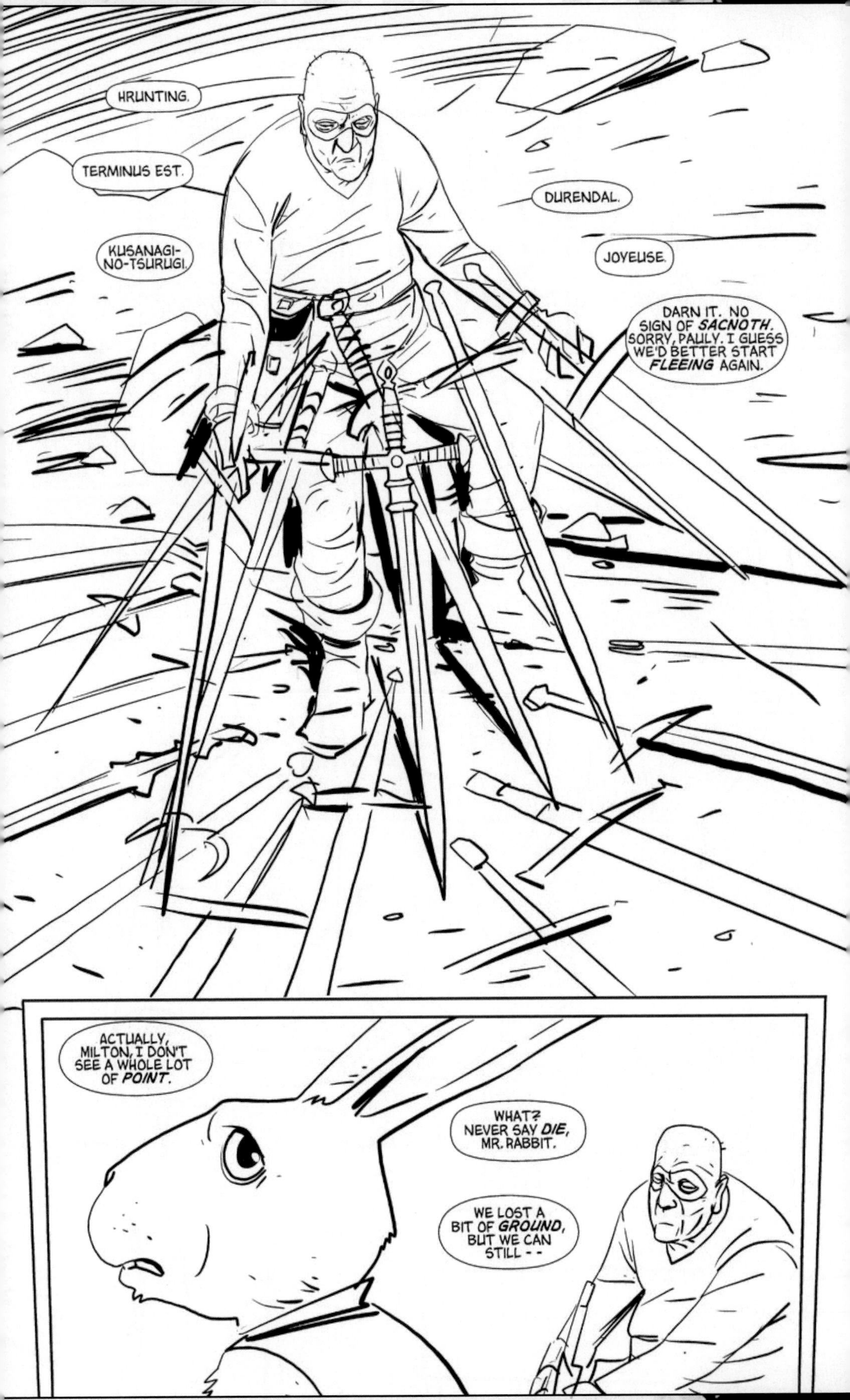
HRUNTING.
TERMINUS EST.
KUSANAGI-NO-TSURUGI.
DURENDAL.
JOYEUSE.
DARN IT. NO SIGN OF *SACNOTH*. SORRY, PAULY. I GUESS WE'D BETTER START *FLEEING* AGAIN.
ACTUALLY, MILTON, I DON'T SEE A WHOLE LOT OF *POINT*.
WHAT? NEVER SAY *DIE*, MR. RABBIT.
WE LOST A BIT OF *GROUND*, BUT WE CAN STILL - -

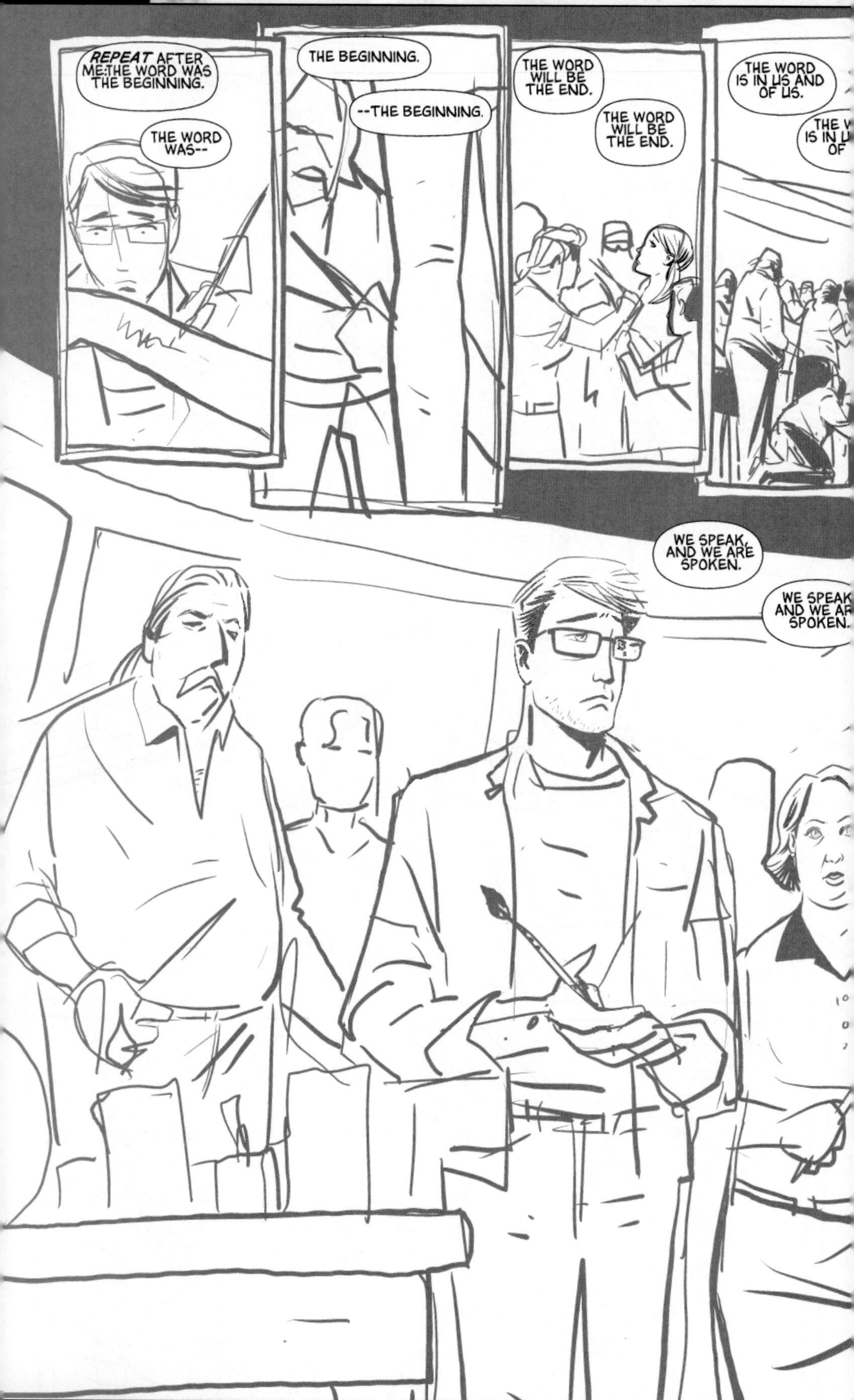
REPEAT AFTER ME:THE WORD WAS THE BEGINNING.
THE WORD WAS--
THE BEGINNING.
--THE BEGINNING.
THE WORD WILL BE THE END.
THE WORD WILL BE THE END.
THE WORD IS IN US AND OF US.
WE SPEAK, AND WE ARE SPOKEN.

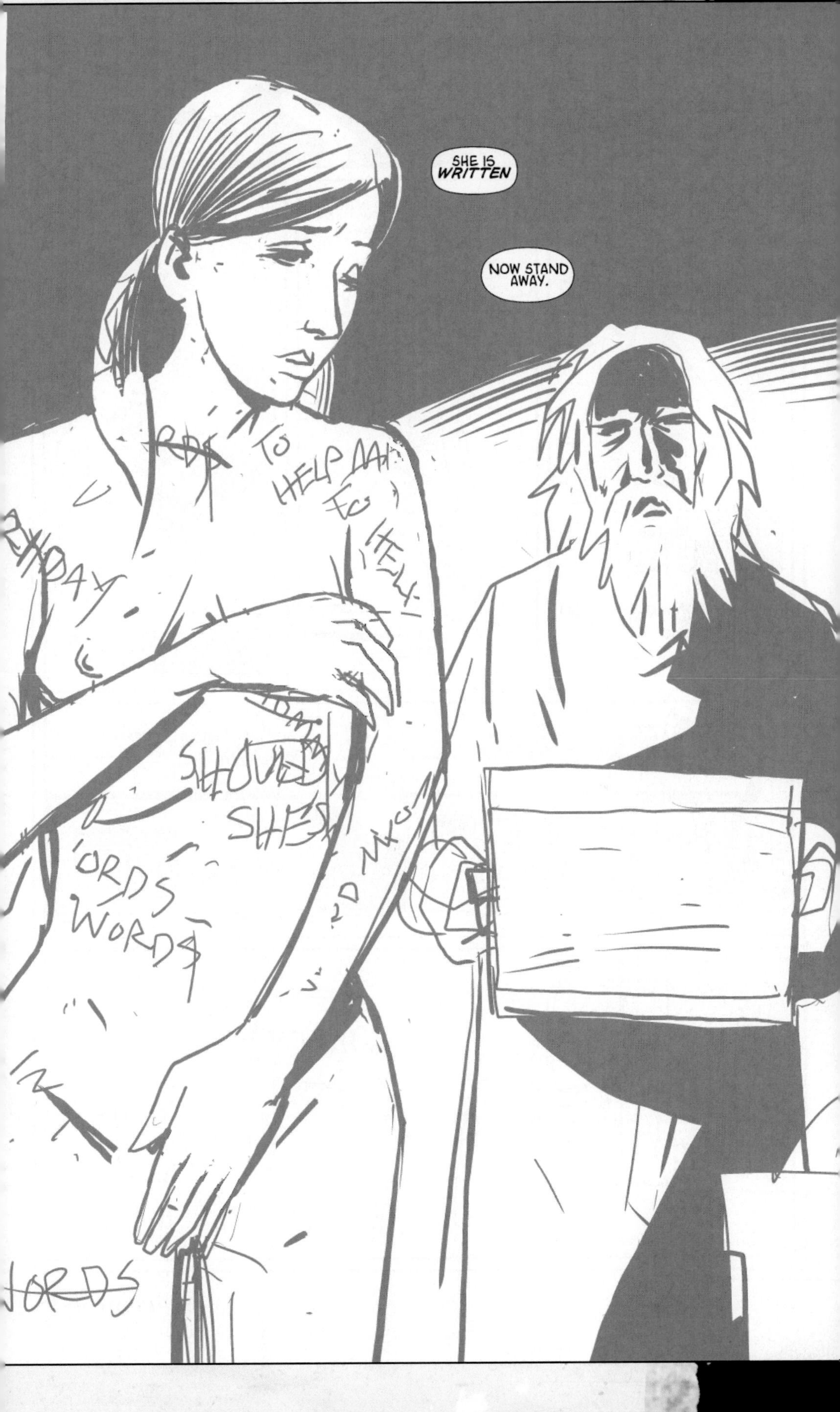
SHE IS WRITTEN
NOW STAND AWAY.

Issue #38

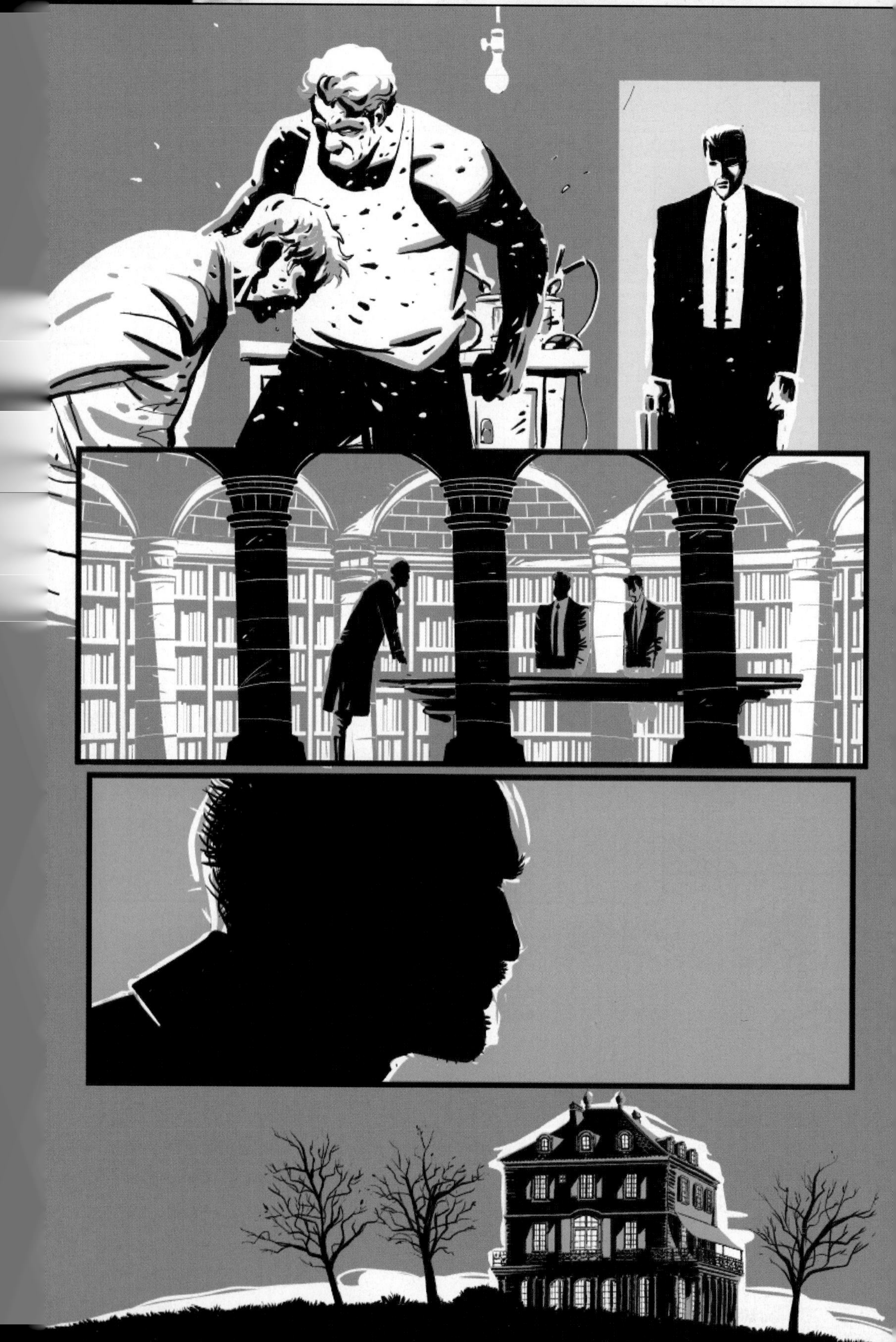

Issue #39